THE HISTORIANS OF GREECE AND ROME

THE HISTORIES OF GREECE AND ROME

The Historians
of
Greece and Rome

by

STEPHEN USHER

Bristol Classical Press

Cover illustration: bust of Herodotus, reproduced by courtesy of the
Metropolitan Museum of Art, New York (gift of George F. Baker, 1891).

First printed in hardback (1969) by Hamish Hamilton Ltd
and in paperback (1970) by Methuen and Co. Ltd

Reprinted, with minor corrections and new bibliography (1985)
by Bristol Classical Press by permission of Hamish Hamilton Ltd

Bristol Classical Press
an imprint of
Gerald Duckworth & Co. Ltd
The Old Piano Factory
48 Hoxton Square, London N1 6PB

A catalogue record for this book is available
from the British Library

ISBN 0-86292-152-X

Printed in Great Britain by
Short Run Press Ltd, Exeter, Devon

Contents

Acknowledgments

The quotations from Sallust's *Catiline* and *Jugurthine War*, and from Livy, Velleius, Appian, Arrian and Ammianus, are from the Loeb Classical Library editions; those from Xenophon and from Tacitus's *Annals of Imperial Rome* and *Histories*, translated respectively by Warner, Grant and Wellesley, are from the Penguin Books editions.

Preface to Second Edition

Readers of the kind originally envisaged for this book have multiplied since its publication in 1969, with the growing number of university and school courses for non-linguists and students of Classical Literature and Civilisation. For this new edition changes have been confined to correction of misprints and minor errors. The bibliography (pp. 264–7) has been revised to take account of work published in the last twelve years.

I wish to express my thanks to John Betts of Bristol Classical Press and to the University of Oklahoma Press for undertaking republication of the book.

Stephen Usher
1982

Introduction

THE STUDY of the early evolution of any literary form has an intrinsic fascination. But when that form is a late arrival on the cultural scene, and has to struggle for an independent identity, the course of this struggle, when viewed against the historical background, has an added interest, since it reveals the relative strength and endurance of the contending influences. Such was the experience of historiography. Although Herodotus's literary skill ensured that his history was artistically accomplished, it came nowhere near to resolving the struggle: epic, dramatic and scientific elements compete with what would today be accepted as historical material; and the battle continued to rage down the centuries, with fluctuating fortunes but surprisingly few casualties. Even in the hands of Thucydides, who self-consciously strove to purify the genre and define its field of operation, history retained a certain hybrid quality which enabled one scholar to argue that his work was tragic drama in disguise, and another, with equal conviction, that it was written in the same spirit as contemporary Hippocratic and other scientific tracts. Again, those historians who, like Polybius, tried to distinguish their profession by its serious educative purpose, nevertheless used a variety of devices the purpose of which can only have been to add literary colour.

In the end, the demands of artistry gained precedence over those of science. Cicero said that historiography was a branch of rhetoric, and subsequent historians ignored this dictum only at the risk of oblivion. Sallust, Livy and Tacitus were all primarily literary artists, only secondarily chroniclers of events: otherwise their work would not have been read in their own time, still less preserved for posterity. In Greece and Rome, the same education which conferred literacy also taught and conditioned its pupils in the art of persuasion. Literary merit was consequently identified with rhetorical effectiveness. All ancient literature had to submit to the test of oral delivery: the Greeks and Romans read aloud even when alone, so that the historian who eschewed the

ix

public performance of his work might expect no indulgence for any faults of style at the hands of his private readers. Indeed, with circulation small and copies expensive, almost every customer was a literary critic; and the standard of criticism was very exacting. Because poetry preceded prose, the latter tended to be subjected to some of the same rules of composition: attention to stress (and hence the attachment of paramount importance to the order of words), quantity, balance and rhythm; indeed, in its most stylized form, prose differed from poetry only in its lack of a regular metrical scheme. Such devices had the power to beguile the ancient ear, which responded sensuously to the spoken word in a degree which cannot today be imagined.

With the importance of style thus established, we are in a better position to understand the ancient historian's attitude to what the modern critic would regard as the basic instruments of his trade: his sources and his criteria. In most cases we are told little about either. Although the earliest historians admitted that their prime duty was to discover and tell the truth, few at any age considered it essential, or even desirable, to obtain information at first hand. Again, although many claim to be impartial, or are ingenuous enough to make their prejudices plain, they all make serious omissions and exaggerations. The commonest tendency is to dwell on episodes which illustrate some particular interest of the historian, or which simply have the quality of a good story. A further weakness of ancient historians is their disregard for economic factors, which has left the field open for a plethora of modern theories of 'real causes', based on commercial, agricultural and mineral interests, whose validity depends largely on conjecture. Economics lack palpable rhetoric: the ancient historian had to think of his public, who looked to him for moral edification couched in persuasive language.

For all these limitations, the historians are immeasurably superior to all other sources for Greek and Roman history; while through their concern for literary form and content they deserve the attention of a much wider reading public. The tense, vivid narrative, the static scene of horror or pathos, the cool, balanced judgment of personal talent and achievement, the enigmatic manifestations of divine interest or agency, the moralizing epilogue coloured by praise and blame: all these were invented and perfected by the Classical historians. Their successors added little to historiography as an art, and benefited greatly from the adumbrations of scientific method that they found in the earlier writers. Meanwhile, in the interval of time between them, human nature, the one constant factor in history, has remained fundamentally unchanged, so that the generalizations about it, in which the ancient historians delighted, are as valid today as when they were made.

In the following chapters the historians will be treated chronologically, in keeping with the purpose of relating them to their historical background. Because of the different character of Greek and Roman civilization a uniform development passing smoothly from one to the other is not to be expected; rather we shall see constantly the recurrence of old influences in new environments, giving rise to an endless variety of approaches to the problem of how history should be written.

CHAPTER I

Herodotus

OUR KNOWLEDGE of Aegean civilization before Homer is obtained from archaeological remains found in Crete, Pylos, Mycenae and elsewhere. The recent decipherment of the language which appears on the clay tablets found at certain sites has added considerably to our understanding of this prehistoric world. But many fundamental questions remain unanswered, and the whole period still affords wide scope for conflicting theories and imaginative reconstructions. It is thought, for example, that Pylos was preparing for a great invasion when its collection of tablets was written; but since the tablets record not events but, like the Domesday Book, lists of property and available resources, the identity of the enemy, the nature of the preparations to meet him, and the feelings of the citizens at the prospect of war all remain a mystery. How much more could be understood, and yet more deduced, if among the thousands of documents a few had survived which recorded historical events! We have a clearer picture of the Heroic Age which followed, because Homer's *Iliad* and *Odyssey* are set in this period; but we cannot ascertain whether Achilles, Agamemnon, Menelaus, Odysseus and the rest really existed; and we leave Homer unconvinced that Helen was the cause of the Trojan War, or that it could have lasted ten years. Homer was a poet, an idealizer of men's actions and motives, whose purpose was to extol the deeds of heroes for the entertainment, and to a lesser extent the edification, of men of substance at banquets. The truth about the war may have been wanting in entertainment value, and Homer is not to be criticized for embroidering it (always assuming that he knew it).

Poetry remained the sole literary medium for over two centuries after Homer. His successors did not write only epics. Hesiod wrote of the gods and of agriculture and rural life; Parmenides committed his philosophical theories to verse; and a

I

host of lyric poets wrote of love, wine and war. All claimed their audiences' attention, implicitly or explicitly, by virtue of the inspiration of the Muse. But not all writing was literary, nor all men who wrote inspired. From early times records had been kept (witness the Pylos tablets): temple records, civic records and palace records held by princes and kings. These records were factual, and their authors were devoid of literary inspiration; the subject was prosaic, and the medium was prose. During the sixth century B.C. there began a new age of philosophic and scientific speculation. Little of what was written has survived, but some of the most important fragments are from the works of Hecataeus of Miletus; and these are written in prose. Hecataeus was a practical man of affairs, whose knowledge of ethnology enabled him to advise his fellow-citizens against provoking a war with Darius, the Persian king. He recited to them a catalogue of the nations over which Darius held sway. On failing to persuade them, he advised them to take control of the sea, but again his advice was rejected. The Ionian Revolt ended as he had foretold, and the destiny of Greeks and Persians remained intertwined for the next three centuries.

The fragments of the writings of Hecataeus reflect the contemporary interest in man's place in the world. They embrace genealogy, ethnology, demography and history. They appear to be derived from two works, the *Genealogies*, which trace family trees (including his own) back to the mythological pantheon; and the *Periegesis*, an account of the places which he visited in the course of his wide travels over the inhabited world. The interest of the two works was fundamentally the same: man, his background and his environment. Both before and after his time this subject, with its various ramifications, was thought to be a suitable subject for poetry: Hecataeus employed prose because he was writing in a spirit of scientific inquiry and with the purpose of presenting factual material, not of exercising creative imagination. But it is not in this departure from literary tradition that his main importance lies: he possessed the chief quality which distinguishes the mere story-teller from the true historian —scepticism. He undertakes to tell only what seems to him credible for, as he says, 'the stories of the Greeks are many and ridiculous, as it seems to me'. In practice, the principle turns out to be more impressive than its application, so that on occasion

Hecataeus seemed gullible and naïve even to his contemporaries, like Heraclitus, who includes Hecataeus in the company of men who illustrate his dictum 'Much learning does not teach common sense'. However, it is probably not an exaggeration to credit Hecataeus with the first attempt at reconciling mythology with history in his *Genealogies*, and of being the first writer to observe and record systematically the topography and historical traditions of the several cities of the Greek world. Thus when Herodotus made his enquiries later, often the first thing he did was to ask whether the tradition recorded by Hecataeus was true. He takes every opportunity to discredit Hecataeus and to sneer at his credulity, but also uses much of Hecataeus's material without acknowledgment (in the accepted ancient manner, but in this case, perhaps rather ungraciously). The truth of the matter probably was that Hecataeus had covered the ground as thoroughly as either historian was equipped to do.

The remaining early historians are little more than names to us.[1] We know that Xanthus wrote a Lydian history, and that it contained many strange tales, including that of the Lydian king who devoured his own wife, then waking up in the morning to find her hand in his mouth, killed himself. He was thus not, apparently, in advance of Hecataeus in the matter of credulity; but he had a taste for curious stories, especially those with an oriental flavour, which Herodotus inherited. Another name is that of Charon of Lampsacus, a contemporary of Herodotus, who wrote about the Persian Wars; but little can be deduced from the very scanty fragments of his history, except that his method probably resembled that of Herodotus more closely than that of Xanthus or Hecataeus.

In approaching Herodotus through these shadowy forerunners, we are equipped only to a limited extent to assess the degree of his originality. Among ancient critics, who were in a better position to make comparisons, most of those who disparage Herodotus do so for partisan reasons, while those who praise him are mostly literary critics, who judge his work chiefly from a stylistic standpoint. Our concern must be to try to discover in what ways he laid the foundations for the subsequent development of Greek historiography; but it is as well to begin with the known facts concerning his life.

Herodotus was born at Halicarnassus, on the south-west coast

of Asia Minor. The best evidence we have points to the year
484 B.C., which means that he was born six years after the battle
of Marathon, in which the first Persian expedition was repelled,
and four years before the second, and greater invasion under
King Xerxes. He was thus born into an atmosphere of conflict
between Greeks and Persians, and the surprising defeat of the
Persians may have been one of his earliest childhood memories.
Little for certain is known of his life. Trouble at Halicarnassus
seems to have driven him to Samos, and thence to Athens. From
there he travelled widely, going to Egypt, Scythia and Cyrene,
and to the new pan-Hellenic colony of Thurii which the Athenians founded in south Italy. But Athens became his second home,
and it was there that he read parts of his *History* to admiring
audiences, and won the friendship of some of her famous men.
No firm date can be given for his death, but he was probably
alive at the beginning of the Peloponnesian War (431 B.C.).

The division of the *History* into nine books is the work of a
later librarian, not of the author, but it effectively reflects the
tripartite structure of the whole. Broadly speaking, Books I to III
deal with the events which led to the establishment of Persia as
the greatest power in the Greek world; in Books IV to VI we
read how King Darius was thwarted in his wider ambitions for
conquest, and how the Ionian Greeks chafed under his yoke,
involving in the process their kinsmen on the Greek mainland,
who defied the king successfully. Books VII to IX tell how
King Xerxes, who inherited the unsettled score from his father,
deliberated, decided and proceeded on the full-scale invasion of
Greece and met with defeat, personally at Salamis and vicariously
at Plataea and Mycale. This arrangement of events has been
likened to the trilogies of tragic drama; for our purpose, however,
it is necessary only to recognize it as a planned narrative with a
climax in order to establish Herodotus as the first historian who
was a mature literary artist.

Herodotus defines the scope and purpose of his *History* in his
introduction:[2]

> The following is an exposé of the researches of Herodotus the
> Halicarnassian, in order that the memory of men's actions may not be
> erased by the passage of time, nor the mighty and wonderful deeds
> of both Greeks and barbarians be without glory; and in particular
> it is my purpose to establish the cause of their conflict.

In this introduction three distinct, and progressively more specific, aims may be discerned: a general concern with the preservation of records of human affairs; the more particular interest in the deeds of Greeks and barbarians; and the aetiological or scientific interest in discovering the cause of this conflict.

The first aim raises the question of the scope of Herodotus's *History*. The antagonists in the final conflict do not meet until halfway through the work, and even after they have met the narrative of their struggle is frequently interrupted by digressions. In the course of his travels Herodotus was told many stories of 'men's actions' by informants who had had little or no part in the central struggle. He solicited and recorded these stories as he proceeded, and their ultimate inclusion in the *History* was determined by one criterion only—that they were worth the telling. To talk of relevance in Herodotus is thus itself an irrelevancy. But a reader of history, as distinct from mythology, is entitled to ask whether his author shows sufficient concern for verisimilitude. Herodotus gives his answer to this question in two passages. In the first of these he states:[3]

> Any person who finds such stories credible may adopt the account given by the Egyptians: for my part, it is my principle throughout the whole history to record what I have heard said by each of my informants.

A similar attitude is found in the second passage:[4]

> I feel obliged to tell what is told to me, but I do not feel at all obliged to believe it: let this hold as the governing principle for the whole history.

Herodotus, unlike Hecataeus, feels no firm obligation to attempt an assessment of the truth of his stories, and cannot be accused of credulity when some of them seem far-fetched. The decision to believe or to disbelieve rests ultimately with each of his readers, who will vary in their tolerance of strain on their credulity: but in practice Herodotus quite frequently tries to relieve that strain by venturing an opinion of his own. The stories in question vary considerably in their intrinsic credibility. Thus we find him dismissing, in a solemn manner which brings a smile to the face of the modern reader, such preposterous tales as that of Scyllias of Scione, the famous diver who was said to have joined the

Greek forces before the sea-battle of Artemisium by submerging at Aphetae and swimming underwater for ten miles: Herodotus offers it as his considered opinion that Scyllias accomplished the journey in a boat.[5] Elsewhere he raises doubts about the existence of races of men born one-eyed,[6] or with goats' feet.[7] Often he expresses positive dissent and corrects false beliefs: he contradicts the opinion of the Caunians as to their own origin,[8] and repudiates the claim of the Egyptians that the Persian king Cambyses was born of an Egyptian princess;[9] and we read, to our edification, that it is the Massagetae, and not the Scythians, who are promiscuous.[10] Occasionally he exercises real judgment in dealing with stories which might have been true. He was probably contradicting a body of informed opinion when he doubted the report that the Alcmaeonids, the most powerful family group in Athens, were conspiring for a Persian victory at the time of the battle of Marathon, and signalled by means of a flashing shield to the Persian fleet.[11] In some cases he finds it impossible to adjudicate between rival accounts: thus he confesses that he is uncertain whether the cup, the golden bowl and the sword which king Xerxes threw into the Hellespont were intended as a sacrifice to the sun or as a propitiation of the waters which he had insulted.[12] Likewise many discussions end inconclusively, such as the argument between Greeks, Persians and Phoenicians concerning the origins of the enmity between Greeks and barbarians.[13]

But beside the rational scepticism which he exercises in the above cases, many exaggerations and naïveties seem to have escaped his notice, whose presence may be only partly explained by his own disavowal of responsibility for them. Few, if any historians now accept his figure of three million as the number of men participating in the great expedition of king Xerxes.[14] Scarcely more credible is his account of the reason for the change which came over the reign of Periander, the tyrant of Corinth. We are asked to believe that Periander sent an emissary to Thrasybulus, tyrant of Miletus, to seek advice on the best way to maintain his tyrannical power; that Thrasybulus led the emissary into a field of standing corn, and cut off those ears which stood taller than the rest; and that Periander, in accordance with this allegorical advice, and without provocation, set about murdering his most eminent citizens.[15] So also in matters of fact:

we read that the hare can conceive again during gestation, while the lioness conceives only once in her life, because her first whelp tears out her womb with its claws.[16]

These and other improbable stories lead on to the next clause of Herodotus's introduction

> ... nor the mighty and wonderful deeds of both Greeks and barbarians be without glory.

His first concern has been purely historical—to preserve records. His second concern is literary and artistic—the glorification of the deeds of men. In this respect his position is close to that of the poets, especially Homer; it is the function to which later classical writers like Sallust and Cicero were alluding when they said that the fame of any age is only as great as the skill of the historian who chronicles it. The single quality which makes Herodotus one of the most readable of ancient writers is the constant alternation between material of factual and scientific interest (which he often analyses and criticizes), and that of phenomena which excite our imagination (to which he applies no such tests). These latter are the wonders of the physical world and of human achievement. They take many forms. Physical size plays an important part in some of them. Xerxes's great army, we are told, drank dry all but the greatest rivers.[17] The man-made mountain, the harbour-works and the city water-supply constructed by the Samians,[18] and the huge scale of building in the city of Babylon,[19] are described in the same spirit of wonderment at physical size. But equally calculated to titillate the imagination are many curious tales, like that of Polycrates the tyrant of Samos who, on the advice of Amasis, king of Egypt, tried to avert divine wrath at his unbroken prosperity by throwing his most treasured possession, an emerald inset in gold, into the sea.[20] The ring was found six days later in the stomach of a fish that was being prepared for the king's table. The tale of Arion, the poet and musician, who was carried over the sea to Taenarus on the back of a dolphin;[21] the story of the treasure of king Rhampsinitus, and the thief who finally earned the king's pardon by repeatedly outdoing him in cunning;[22] the account of the succession of Darius to the Persian throne, which came about through the ingenuity of his groom:[23] these and many other tales are not for readers with the narrow, if serious purpose of assimilating historical knowledge and exercising historical judgment; they are for our entertainment and our aesthetic pleasure, and closely resemble the themes found in the lyric poems of Pindar and Bacchylides. Within the framework of Herodotus's *History*, they perform the artistic function of providing variety, allowing the reader's critical faculty intervals of repose between periods of more serious activity.

From a general interest in recording the deeds of men viewed as both a scientific and an artistic exercise, we turn to Herodotus's particular interest in Greeks and barbarians. Since, to a Greek, all foreigners were 'barbarians' (the word itself being an onomatopoeia to represent the babblings of those who could not speak Greek), it may be objected that an interest in 'Greeks and barbarians' is not 'particular', because it must comprise the whole of the inhabited world; and indeed, Herodotus includes as much of the world as he knows in his history. But it becomes clear from a comprehensive study that it is his purpose not merely to describe but to contrast. Writing as a Greek whose countrymen had suffered, more or less directly, from Persian rule, and who had himself enjoyed the growing prosperity of Athens, which was one of the most important results of the Greek victory, Herodotus undoubtedly looked upon the success of the Greeks in the Great Wars with satisfaction. The Greeks stood for freedom; the barbarians preferred slavery: from this difference sprang many things. Freedom had to be guarded and fought for; but it was an ideal which did not necessarily bring material rewards. Slavery could be accepted without exertion, and often brought a life of luxurious, if precarious ease. Freedom implied individuality, which in turn could lead to differences of opinion and even strife; slavery to a single master ensured that one man's interests were served with complete unanimity. Finally, freedom of the individual demanded, for the continued existence of ordered society, that there be laws to which everyone willingly adhered; monarchy on the Persian pattern meant the arbitrary exercise of power by one man. Herodotus expatiates on all these differences. In one passage in Book VII (the most important book from the structural point of view), he touches on every single one. It is a conversation between Demaratus, a distinguished Spartan exile, and the Persian king Xerxes. Demaratus has been asked whether he thinks that the Greeks, with their slender resources and their disunity, will offer resistance to the united might of Persia. He replies:[24]

> O king, since you positively order me to speak the truth, my words will be such that nobody who later repeats them will be found guilty of falsehood by you. In Greece poverty is endemic, but they have succeeded, through wisdom and the binding force of law, in introducing virtue; with the aid of which she keeps at bay both poverty and tyranny. I naturally commend all those Greeks who dwell around those Doric regions, but what I am about to say concerns not all of these, but the Spartans alone. Firstly, it is unthinkable that they will listen to conditions from you which bring slavery to Greece. Secondly, they will oppose you in battle even if the rest of Greece takes your side. Do not ask how many of them there are, that they are able to do this: their numbers are irrelevant; for whether a thousand, or more, or even less should march out against you, they will give you battle.

Xerxes good-humouredly dismisses this as an idle boast, and says further:[25]

> Come, let me explore the limits of probability: how could a thousand men, or even ten thousand, or even fifty thousand, when they are free and not subject to the command of one leader, withstand such an army as this; for if they are five thousand, we are more than a thousand against one. They might, if subject to one man's leadership, after our own fashion, exceed their natural courage: forced by the whiplash, they might attack a greater number in spite of their smaller own numbers; but now, being left to their own free will they will do none of these things.

He then goes on to say that his own best troops are individually a match for the best that the Greeks can put in the field. But Demaratus reaffirms the prowess of his countrymen, and ends with the following words:[26]

> The Spartans are inferior to none in single combat, but together they are the bravest of men; for, though free, they are not entirely free: there rules over them a master, the law, which they fear much more than your subjects fear you. Thus they do all that it commands; and one of its consistent commands is not to retreat before any number of men in battle, but to remain in their ranks and conquer or perish.

The Spartans are admittedly exceptional in their courage; but it is clear that they are here singled out in order to draw the extremest possible contrast between the Greek and the Persian view of life. When the testing-time comes they are not left to face the Persians alone, in spite of certain misunderstandings which were largely of their own making.

Thus the acceptance of slavery is unthinkable to a Greek, while the barbarian cannot understand how men can be prepared to sacrifice their lives for an ideal, or indeed fight effectively at all except under the compulsion of a single master's lash. The contrast between Greek idealism and barbarian materialism, which is incidental to the dialogue between Xerxes and Demaratus, recurs elsewhere in a more overt form. It is the main theme of the famous dialogue between Solon, the Athenian poet and statesman, who was later numbered among the Seven Wise Men of Greece, and Croesus, the wealthy and powerful king of Lydia. Herodotus gives the following account of their conversation:[27]

On his arrival, Solon was entertained by Croesus in his palace, and later, on the third or fourth day, Croesus bade his attendants conduct him around his treasury; and they showed it to him in all its wealth and splendour. And after he had viewed and taken in all its contents sufficiently, Croesus posed him this question: 'My Athenian guest, word has reached me of your wisdom and your wide travels, how in your love of learning you have journeyed widely as an observer. I therefore desire now to ask you whether you have seen the happiest man in the world.' He asked this question believing that he was himself that man; but Solon replied truthfully and without flattery, saying, 'Tellus the Athenian, O king!' Surprised at this statement, Croesus questioned him closely: 'Why do you consider Tellus the happiest?' Solon replied: 'In the first place, Tellus lived in a well-governed city and had fine sons; he saw them all produce children, and these all survived; secondly, after living as good a life as the human condition permits, he ended it in a most glorious manner: he assisted the Athenians in a battle against their neighbours of Eleusis, and after putting the enemy to flight he died nobly; and the Athenians buried him at public expense where he fell and did him great honour.' When Solon had aroused Croesus's interest by recounting the various aspects of Tellus's good fortune, Croesus, expecting at least to gain second place, asked whom he had seen next to him. He replied: 'Cleobis and Biton. These men, who were natives of Argos, besides having sufficient livelihood, possessed such physical strength that they both took prizes in the games. Moreover, this story is told concerning them: when the Argives were holding the festival of Hera it was required that their mother be drawn to the temple in a waggon but the oxen did not come from the fields in time; being pressed for time the young men yoked themselves to the waggon, and after pulling it for over five miles brought their mother to the temple. After they had been seen doing this by the assembled multitude, a most happy end was put to their lives. The men of Argos stood round and admired the strength of the young men, while the women blessed the mother for having such sons. But the mother herself, being overjoyed at the deed and the glory, stood before the statue of the goddess and prayed that she would grant to her sons Cleobis and Biton, who had honoured her so highly, the greatest blessing possible for man. After this prayer and the sacrifices and festivities, the young men fell asleep in the temple itself and never woke up, but met their end there. And the Argives had statues made to them and dedicated at Delphi in memory of their piety.' Thus Solon accorded these men the second place of good fortune.

Croesus is unconvinced, and the dialogue concludes on the theme of the fickleness of human fortune. Solon points out that he cannot make a pronouncement concerning Croesus's fortune until he has heard that he has ended his life happily. Without continuous good fortune, wealth is useless, because its loss will bring more pain than its enjoyment will bring pleasure; it is better to have the more permanent source of human joy— health, a good family life and the respect of one's fellow men.

Since human fortune is unstable, it is unwise to lay too much store by those aspects of it which are themselves most subject to loss or diminution: this, in short, is the theme of the dialogue between Croesus and Solon. The Persians are also materialistic, and their mentality is nowhere better illustrated than when they hear that the prize at the Olympic games is an olive crown. A young noble, Tritantaechmes, exclaims:[28]

> What manner of men are these that you have brought us to fight against, Mardonius, who compete not for money but for honour?

The Persian kings are constantly boasting about their wealth; but the history of their own country should have reminded them that a nation's fighting qualities decrease in proportion to the growth of its material prosperity. Herodotus's description of the Persians before they embarked on their career of conquest is that of a hardy, frugal people; and his *History* concludes with a reference to the decision of Cyrus, the first king of the Persian empire, to make his subjects live in the barren rather than the fertile parts of the country in order that their fighting qualities might not be sapped.[29] Cyrus's successors reversed his policy, but found that materialism goads its victim ceaselessly to add to his possessions; and since this is the nature which has become ingrained in his subjects, the king must, by constantly adding to his empire, foster the illusion of its increasing prosperity. When he has subdued his weaker neighbours, he must challenge stronger opponents, and some of these exhibit the same rugged qualities which made the Persians great. Thus the Scythian king tells Darius that his people have no cities or land which compel them to stand and fight; they will, however, fight to defend the tombs of their ancestors; but he doubts whether the Persians will find them.[30] The Greeks find Persian ambitions inexplicable, as is illustrated by the story which Herodotus tells about Pausanias, the commander of the victorious Greeks at the battle of Plataea. When the Persian camp was captured after the battle, quantities of gold and silver and other finery were found. Pausanias ordered the Persian bakers and cooks to prepare a meal as for Mardonius, their dead commander, and when this had been done he ordered his own attendants to prepare a Spartan meal. He then called in his fellow-generals and said:[31]

> Men of Greece, I have called you together for this reason, to show you the folly of the Persian general, who had such luxury, and yet came to deprive us of our meagre fare!

But the Persian empire possesses real strength, and Herodotus does not underestimate it. Its unified command is an important factor. In addition to allowing clear decisions and positive action, it had certain psychological advantages. Every subject owed personal allegiance to the king, whose slave he was. This led to many deeds of valour in battle, and these Herodotus does not stint to recount; but one of the most striking stories of devotion is one of the versions which he gives of Xerxes's return home after the battle of Salamis. The king's ship, overloaded with his effects and his entourage, was caught up in a storm, and Xerxes, on being told by the captain that the only hope of safety lay in removing some of the passengers, called upon volunteers to jump overboard and so save the king; whereupon his entire staff paid him homage and leapt into the sea.[32] (It should be added, however, in fairness to Herodotus, that he preferred the other version, which states that Xerxes returned by land.)[33] But the anxiety of his subjects to please him had two serious consequences. In counsel, his advisers mostly tried to guess what he wanted to do before offering their opinions. Thus, after the seeds of the enterprise had been sown in the mind of Xerxes by Mardonius, and it was generally believed that he was resolved to invade Greece, only Xerxes's uncle Artabarnus had the courage to advise him against it; and in the deliberations before Salamis the other leaders voted to give battle because they conceived this to be the king's will, and when the Carian queen Artemisia advised against battle they expected her to be punished.[34] Xerxes, however, admiring her independence of mind, did not punish her; but he nevertheless followed the 'majority opinion' with disastrous results. In battle, and in the battle of Salamis in particular, desire to please the king could have equally unfortunate consequences: in that battle the smaller number of the Greek ships succeeded in hemming in the barbarians against the shore; and in these conditions, with the king watching from his throne on Mount Aegaleos behind them, the captains of the ships in the rear, in their anxiety to be seen performing deeds of valour, pushed forward and fell foul upon those in front; and the resourceful Artemisia, correctly relying on the assumption that Xerxes was not long-sighted, won his approval by ramming a friendly ship.[35] The individual bravery of the barbarians in battle is no match for the disciplined skill of the Greeks who, according to Herodotus, won the only large-scale land-battle of the campaign, at Plataea, in spite of misunderstandings and obstinacy among their commanders, because they kept their ranks. He also mentions a specific advantage which they enjoyed, that of heavier arms and armour.[36]

On the Greek side, the war effort is severely hampered at every stage by disunity. They fail to settle their internal quarrels until the invading Persian army is nearly upon them; and even after losing Northern Greece through selfish short-sightedness, they still quarrel over the command of their forces until they are silenced by the magnanimity of the Athenians, who withdraw their claim to the command of the fleet in the interests of unity. Earlier the Ionian Greeks have been even more culpable in actually losing the sea battle of Ladé through divided loyalties. And yet uniting sentiments could be appealed to. We read that the Athenians felt such a strong bond of kinship with the Ionians, that when Miletus fell to the Persians they deemed it a domestic misfortune, and fined one of their poets, Phrynichus, for reminding them of it in his play *The Capture of Miletus*.[37]

In political terms, the form of government which comes nearest to safeguarding personal freedom is democracy, while the one which connotes the subjection of all to one man's arbitrary will is tyranny. Herodotus discusses both as phenomena of his own time. Democracy is a peculiarly Greek concept (though not all Greek states are democracies), and its effects are to be observed in the Greek states which have adopted it. Of these Athens is the conspicuous example. Herodotus asserts that the Athenians became superior to their neighbours after they embraced democracy, because each man realized that he had a personal stake in the city's destiny.[38] He also tells how the Spartans viewed the growth of Athens with alarm, and sought unsuccessfully to impede it by restoring the tyrant Hippias.[39] Herodotus is pro-Athenian, and does not criticize democracy as practised by Athens; but in a passage in which the Persian nobles discuss the form of government to adopt after the death of king Cambyses, the weakness of democracy is exposed—that it involves entrusting the conduct of affairs to men who lack education and a sense of responsibility, and that it is easier for a persuasive speaker to impose his will upon a multitude than upon a single man.[40] Of tyranny Herodotus has nothing good to say: he echoes the popular view that tyrants are evil by the very nature of their power, which is absolute and uncontrolled. He regards the Persian monarchs as guilty of the same excesses as the Greek tyrants: the only difference is that they can feel safer on their thrones because their subjects are more amenable to the rule of one man. But we read more of the cruelties of Persian than of Greek monarchs, and of these none is more gruesome than the punishment of the wealthy Pythius of Sardis, who, in return for his hospitality to Xerxes, asked that his eldest son be excused from participating in the expedition to Greece. Xerxes had this son's body cut in half, and the halves set on each side of the city gate as the army marched through.[41] Unpredictability is another characteristic of Persian kings, and of Xerxes in particular. Thus he praises Artemisia for offering frank advice[42] after showing anger against Artabanus for doing the same,[43] and he presents the pilot of the ship which brought him home after the storm with a golden crown for saving him, then has his head struck off for causing the loss of so many Persians.[44]

The character of absolute monarchy and its effect upon its holders has a crucial bearing on the last question which Herodotus proposes for himself in his introduction—the reason why Greeks and barbarians fought. We have seen how their attitude to some of the fundamental problems of human life differed; but this in itself hardly provides a motive for war. According to Herodotus, the Persians trace the origin of their enmity with the Greeks back to the Trojan War: they blame the Greeks for this, claiming that since no woman allows herself to be abducted unless she wants to be, they were guilty of pettiness when they made the rape of Helen a *casus belli*. He begins his own account more realistically at a point in more recent history—the reign of king Croesus of Lydia. From this point onwards a succession of kings make war on the Greeks and their neighbours, but their motives for doing so are basically two—pure lust for conquest and desire for revenge. With regard to the first of these Herodotus, unlike Thucydides, believed that monarchs tend to be expansionist because they depend upon conquest for the maintenance of their superhuman image. They must not only keep their fighting men occupied: they must also rival the conquests of their predecessors in order to compare favourably with them in the eyes of the common people. But if desire for conquest is a reason, it could never be advanced as a pretext. Revenge, however, is a perfectly acceptable pretext, since it implies that the enemy has committed the first wrong, and therefore war can be undertaken in the assurance that the gods will be favourable. Both Croesus and Xerxes speak of revenge; and Cambyses invaded Egypt, Darius made war on the Scythians, and the Athenians determined to remain at war with Persia after Salamis, all from avowed motives of revenge. The difference between the Greek and the Persian attitude to revenge is that, in the latter case, revenge is no more than an aspect of the king's exercise of power, in that it is as important for him to take cognizance of all insults against him as it is for him to increase his prestige by conquest. It is for this reason that Darius instructs one of his

servants to remind him before each meal to 'Remember the
Athenians' after they have contributed twenty ships to the revolt
of his Ionian subjects.[45] The Greek motive, by contrast, is the
righteous one of avenging the sacrilege committed against their
cities and the shrines of their gods.

Out of the frequency with which Herodotus assigns motives
of power-lust and revenge to his leading characters arises the
general question of personal motivation. Herodotus has been
criticized for being too ready to accept the whims of potentates
as the sole grounds for actions which change the whole course of
history, to the exclusion of rational motives based on economic
or political considerations. In certain cases this criticism has
some substance, as when we are asked to believe that the Athenian
legislator Cleisthenes conceived his constitutional reforms in
emulation of his maternal grandfather.[46] But to insist on the
existence of rational motives or long-term plans in the minds
of such palpably capricious men as Cambyses, who was mad, and
Xerxes, who was very young, is unrealistic. Herodotus's *History*
concerns an age in which absolute rulers figured largely. These
men regarded their dominions as their personal property,
symbols of their prestige to be augmented as opportunities
presented themselves. On the Greek side, those who believe
that love of freedom alone could not have caused the Greeks to
withstand the overwhelming might of Persia would do well to
study the record of the Greek resistance against Nazi Germany
in the Second World War, which reveals the same indifference
to prospects of success as that portrayed by Herodotus through
the mouth of Demaratus.

Our confidence in Herodotus's grasp of motivation is enhanced
by the realism with which he portrays the conflicting emotions of
his characters. Thus the battle of Salamis took place not because
of the single-minded resolution of the Greek captains to stand
and fight, but because Themistocles anticipated their fears and
arranged that retreat should be impossible by secretly advising
the Persians to block the western channel. Nevertheless, the
Greeks could have surrendered both at Salamis and at Thermopylae, but chose to fight in both cases. Fear, such as that which was
felt throughout Greece at the news of the Persian invasion, is a
natural human emotion; and by admitting its presence in men's
minds at the time Herodotus makes us admire the ability of

leaders like Leonidas and Themistocles to make cool decisions which apparently discounted the odds. Realism may be seen also in the balanced characterization of some of the leading men. Themistocles, for example, whom Herodotus obviously admired, is nevertheless charged with greed;[47] and the character of Periander is a mixture of intemperance and compassion. But the most complex character is that of the central figure of the final drama, king Xerxes himself. He is arrogant and impious when he whips the Hellespont, and cruel in his treatment of his host Pythius; but he is also generous on many occasions, and shows a deeper human side when he laments the mortality of man as he reviews his vast army at Abydos and observes that they will all be dead a hundred years hence.[48] He also combines the headstrong nature of a young man with an obvious dependence upon the advice of his elders.

As a conclusion to any discussion of the rational element in Herodotus it is appropriate, since the *History* is chiefly about war, to consider what account he takes of strategic matters. In general, it must be said, very little. But he gives a clear explanation of the importance of sea power to the Greeks, by showing that without it the building of a defensive wall across the Isthmus of Corinth (the plan favoured by the Peloponnesians) would be useless, because the Persians could choose any favourable spot along the coast of the Peloponnese on which to land and begin an encircling movement.[49] It is also clear from his narrative that Persian strategy was based on the combined operation of army and navy, as when we read how the navy awaits the arrival of the army at a corresponding point on land before proceeding further. We also receive, through the mouth of Artabanus when he warns Xerxes of the difficulties of victualling such a vast host in hostile territory, a notion of Persian administrative and logistic problems; but we hear little of the manner in which the problems were overcome in practice. Nor does Herodotus, who probably saw no active service himself, show much knowledge of tactics, in spite of the special study which he appears to have made of the battle of Plataea *in situ*. But his descriptions of what actually happened in battles (especially land battles) are usually lucid and convincing, and they are embellished by accounts of individual valour in the Homeric tradition.

In spite of his concern for rationalism and realism, Herodotus was far from believing that everything was explicable in human terms. Religion plays a paramount part in his scheme of things. He reports conscientiously the utterances of oracles before important events. One of these, the oracle of Bacis, made the following prediction before the battle of Salamis:[50]

> When they [the Persians] bridge with their ships the sacred shore of Artemis of the golden sword [Salamis], having destroyed in frenzied hope the brilliant city of Athens, then divine Justice shall quench strong Excess, the son of Arrogance, who has in his eagerness supposed he will overcome all who resist him. Bronze shall clash with bronze, and Ares shall redden the sea with blood. Then shall the far-seeing son of Cronus and Queen Victory bring to Greece her day of freedom.

Regarding this prediction in the light of events, Herodotus makes the following unequivocal statement:

> As I view such occurrences and consider the clear statement of Bacis, I neither venture myself to say anything to contradict oracles, nor do I allow others to do so.

This attitude is essentially rational: events have turned out as the oracle predicted; hence it is foolish to ignore oracles. They are the earthly pronouncements of the gods: the fact that their predictions are fulfilled suggests that the gods play an important part in human affairs, and perhaps even control the destiny of man. Portents are another means by which the gods informed man of the future, and Herodotus shows a similar respect for them. The portents which are revealed to Xerxes as his army crosses the Hellespont, and which he ignores, are of special interest. Herodotus reports that a mare foaled a hare, and a mule brought forth a hermaphrodite colt.[51] Later, as the Persian army approached the sacred shrine of Apollo at Delphi, we are told that the oracle forbade the god's servants to remove his treasure, as 'the god was able to protect his own'.[52]

The narrative continues:[53]

> As the barbarians advanced, and could see the temple in the distance, at that point the prophet, whose name was Aceratus, saw that the sacred weapons, which no mortal was permitted to touch, had been brought out from within the shrine and laid before the temple. He therefore went to inform those Delphians who were present of the prodigy; but what happened as the barbarians reached

the temple of Athene Pronaea, marching at full speed, was even more remarkable. It is indeed a great miracle, that weapons of war should appear before the temple of their own accord; but what followed upon this ranks above all other portents in its miraculous quality. For when the barbarians had advanced near the temple of Athene Pronaea, at that moment thunder burst upon them from heaven, and two peaks broke off from Mount Parnassus and bore down upon them with a mighty crash, crushing many of them to death; and a war-cry and a shout of victory were heard from Athene's temple. As all this happened at once, the barbarians were stricken with fear, and turned tail; whereupon the Delphians came down from the mountains and killed a considerable number of them. The survivors made straight for Boeotia, and of these, I am informed, some saw other divine prodigies: they say that two superhuman warriors in heavy armour followed them, wreaking slaughter. The Delphians say that these were two local heroes, Phylacus and Autonous, whose precincts are near the temple: that of Phylacus is by the roadside, above the temple of Athene; and that of Autonous is near the Castalian spring beneath the summit of Hyampeia. The rocks which fell from Parnassus still survive in my time, lying in the grounds of Athene's temple, where they fell as they ploughed through the ranks of the barbarians. Such, then, was the retreat of these men from the temple.

Most of the details of this story are explicable in terms of human or natural agency, and it must be admitted that Herodotus does not actually say that he believes that the gods took a direct hand in the defence of their sanctuaries. But the concluding sentence certainly suggests that he accepts the substance of the story in the same uncritical spirit as he accepts that of the incredible parturitions which attended Xerxes's crossing of the Hellespont. His belief in divine intervention is established on an even firmer basis by another passage, in which we are informed that the battles of Plataea and Mycale took place on the same day, and that the combatants in the latter received news of the victory in the former before they engaged the enemy. We read:[54]

When, therefore, the Greeks were ready, they advanced towards the barbarians; and as they were marching, a rumour flew through the whole army, and a herald's wand appeared lying on the beach. The rumour which spread among them was this, that the Greeks had fought and conquered the army of Mardonius in Boeotia. Thus there is plain and substantial evidence of the operation of divine power, that on the same day on which the defeat at Plataea took place, and the battle of Mycale was about to be fought, news should reach the Greeks in the latter place, so that the army was inspired with much greater courage, and was more eager to meet danger.

This passage, together with Herodotus's statement about oracles, makes his attitude to the gods clear beyond reasonable doubt. He believed that they intervened in human affairs, and that when they did their actions could defy natural laws, and hence rational explanation.[55] But their actions are to be sharply distinguished from the many prodigies and marvels which are recounted for their entertainment value. The gods intervene with a purpose: they take a hand in events in order to ensure that these turn out according to their will. But they are not the authors of any long-term programme of history: their interest is rather in the behaviour of individuals, and of groups of men when these are acting in concert. The frailty of the human condition, which, as we have seen, is the underlying theme of the dialogue between Solon and Croesus, is a fact of which men need constantly to be reminded. The gods, from mixed motives of philanthropy and jealousy, are displeased when men enjoy too much success. Polycrates of Samos was extremely successful, but his success was viewed with alarm by the friendly king Amasis of Egypt, who sent him the following message:[56]

> It is pleasant to hear of the successes of a friend and ally; but yours are so great as to give me no pleasure, knowing as I do that the gods are jealous. For myself, and for those whose interests I have at heart, I would choose partial success and partial failure in our undertakings; thus we should pass through life with changing fortunes, rather than with uniform success. I know of no man, who, after a life of unbroken success, did not suffer an utterly wretched end.

But Polycrates was marked out by the gods in consequence of his success, and no artificial means which he or his friend might devise could undo the damage. His most valuable possession, which he threw away in order to avert divine jealousy, was returned to him in the belly of a fish; and the manner of his death was such that even Herodotus will not describe it in detail.

Success may come unbidden; but more often it comes through the exertions of men who are naturally superior to their fellows. If the gods are jealous of success itself, they are even more jealous of its excessive exploitation. *Hybris* ('arrogance') is always followed by *Nemesis* ('retribution'), whether in the short term, as in the case of the Spartans who invaded Tegea with a view to enslaving the population,[57] or in the long term, as in the case of king Xerxes, who flogged the Hellespont (which was a god) for destroying his first pontoon bridge,[58] and later suffered defeat at Salamis. The importance of the *hybris-nemesis* nexus in Herodotus's scheme of things has given rise to much speculation as to his relationship to the Athenian tragic poets, since this is also an essential ingredient of most of their plays. It is a historical fact that Herodotus struck up a friendship with Sophocles, and parallel situations arise in the plays and the *History*. The dominant theme of the *Persians* of Aeschylus is the downfall of a man who is the victim of overweening pride. The contemporary lyric poet Pindar also speaks of 'inability to stomach great success'.[59] The fifth century was an age in which the old religious beliefs were widely questioned by intellectuals, but the majority of the poets' audiences still accepted them, and few poets would risk loss of popularity by trying to disabuse them. Herodotus does not seek to detach history from the common literary tradition by divesting it of popular beliefs; but in his case we must probably add genuine religious belief to conformity to popular literary taste as the reason for his adherence. He seems sincerely to have believed that the gods are active in human affairs, and that there is a whole range of phenomena which cannot usefully be subjected to the tests of reason and probability; and in this belief he has many supporters at the present day.

The task of assessing the achievement of a pioneer is never easy; when he is an artist at once as gifted and as enigmatic as Herodotus the task becomes formidable. His debts to earlier and to contemporary writers in other genres are manifold. Homer was his spiritual forebear in that he described a great war in which warriors on both sides performed deeds of valour, and in which the gods took an active part (though Herodotus's heroes are richer in human foibles, and his gods less capricious and less personally involved than Homer's). Homer is also recalled when the epic scale and the episodic variety with which Herodotus treats his great theme are considered. His interest in man's problem of making for himself an acceptable life which does not violate divine ordinances relates him to the tragic poets of his own day, a relationship which he would probably have been prepared to admit. The originality of Herodotus lies in the manner in which he incorporated the tractable elements from disparate poetic traditions in a prose medium, and judiciously adapted them to a single contemporary theme—the confrontation of East and West. This theme inspired in Herodotus not poetic and imaginative impulses, but an insatiable appetite for travel and inquiry, with the purpose of finding out as much as he could about the Greek and barbarian worlds. He concludes that the differences between the two worlds are such that they could never live side by side in harmony. The Greeks accept no human being as all-powerful: such is the attitude of the Spartan envoys to the king of Persia, to whom they refuse to abase themselves.[60] The barbarians, and in particular the Persians, are ruled by absolute monarchs who feel compelled to carry out campaigns of conquest regardless of the risks involved: thus Xerxes dismisses the reasoned warnings of Artabanus with the sentiment that meticulous calculation leads inevitably to indecision, and that even the best-laid plans often misfire.[61] The two sides are thus bent upon a collision course as soon as their lands become conterminous. The great area over which the historian casts his net serves to underline both the alien character of all barbarians, and the obsession of the Persians with conquest, regardless of its rewards. On the Greek side, external vigilance and a minimum of internal discord are essential. Such was the world as Herodotus saw it and portrayed it, diversifying his narrative by recounting speeches and conversations, real or imaginary, and enriching it with stories which excite wonder or give rise to general reflections on the human condition.

CHAPTER 2

Thucydides

WHILE HERODOTUS was residing at Athens, he gave public readings from the completed portions of his history. One of these was attended by Thucydides, who is said to have left the performance in tears. In conversation afterwards with the young man's father, Herodotus attributed this display of emotion to his desire to learn, which had been over-stimulated by the wealth of information that had been placed before him. However this may be, when Thucydides later came to write history, he showed little inclination to imitate his predecessor. The difference in form, spirit and style between the two works is too great to be explicable solely by difference of environment, a factor which itself should not be exaggerated. Herodotus was subjected to most of the cultural influences that Thucydides underwent, but responded to different ones. One must therefore give precedence to character and temperament (though not, it should be emphasized, to different levels of intelligence) in an ultimate explanation of their extreme dissimilarity, and perhaps reinterpret the young listener's tears.

In one respect, however, background played an important part. The family of Thucydides's father Olorus had Thracian connections which brought him wealth through access to the rich gold and silver mines of that region. He was also related to the illustrious Philaidae, a family which included Miltiades, the victor of Marathon, and Cimon the conqueror of the Persians in the battle of the Eurymedon. With these advantages Thucydides could choose from several alternative media in which to exercise his considerable intellectual powers. We do not know how he spent his time until the outbreak of the Peloponnesian War in 431, when he was probably approaching his thirtieth year; but it is plain from the first sentence of his history that this event decided his vocation, and perhaps gave him the practical opportunity to study one of the main problems that had been

engaging his mind ever since he had listened to Herodotus—
that of the nature of history. Anticipating, with a foresight that is
in itself remarkable, that the war would be great, he resolved to
examine its origins and plot its course from beginning to end.
This was a completely new idea: until then the past, not the
present, had been regarded as the historian's proper province;
but Thucydides sought above all to discover the truth, which he
found to be difficult enough to extract from conflicting accounts
of contemporary events, and therefore impossibly elusive if
sought in those of the remoter past.

Active service in the war took him to his ancestral Thrace,
where he had the misfortune to be late in answering a call to
relieve Amphipolis in 424 from the assault of a Spartan force
under Brasidas. With his squadron of seven ships he secured
neighbouring Eion, but this success was not enough to save him
from disgrace. He was exiled, and probably lived out the rest of
his life abroad. He died soon after the war ended in 404 B.C.
Because he was an honest man, his experience of being both
participant and observer equipped him admirably for his task.
His narrative of battles and campaigns has a professional
authenticity, but is laudably free from the malice and self-
righteousness that the memoirs of generals so frequently contain,
and for which in the circumstances he might be excused.

Thucydides's *History of the Peloponnesian War* comprises
eight books, the last seven of which cover the first twenty years
of the war, the years 431 to 411 B.C. Book I is introductory: it
outlines the immediate and antecedent causes of the war and the
principles which the historian has adopted in his composition.
Book II takes us down to spring of the year 428, and includes the
Theban attack on Plataea, the Plague at Athens, the Funeral
Speech of Pericles and his death, and the naval exploits of the
Athenians under Phormio. Book III covers the next three years
down to spring 425, and includes the revolt of Mytilene, the
surrender of Plataea, the sedition in Corcyra, the first Athenian
expedition to Sicily and Athenian operations in the north-west.
In Book IV Spartan peace proposals are rejected and the
Athenians capture Pylos and Sphacteria and the island of Cythera;
but these successes are cancelled out by the exploits of Brasidas
in the north-east and the Battle of Delium. Book V begins in the
spring of 422, and contains the operations that led to the death

of Cleon and Brasidas and the conclusion of the Peace of Nicias; these are followed by the Argive policy of Alcibiades, and the Athenian capture of Melos in 416. Books VI and VII cover the years 415 to 413, and describe the Sicilian Expedition from beginning to end. Book VIII carries the renewed war in the Aegean theatre down to 411, and breaks off abruptly. It is certain that the work was not completed, since Thucydides declares his intention to follow the war to its conclusion; moreover Books V and VIII, which lack speeches and are in other respects less polished than the remaining books, are probably unfinished. Their contents may explain this. In the case of Book V, the first part of the war ends with the Peace of Nicias near the beginning: it is thus quite likely, in spite of the historian's reproval of those who regard the period during which Sparta and Athens were not in direct conflict as one of 'peace', that the events in Book V seemed to him to require less urgent attention when he was revising. The unpolished state of Book VIII is easily explained by the fact that it is the last book, which the author did not reach, for reasons we shall never know, in his revision. It is, however, certain that he survived the war and composed certain important passages in the narrative after the final defeat; and most scholars agree that many of the speeches were written some considerable time after the narrative which surrounds them. A partial explanation of the unsatisfactory state of the work may therefore be that Thucydides recorded events down to 411, then applied himself to the task of writing speeches for the whole history, a task on which he was engaged until the end of the war, which he survived only long enough to add a few further reflective passages. However, this still leaves unanswered the question why he stopped so abruptly in mid-campaign in 411; but on this point conjecture is useless.

The historian's obligation to assign events to their time of occurrence was ignored by Herodotus but accepted by Hecataeus, whose concern with genealogy rendered some chronological framework essential, and later by Thucydides's contemporary Hellanicus. The latter was, indeed, more a chronicler than a historian, so far as we can deduce, and therefore has no place in this study. He used the year as his unit of time, and identified each according to the name of the annual Athenian *archon eponymus*. But the Greek calendar was anything but accurate:

there was a confusion between the solar and the lunar year, which made precise dating impossible. Thucydides chose to refer the reader to a fixed point in time—the beginning of the war—and to count the solar years from that point, dividing them into seasons and referring to shorter periods with such descriptive phrases as 'when the corn was ripe' and 'when the summer was at its height' (in other words when it was hottest, a fairly accurate delimitation in a Mediterranean climate). This method of chronology was well suited to a narrative in which military operations played so large a part, and provided a sound practical framework in which to view the sequence of events.

The last topic to deal with concerning the composition of the *History* is his *modus operandi*. Thucydides gives us virtually no access to his workshop, and no insight into his methods of research or the criteria on which he chooses his final version of any particular episode. After once assuring us that his task has been difficult, he spares us the agony of his gestation and presents us with a progeny that bears no signs of a struggle. No informants are named, and no reasons given for choosing one version of a story rather than another. Up to the time of his exile we may assume autopsy of much that he narrates; but he does not tell us when he was an eyewitness and when he was not. Even in the narrative of an event in which he is known to have participated, the fall of Amphipolis, there is no perceptible increase in vividness or detail: such effects, of which he was the master when he chose to use them, he reserved for events of especial importance, like the Plague at Athens and the battle in the Great Harbour of Syracuse. After his exile he had access to a wider selection of sources, but while admitting that he obtained information from the Peloponnesians, he remains silent as to their individual identity. In a lesser historian this editorializing uniformity might reasonably be viewed with suspicion; but Thucydides is rarely to be found at fault in the matter either of judgment or bias. By thus relieving the reader of the burden of discrimination as to fact, he leaves him with his mind free to concentrate on weightier issues.

Thucydides's decision to write contemporary history enabled him to satisfy his intellectual appetite; but the precise manner in which he dealt with the various historical problems was dictated by two of the educative influences which enjoyed vogue in his day. The first of these was the Sophistic movement, the temper of which was established by the dictum of its founder Protagoras —'Man is the measure of all things'. The teachings of the Sophists aimed in general to encourage men to have confidence in their own mental powers, even to the extent of throwing back the frontiers of Zeus's Olympian kingdom. On a practical level, they undertook, for a fee, to enrich their pupils' lives by teaching them proficiency in a wide range of accomplishments. The more unscrupulous sophists exaggerated their powers and so brought the movement into disrepute; but its influence was, on balance, progressive and beneficial. In the political field, they concentrated on the spoken word, with the purpose of enabling citizens in a democratic society to participate by argument and persuasion in the deliberations of its sovereign assembly. They taught that in every dispute at least two viewpoints must exist, so that at least two arguments must be considered before a case can be decided.

Thucydides was profoundly influenced by this mode of thought. Political speeches form a large part of his history; and while their original inclusion may have been due mainly to literary convention, the form in which the arguments are cast in most of them owes much to sophistic method. In the examination of historical causes and grievances this method had much to recommend it, since it allowed a balanced and impartial presentation of the case for each of the contending sides. In a more general sense it encouraged open discussion, on a pragmatic level, of political and moral issues unimpeded by the prejudice imposed by custom or religious belief; and this was a further aspect of sophistic teaching that was to Thucydides's taste. Indeed, it is with his many reflections on war in general, and the Peloponnesian War in particular, viewed as an aspect of human experience, that much of this discussion will be concerned.

The other influence which coloured Thucydides's attitude to history was the growing science of medicine. The considerable volume of medical literature that was in circulation in his time embraced a wide range of topics more or less concerned with the physical and mental condition of man. Conclusions as to the identity of diseases were reached by the careful observation of symptoms; comparison with previously observed cases was followed by treatment where this was known, and a prognosis of the patient's likely future health was made; and, most relevant to the study of history, particular attention was paid to the conditions and environment in which the different illnesses occurred. The possibility of applying such methods to history was not lost on Herodotus, but he never used them systematically. To Thucydides their attraction was irresistible; and as a corrective to one of the more sinister consequences of sophistic teaching—the proposition that absolute truth is unattainable, because of the two-sided nature of all problems—their influence was salutary. The Hippocratics, as this anonymous body of medical writers is called, by affirming the attainability of practically useful knowledge by empirical means, gave Thucydides a sound foundation on which to build an entirely new conception of historiography.

The historian's duty is to discover the truth and to convey its significance to his readers: this is Thucydides's basic proposition. Its consequences and implications are enucleated in a crucial passage in Book I, in which the substance of the argument is as follows:[1]

> Most men receive and pass on information in an uncritical spirit. Hence most Athenians are misinformed even concerning comparatively recent events in their own history; and because historical events are legitimate material for poets and others, who are more concerned to adorn and exaggerate than to present them truthfully, they become irretrievably lost to posterity. Therefore no realistic historian who cares for the truth will attempt to describe events of which he does not either have first-hand knowledge or reliable informants whose accounts he can check. This has been my principle, though it has not made my task easy. It has produced a work which will give but little pleasure to those who seek mere romance and sensationalism; but if it is of some use to those who wish to have a clear view of the past, and through it a guide to the future, since human nature is a constant factor, I shall be satisfied. It is composed as a possession for ever, not as an occasional piece for a single hearing.

Two important points are raised here. Contemporary history is the only history worthy of the name, because it is the only form in which the historian has a reasonable chance of discovering the truth. In practice Thucydides makes a number of excursions into past history, but apart from one instance which he uses as an illustration of false opinions held about past events,[2] he concerns himself only with generally accepted facts about earlier periods which he uses to highlight a particular point. The second matter concerns his purpose in writing history. It has often been suggested that he is here claiming a specific didactic power: that men of affairs who read his history will be able to shape the future by observing the occurrence of parallel situations to their own in his pages, and avoiding the mistakes of the past. But Thucydides makes no such claims, and thus warns us not to carry our comparison with the Hippocratics too far. He offers no cures where none are to be found; and this is a property which human nature and the Plague at Athens have in common. Nowhere is the influence of the Hippocratics more plainly visible than in his detailed, clinically technical description of the symptoms of the disease which ravaged Athens for two summers in 430 and 429;[3] but on the subject of treatment, he merely observes that none of the remedies applied at the time was universally efficacious. Moreover he gives no details of these remedies, but adds that eventual recovery seemed to depend more upon chance than medical care. His sole purpose in giving precise details is to afford the means of future recognition. No less pessimistic in tone, and for the same reason, is the famous excursus in Book III on the effects of revolution and war.[4] As an analysis of the symptoms of a malady it has obvious points of contact with the description of the plague; but it is of greater significance from the historical point of view because it describes a commoner and more destructive condition of man. War destroys prosperity and upsets human values. Qualities that were formerly esteemed are despised and identified with their baser counterparts: circumspection, moderation and intelligence are equated with cowardice, spinelessness and laziness. Revolutionaries and conspirators become the most respected of men, while those who uphold the institutions by which political stability is maintained—the laws, the gods and family ties—are held in no regard. Greed, ambition and personal animosities are given unbridled licence, so that calculations based on the normal course of events in a settled world are no longer of any assistance in predicting the future. Compared with this picture of the world at odds with itself, Athens in the toils of the Plague is like a microcosm, experiencing the same symptoms of social and moral disintegration but on a smaller scale of space and time. As the disease takes hold of the city, religious observances are the first to be disregarded, especially those concerning burial: men are dying in such large numbers that there is no time to perform the proper obsequies. But on the psychological level also religion loses ground, because men see that the impious and the devout are being struck down indiscriminately. Human law likewise has no power to withstand the pervading moral corruption that follows in the wake of social upheaval. Men show greater audacity, openly doing things that they formerly took pains to conceal, and ignoring possible penalties on the assumption that they will not live to pay them. For the same reason, they seek the pleasure of the moment rather than the long-term course of honour. The only differences between this and the previous description are the speed of the disaster and its immediate physical consequences: otherwise the symptoms are recognizably similar, and are governed by the one factor that is constant in all such situations—human nature. It is upon the immutability of man's collective character, and hence the predictability of his reactions to classic situations, that Thucydides rests part of his claim for the permanent value of his history.

No less important than the interest in human pathology seen in the above passages is the study of the active elements in man's character which can become the cause of wars and seditions. Thucydides distinguishes two in particular: the desire to dominate other men and the sanguine hope that leads them to undertake enterprises beyond their means. Both these ideas are found in Book IV, in the first speech of the Syracusan leader Hermocrates, referring to the threatened interference of the Athenians in Sicilian affairs. Instead of deploring their rapacity, he admits to a certain understanding of their motives: it is a part of human nature always to rule over a neighbour who yields; therefore those who do not wish to be dominated by others should take the necessary measures to provide for their defence.[5] (In cases where lack of resources rules out such a course, the weak have no choice but to yield to the strong; but this raises the problem of the exercise of power, which will be considered later.) Secondly, irrational hopes are the mainspring of many human actions. Possible gains, as Hermocrates says, often seem greater than the dangers involved.[6] This characteristic is well illustrated in the Athenian debate in which Nicias tries to discourage the assembly from undertaking the Sicilian expedition by exaggerating the strength of the armament that would be needed. Far from having the desired effect, his advice reassures them: with such numbers as he advocates, failure seems out of the question.[7] In this mood of elation and optimism, nobody contemplates the greater loss in the event of defeat. In another passage, at the beginning of Book VIII,[8] the Spartans, normally the most phlegmatic of men, react to the news of the Athenian defeat in Sicily with premature visions of dominion over the Greek world, thus displaying the two characteristics at the same time. Irrational hopes and desire for conquest are a destructive combination: how can men ever live in peace? By ensuring that they are strong, and by abstaining from injuring their equals at a time when they are enjoying a temporary advantage. Such is the advice that Thucydides puts in the mouths of the Corinthian envoys when they warn the Athenians to reject the Corcyrean alliance which led to the war: do not disturb the balance of power as an aggressor, or allow it to be disturbed by passively neglecting the measures necessary for self-defence.[8(a)]

Human desires are proportionately more violent and irrational as the number of men deliberating together is increased. At Athens the Popular Assembly was sovereign, and was therefore ultimately responsible for the aggressive policies which led to the Peloponnesian War. Every male citizen over the age of eighteen had the right, indeed the duty, to exercise a direct vote on all major matters of policy. Thucydides was therefore quite right to make its character and behaviour central to his view of the war. The people, he says, are ignorant, and therefore gullible; their emotions are easily roused, and they are prone to act upon them precipitately; they do not deliberate in the true sense, but adjudicate between the performances of the several orators who address them.[9] The effect of this latter weakness upon the less scrupulous politicians is anything but salutary, for they tend to advocate those policies which they think will please the people rather than those which will benefit the state. This serious fault of Athenian democracy was overcome only when the assembly was held in voluntary subjection by a man with the force of personality to impose unpopular but necessary policies upon it. Such a man was Pericles, for whom Thucydides had a special regard. Democracy under Pericles was in one sense a paradox, for it was in reality the rule of the first citizen, who led the people instead of following them. But he ruled them freely: they could dispense with his services any time they chose; yet such was his moral ascendancy over them that he was able to implement the most unpopular policies without losing their trust.[10] This, to Thucydides, is an ideal democracy; but there was only one Pericles. His successors, lesser men, were in constant danger, for while the assembly was easy to persuade, it habitually made scapegoats of speakers whose proposals misfired, 'as if,' as Thucydides says, 'they had not themselves ratified them.'[11] In fact, demagogues were afflicted with two kinds of fear, which drew them in opposite directions. The first caused them to be over-cautious, and was a major reason for the desultory nature of much of the first part of the war (the so-called Ten Years' or Archidamian War, 431–421). Because of it the Athenians missed a good opportunity of capturing Megara; and their most brilliant success of this period, the capture of Pylos and Sphacteria, came about by chance. Earlier than this Demosthenes, and later Nicias, were afraid to face the Assembly after suffering defeat, the latter even ill-advisedly delaying his decision to leave Sicily because he feared the Athenians more than the enemy.

The other fear which constantly goaded Athenian politicians was related to the standing of their rivals. Measures were never proposed *in vacuo*, but were conceived in the context of political competition. It was also a legitimate part of the game to discredit a rival, and to oppose him even when he was acting in the state's best interests. In a famous passage which serves as an epitaph to Pericles, Thucydides makes this sweeping indictment of his political heirs:[12]

> His successors, being more on a level with one another, and each striving for supremacy, pandered to the pleasures of the mob and betrayed the state's interests. As a result many mistakes were made, as happens when a city is great and rules an empire; and in particular there was the disaster of the Sicilian expedition. This was not so much an error of judgment as to the strength of the enemy, as a case of subsequent mishandling by the home government, which failed to make adequate provision for it after it had set out, but instead became involved in campaigns of mutual denigration in private contests for political leadership. In so doing the politicians concerned impaired the efficiency of the military operations, and thus for the first time involved the city in their own confusion of interests.

None of Pericles's successors could so dominate the *demos* that he could pursue the best policy without regard for its popularity. With the death of Pericles Athenian statesmanship lost all its consistency and all its poise, because power was constantly changing hands and politicians were always looking over their shoulders. The Sicilian expedition was not ill-conceived: it was never given a chance of success because political rivalry deprived the city of the services of the one man who might have made it succeed—Alcibiades, who was driven into the enemy camp by the slanders of his enemies.

Where does Thucydides stand in the political spectrum? Appealing to the several scornful references he makes to the Athenian mob and its excesses, commentators have too readily identified him as a confirmed oligarch. At first sight this opinion is corroborated in the first sentence of a passage in Book VIII,[13] in which he passes the following judgment on the oligarchic revolution of 411 B.C.: 'This is absolutely the first time during my life that the Athenians seem to me to have adopted a good constitution.' But we should also read the prelude and the sequel: the former is a statement that important democratic elements survived the revolution—the assembly still met frequently and appointed officials; and in the latter he describes the new constitution as 'a balanced distribution of power between the few and the many'. This may be compared with the words ascribed to the Syracusan democrat Athenagoras:[14] 'I say firstly that "the people" is the name of the whole state, "the few" is that of a part; that the best guardians of property are the wealthy, that our best counsellors are the intelligent, while the populace are best fitted to listen to their deliberations and decide: and it is in a democracy that these three elements have an equal share and an individual part to play.' To those who may doubt whether Thucydides would make a Syracusan demagogue the spokesman of his own views, it is pertinent to point out that the passage quoted has a moderate and balanced tone that highlights it and distinguishes it in a speech which otherwise contains mostly bad advice.

Thus Thucydides probably favoured a balanced constitution; but the paucity of evidence as to his views has its own significance. Taken as a whole, this leads to the conclusion that he was prepared to accept any constitution that worked in practice and promoted the state's prosperity. The government under Pericles was neither democratic nor oligarchic, but monarchic; but it worked, and therefore won his approval. He was not interested, as some of his contemporaries and successors were, in the theory of constitutions. Indeed, it has been correctly observed that he was more interested in foreign policy than in domestic politics, and gives us a very incomplete picture of the political scene at Athens. But in relation to this particular war, the fact that the Athenians chose to be governed by a democracy had a decisive effect on her policy towards her neighbours, and it is for this reason that he devotes so much space to discussion of its character.

The Peloponnesian War involved more cities and lasted longer than any previous war. It began in 431 and ended in 404 B.C. Although a formal peace was signed in 421, Thucydides realistically ignores it and counts the years of uneasy quiet as if the war was still going on. He precedes his narrative of the events which led to the outbreak of hostilities by a review of earlier history, called the *Archaeologia*.[15] The main purpose of this review, in fact its *raison d'être*, is to show the inferiority in size and destructiveness of all previous wars. Even the Trojan War, he assures us, could not have matched the present conflict in scale, for ancient cities were relatively poor in material resources. Before that time King Minos had shown the way to prosperity and empire by taking control of the sea, which Thucydides regards as the key to progress. Minos largely suppressed piracy and thus gave added stimulus to trade, which in turn increased wealth. But this was still not great enough in Agamemnon's time to enable him to provide adequately for his forces. Hence the length of the Trojan War: the army had to expend its energies in providing for its physical needs, resorting to brigandage and even agriculture (Thucydides is supplementing Homer with other sources); so that the Trojans were able easily to ward off the contingents which actually engaged them in battle, and to prolong the war to ten years.

Greece went through an unsettled period after the Trojan War, but subsequently a fresh influx of wealth coincided with a renascence of maritime activity, both peaceful and hostile. Sea-power emerges as the *leitmotif* which links earlier with more recent history, while incidentally serving as an illustration of the instruction that can be derived from a study of the past. After the Persian War (which, like the other earlier wars, was inferior in length and in destructiveness to the Peloponnesian War), the Athenians resolved to take to the sea; and their rise to power is traceable from that decision. Subsequently discontented subject-allies gave them the practice in war that put them in a state of preparedness for the great contest that was to come.

In his narrative Thucydides deals with the *Pentekontaetia*, the 'half-century' which separated the Persian from the Peloponnesian War (479 to 431, to be precise), in chapters 89 to 118 of Book I, having briefly summarized these years in chapters 18 and 19 at the end of his *Archaeologia*. Although these two excursuses cover consecutive periods, there is a good reason for their separation. Thucydides, as has been said, was convinced that serious historical writing should, in so far as it is concerned with events, be concentrated on the present. We may therefore believe that it was in reluctant acceptance of necessity that he wrote his account of the *Pentekontaetia*, and inserted it after his description of the immediate causes of the war, in order to provide his readers with a broader aetiology, with the growth of Athenian power as its central theme. Not surprisingly, historians have found his account of these years deficient in many respects; and we can sympathize with their frustration the more when we recall that this period has fared badly at the hands of other ancient historians. But when considered in the light of its limited purpose, and of Thucydides's own mistrust of non-contemporary sources, his narrative of these years, jejune and incomplete though it is, is seen to provide an essential link between the past and the present.

The purpose of the *Archaeologia* is quite different: it is concerned not with amplifying the historical background, but with making certain generalizations about the growth of civilization, and showing how Athens has followed a pattern of progress that is comparable with those of earlier empires. By placing it at the beginning, Thucydides gives us an early insight into his history's novel character, and an illustration of his personal conception of the proper purpose of history, which follows immediately after it. This treatment of earlier history is in no way stultified by his statement that contemporary events are the proper subject of serious history, because he is concerned in the *Archaeologia* only

with generally accepted facts, for instance that there was a
Cretan thalassocracy, and a Trojan War, upon which he builds
hypotheses. Society progresses through the increase of wealth,
which can be achieved to a certain degree through commerce; but
in order to reach a higher level of prosperity small communities
must become united. This can happen when a single state out-
strips its neighbours, who then submit to her, either willingly
or under duress. Minos built his empire in this way; it was
through his superior power that Agamemnon was able to convoke
the mighty host of Aulis (not because of any suitors' oaths—mere
romantic nonsense); and the Athenians won their hegemony by
similarly pursuing an active foreign policy based on sea power.
In the *Archaeologia* Thucydides names Minos and Agamemnon
as if they were real persons (a question which he was in no better
position to answer than we are), but in fact he was not primarily
interested in their historical identity: for him it was merely
convenient to use the names popularly ascribed to the leaders of
two civilizations which he (and we) regard as historical. But
Thucydides's most striking achievement in the *Archaeologia*
consists in the first instance in his application of reason to
mythology, and secondly in his discovery of the operation of
general historical trends in events which were thought to be the
material of epic and tragic poetry. Moreover, most of his conclusions are in broad agreement with the opinion of modern
scholarship on the early history of Greece, which is able to draw
upon archaeological evidence to which Thucydides could not
have had access. There could be no greater tribute to his breadth
of vision, and to the general validity of the theory he pro-
pounds.

The most important development in the *Pentekontaetia* is the
growth of Athenian power, which we are now in a better position
to study intelligently. It began immediately after the departure
of the Persians. The Athenians had to rebuild their ruined city,
but their large navy was still intact. Sparta was immediately
suspicious, for this was now the only force in the Greek world
that was in a state of war-readiness; and the rebuilding of the
walls of Athens, in which her citizens were now engaged with
characteristic vigour, seemed an added threat to peace, because
it would deprive land powers of the means of effective retaliation
against Athens if she chose to use her navy for hostile purposes.

'The Spartans,' Thucydides says, 'were urged by their allies, who were afraid of the size of the Athenian fleet.'[16] With the insight he has given us into the power that a large navy can give a state, we can readily understand their alarm. But Thucydides goes out of his way to show that these fears were unfounded, and that the maintenance of the fleet was part of a plan of continued hostility to Persia. The author of this policy was Themistocles, who enjoys a place in Thucydides's esteem second only to Pericles, and emerges from this debate with reason on his side. He is made to justify the rebuilding of the walls with the argument that this would put Athens on an equal footing with those cities that had been undamaged in the war. The Spartans, by contrast, 'concealing their suspicions and intentions from the Athenians', use the specious argument that a fortified Athens would provide the Persians with a defensible base from which to fight if they should invade Greece in the future.[17] Themistocles is allowed to reveal the other, and more famous, side of his character when he temporizes with the Spartans until the walls have been built to a defensible height; but we leave the episode with the firm impression that although Themistocles had supplied Athens with the means of empire, he took no hand in their exploitation. He disappears, and is supplanted in Thucydides's account by the man whose career the historian plainly regards as the activating cause of the Athenian empire—Pausanias, the Spartan victor of Plataea.[18] This man abused the trust placed in him by the Ionian Greeks, 'behaving more like a tyrant than a general', and caused them to turn to the Athenians and invite them to assume the leadership of the proposed mission of revenge against Persia. Thucydides's description of the Athenian acceptance of the leadership could hardly be more colourless:[19] 'The Athenians listened to their arguments, and applied their minds to dealing with the situation and to arranging matters in general as seemed best to them.' (Not 'they seized their chance of empire with enthusiasm', or some such hint of imperialist intentions.) But the immediate sequel is of the greatest significance: Sparta, embarrassed by the career of Pausanias and confident in the ability of the Athenians to lead the new alliance, gave up her claims to leadership and withdrew. Unless Thucydides is guilty of inconsistency, we are presumably to understand that the Spartans were strongly predisposed to abandon all overseas commitments, and found in the career of Pausanias an incentive to do so powerful enough to cause them to forget their earlier suspicions.

From Thucydides's narrative it is plain that the effect of this Spartan decision upon the Athenians was immediate and profound. The original purpose of the proposed alliance, a war of revenge upon Persia, now became for them a mere 'pretext' (πρόσχημα)[20] for raising money and centralizing power. The repressive nature of the series of actions which converted the Delian League into an Athenian empire is underlined rather than concealed: Naxos was 'enslaved contrary to the agreement';[21] and the Athenians 'exacted the tribute punctiliously and acted oppressively in imposing compulsion upon men who were unaccustomed to it and did not wish to submit to hardship'. But he concludes this section by observing that the allies had only themselves to blame, for most of them, by choosing to contribute money instead of ships, had left the instruments of power in the hands of the Athenians.[22] We are reminded of the dictum of Hermocrates, which in the present situation applies both to Athens's allies and to Sparta: the latter initially, and the former by a gradual process, abdicated from power; the Athenians merely seized the proffered chance, and in so doing acted in accordance with human nature.

But the question of why Sparta withdrew and Athens became imperialist cannot be left there: Thucydides requires us to take account of a further differentiating factor—national character. This is one of the main themes of the first speech of the Corinthians to the Spartans,[23] the dramatic date of which is over forty years after the first Athenian steps towards empire; but national character does not change much, and the Spartans were already aware of the difference. The Athenians are audacious, revolutionary, and generally fond of activity; the Spartans underestimate their own strength, and are consequently conservative and slow to action even when their vital interests demand it. By attributing this portrayal of radically differing characters to outsiders (the Corinthians) rather than making it part of a mutually recriminative dialogue between Spartans and Athenians, Thucydides shows plainly that he does not intend us to assume the characteristics to be exaggerated. Later, on the Athenian side, we find their own leaders describing them in the same terms. In the debate on the Sicilian expedition, Alcibiades urges them that to act contrary to their nature would be to court ruin through stagnation and decay;[24] while Nicias, who speaks like a Spartan, renounces all hope of changing the Athenian character by means of general arguments against imperialism, and relies instead upon particular practical objections to this enterprise, though with no more success.[25] In Pericles's hands the Athenian character was idealized: desire for fame, honour, renown, glory and a place in history are variously cited as reasons for their ceaseless activity. This Periclean view, which is given at length in the Funeral Speech,[26] is further coloured by the idea that Athenian rule is beneficial to her subjects, so that in that speech we have a picture of universal contentment which is belied by the facts of history and contradicted elsewhere by the same speaker. But once again Thucydides draws us beneath the surface of things. What is it that the Athenians really delight in? Freedom—but freedom of a peculiarly pure kind. He describes it during his narrative of the oligarchic revolution: 'It was difficult for the Athenian *demos*, on the centenary of the expulsion of the tyrants, to renounce their freedom, which had consisted in not merely being subjects of no master, but for over half that time to have enjoyed dominion over others.'[27] The purest form of freedom consists in being able to do what you will both with yourself and to others. It was unfortunate that the Athenians chose to pursue this ideal in Greece. The Persians before them had made the mistake of underestimating the intensity of the Greek passion for personal liberty, as Herodotus demonstrated. Thucydides takes a less romantic view: indeed, instead of the heart-warming stories of staunch loyalty to the cause of Greek freedom and the chivalrous resolve to die rather than face slavery, his cold analysis of human nature leads him to conclude that it is natural for the weaker to yield to the stronger. This principle is seen in operation in his narrative of the *Pentekontaetia*, with the submission of successive states to superior Athenian power. But Sparta illustrates a different though related principle: Thucydides is concerned to show how she never allows herself to be outstripped by Athens, and thus maintains herself in the position to demand 'justice', a quality which can only exist between equals. Yet above all this there remains his statement that Sparta declared war through fear of Athenian power and ambition, being *forced* to do so. The idea

of her possible submission is not entertained: it is as if Thucydides expects his readers to have studied Herodotus.

This discussion of Athenian imperialism leads naturally to the
consideration in a more general context of Thucydides's attitude
to historical causality. Herodotus shows his awareness of its
importance in his introductory sentence; but his history has run
its full course before the causes of the war become fully apparent.
Thucydides discusses them comprehensively at an early stage.
In this discussion he makes a novel and significant contribution
to the study of history by distinguishing between original and
immediate causes. Applying this distinction to the war, he says:
'The true cause of the war, but the one given least publicity, was
the growing strength of Athens, which caused alarm to the
Spartans and forced them to fight. . . .'[28] Contrasting with this
the immediate causes, he continues: '. . . but the publicly alleged
grounds of complaint on both sides, through which they broke
the treaty and declared war, were as follows:' and he relates the
affairs of Corcyra and Potidaea. Prompted once more by his
interest in psychology, Thucydides becomes the first historian to
draw his readers beneath the surface of events. He implies that
Sparta would never have declared war under the influence of
the immediate causes alone, but viewed them against an Athenian
record of aggressiveness, through which Spartan minds had
become conditioned to the eventuality of war. It is for this
reason that he feels obliged, in spite of his distaste for non-
contemporary history, to trace the growth of Athenian power
from its beginnings; while it is the general character of Athenian
imperialism rather than the inciting causes that provides the main
theme in the speeches of the Corinthians and Athenians to the
Spartans, which form the central tableau of this section.

Two aspects of this Thucydidean treatment of causes are
worth considering: its general validity when applied to great
wars, and its application in his history. As a general distinction
it is a useful corrective to superficiality, when applied with
discrimination. Thus, when considering the causes of the Second
World War, we are warned not to stop short at the German
invasions of Austria, Czechoslovakia and Poland, nor even at the
rise of Hitler and the growth of the German war machine, but to
consider the effect of the Treaty of Versailles, which by its harsh
terms sowed the seeds of resentment that found expression in the

resurgence of militant German nationalism. It is reasonable to examine all great upheavals as complex problems, and to be suspicious of the obvious. But not all wars can profitably be treated in this way, simply because for some hidden or long-standing causes do not exist. Mutual misunderstanding and failure in communication were primary causes of the First Punic War; while, in wars involving nations with absolute rulers, the whim of a monarch may be the only discernible cause.

But in the case of the Peloponnesian War most scholars accept Thucydides's analysis as substantially valid. The inciting causes concerned chiefly Corinthian interests, and constituted no direct threat to Sparta; but Sparta, as the leader of a league, had responsibilities to her allies which she could ignore only at the cost of isolation. Assuming, as he does without comment, that she would not accept Athenian dominion, he concludes that she had no alternative but to fight. This much we may accept without demur. But, in giving the greatest weight to this antecedent cause, Thucydides fails to assess the relative importance of the immediate causes. The famous Megarian decree, by which the city of Megara was forbidden to trade in the ports of the Athenian empire, is named by all other ancient sources as the cause of the war. Most modern commentators have decried the shallowness of all but Thucydides; and their judgment must be endorsed to the extent that psychological causes must take precedence. It is nevertheless surprising that the Megarian decree and its effect are not allowed a place in his narrative commensurate with the Corcyrean and Potidaean episodes. This is especially perplexing since its annulment is cited by the Spartans in their final appeal to the Athenians as one of the conditions on which peace could yet be secured.[29] We thus receive from Thucydides the impression that it had propaganda value only; and yet compared with the Athenian alliance with Corcyra, which was defensive in character and remote from Sparta, the intention to bring her neighbour Megara swiftly to her knees by means of economic sanctions, which was what the decree implied, might well be thought to have constituted a greater danger to her security. Yet Thucydides had a good reason for playing down the Megarian decree. The opponents of Pericles, whose brain-child it was, rendered him responsible for the war by his refusal to abandon it; but Thucydides, like Pericles, saw that the removal of individual grievances could only postpone the inevitable conflict, and chose this way of refuting the popular fallacy.

In addition to its importance in the examination of causes, psychology plays a crucial part in the narrative of events. Thucydides is constantly as concerned to show the effects of events upon men's minds as to narrate the events themselves. This preoccupation adds special colour to some of his best battle narratives. The following is an extract from one of the finest of these, his description of the final battle in the great harbour of Syracuse:[30]

> Meanwhile the two armies on shore, while victory hung in the balance, were a prey to the most agonising and conflicting emotions, the natives thirsting for more glory than they had already won, while the invaders feared to find themselves in an even worse plight than before. Since Athenian fortunes depended upon their fleet, their fear for the outcome was like nothing they had ever felt; while their view of the struggle was necessarily as uneven as the battle itself. Close to the scene of the action and not all looking at the same point at once, some saw their friends victorious and took courage, and fell to calling upon heaven not to deprive them of salvation, while others who had their eyes turned upon the losers wailed and cried aloud, and although spectators, were more overcome than the actual combatants. Others again were gazing at some spot where the battle was evenly disputed; as the strife was protracted without a decision, they suffered the worst agony of all as their bodies flinched in vicarious terror at what they saw, as safety and destruction were each a close matter. In short, in that one Athenian army, as long as the sea fight remained doubtful, there was every sound to be heard at once, shrieks, cheers, 'We win', 'We lose', and all the other manifold exclamations that a great host would utter in a great peril.

As any expectant father will confirm, powerlessness to act effectively in a crisis whose outcome is nevertheless of the greatest importance to him imposes a tremendous mental strain on the spectator. In the above battle the spectators are armed men who are not able to fight because there is insufficient room for them on the ships. Their emotional involvement in the battle is therefore as great as it could be, and they follow their comrades through the very motions of combat. Local conditions also play a part; the confined space enhances the general impression of violent activity, to which confusion is added by the scattered disposition of the spectators on the shore around the harbour.

Their intense preoccupation with the outcome has drawn them to the water's edge, from where they can see only a small section of the battle. Moreover, whatever tactics were planned by the opposing admirals beforehand, none appears from Thucydides's description, which immediately precedes this passage, to have been applied uniformly in the battle itself. Thus under his pen the harbour of Syracuse becomes a great cauldron in which human emotions seethe, mingle and agonize in response to the fluctuating fortunes of a battle whose outcome was a vital personal issue to everyone present.

By thus observing psychological factors and making them an essential part of his narrative of great events, Thucydides shows an originality, the extent of which is best measured by comparing the above description with Herodotus's account of the battle of Salamis, a contest of comparable importance fought in somewhat similar conditions. Herodotus's description is 'Homeric', consisting of a collection of encounters between individual captains and including a divine epiphany. Throughout the whole narrative there is no direct reference to the mental state of the combatants, their fear, their anguish, their hope or their dismay. Like Homer's heroes, they appear to be possessed by a super-human battle-fury which has overcome all normal emotions; while the spectators, of which there were many at Salamis, are banished completely from the stage.

In certain other battle-narratives Thucydides devotes several sentences independently of the narrative of the action to the emotional reactions of the participants and the conditions which induce them. In his narrative of the Theban attack on Plataea at the beginning of Book II, the Plataeans are at first terrified by the news that their market-place has been occupied by Theban troops; and the darkness of night causes them to believe that the enemy numbers are greater than they are. Later they discover their actual strength and form a plan in which the darkness will be used to their own advantage, combining with their superior knowledge of the city to destroy the enemy's morale. In the battle which follows, darkness, driving rain and mud, the cries of the Plataean women and slaves, who bombard the intruders with stones and sherds, all contribute to the rout. Later in the same book, Phormio's first naval victory in the Gulf of Corinth (429 B.C.) is a battle of wits and relative confidence from beginning to end.[31] The Peloponnesian admirals fear Athenian seamanship in spite of their own superior numbers, and adopt a defensive formation from the start, arranging their ships like the spokes of a wheel with prows facing outwards. Here the local condition on which Phormio counts for assistance is the dawn wind which blows up from the west. This he proposes to exploit by a tactic of his own. He leads his squadron in single line around the enemy circle, always threatening to ram their jutting, stationary prows, which withdraw inwards, their captains lacking the confidence to call the Athenian bluff. As they concede more and more water, they fall foul upon one another and upon the reserve ships stationed in the inner pool, and, without the necessary seamanship to extricate themselves, they are further disturbed by the rising swell and are forced to ward off their neighbours with their oars; in the course of which there are brisk exchanges of abuse, which prevent them from hearing whatever orders their captains may be issuing.

As a fourth and final example of the psychological element in Thucydidean narrative we may take his account of the Athenian assault on Sphacteria in Book IV.[32] The Athenian general Demosthenes decides not to allow the Spartan garrison to engage his men in hand-to-hand combat, in which they are markedly superior: instead he sets fire to the brushwood surrounding their position, and unleashes against them his light-armed troops, who harry them with darts, stones and arrows. The confused onset of the wood-ash, smoke, and assorted missiles, with a swift-moving enemy striking and making off almost in one movement, creates havoc among the Spartan hoplites, whose training has assumed a formal confrontation with a visible enemy.

To these more spectacular examples of the portrayal of mental reaction to situation may be added many other incidental references to the psychological factor. The Spartan king Archidamus, before the first of the annual Peloponnesian raids, advises his countrymen not to ravage Attic soil, but to keep it 'as a hostage',[33] since ravaging it will only harden the enemy's resistance. In addition to general reflections on the collective nature of man of the kind implied by this example, we find admirable portrayals of the state of mind of individuals and groups of men at a particular time. In 425 the Athenians had sent a fleet of twenty ships to Sicily in response to requests for help from Leontini; but Syracuse had acted decisively and persuaded the Sicilians, Leontini included, to present a united front against all outsiders. The Athenians had no alternative but to return home with their mission unaccomplished. But elsewhere Athens had been enjoying a run of good fortune, which had convinced them of their own invincibility, regardless of the size of the forces they employed. Deducing therefore that their admirals must have been bribed, they punished two of them with exile and the third with a fine.[34] In another example we read of the distinctive behaviour of young men: they are prone to novelty, since a wider range of human experience is new to them. The youth of Athens is a strong force for enterprise and optimism, and plays an important part in promoting the general euphoria at the time of the decision to mount the great Sicilian expedition.[35] But such sections of the community serve only to add weight to certain common human characteristics and to detract from others. In general, human nature is regarded as a single, finite phenomenon, complex but susceptible of analysis, which may reliably be referred to as the gnomon of historical action in an anthropocentric world.

The actions in Thucydides's narrative are thus frequently coloured and embellished by psychological allusion. But men's minds react no less positively to words than to events: in fact the word is prior to the deed in most historical action. Persuasion and deliberation precede decisions and determine them, and therefore form a vital link in every chain of events. Political speeches were thus important historical material; moreover an author who was as preoccupied as Thucydides with the rational element might be expected to give an account of mental processes. But Thucydides does not include only political speeches: he gives us speeches by generals before battles, a funeral speech, a debate in semi-forensic form,[36] and the Melian Dialogue.[37] Moreover, Herodotus, who does not share Thucydides's psychological interest, nevertheless includes speeches. More significantly still, speeches form an important part of the epic poetry of Homer, who thus established the precedent for writers of narrative, whether in poetry or prose, to intersperse live speech with the recital of events. The reasons for this practice were primarily artistic: to provide variety and to enhance dramatic realism, and generally to enrich the emotional content. Historiography was a comparatively new literary form at a time when epic and tragedy were already well established: it was therefore natural that some of the earlier historians should turn for inspiration to the older literary forms. Some, as it turned out, but not all. Hecataeus and Thucydides's contemporary Hellanicus appear to have regarded the recording of facts as their sole function, and thus represent an alternative historiographical tradition that probably paid dearly in terms of popularity for its independence of other literary forms. Herodotus, who desired above all that his history be read, paid due attention to the artistic conventions that had been tested and proved by his predecessors in other genres: Thucydides, in banishing the mythological or romantic element from his history, did not thereby abandon all pretension to literary artistry, but rather gave his new conception of history its best chance of achieving wide acceptance by direct competition with Herodotus on the same literary level. But Thucydides's speeches contain topics and forms of argument which reflect the influence of contemporary rhetoric and sophistic teaching to an extent hitherto not attempted in historical writing, and which makes them the most distinctive feature of his work.

Thucydides composed his speeches separately, and in most cases several years after the surrounding narrative. They are written in a style that makes hardly any concession to the idiosyncrasies of the several speakers, but is remarkably uniform. The arguments are stated in a carefully elaborated manner which betrays a conscious striving after trenchancy and conciseness, an effect which could not have been achieved without much painstaking ratiocination. With this external evidence in mind we can consider what Thucydides himself says about the speeches:[38]

> As for the speeches which politicians made either when the war was imminent or after it had begun, it has been difficult for me to record an accurate account either from my recollection of speeches at which I was present or from the reports of informants on other occasions. The text of my speeches has been determined by my conception of what each speaker in each situation should have said, though I have approximated as nearly as possible to the general purport of what was actually said.

Scholars have understandably found this statement confusing. Thucydides was undoubtedly present at many of the speeches made before he went into exile, though it is impossible to know which. Did he take these down in shorthand and reproduce their substance faithfully, changing only the style? What does 'as nearly as possible' mean in this context? As nearly as he or his informant can recollect, or as nearly as his artistic sense would allow? Did he only choose to record well-composed speeches, or did he make political importance his criterion and doctor a speech which did not in his opinion meet the occasion? To each of the last two questions the latter alternative is much the more likely: Thucydides would never have admitted a bad speech into a work which he intended to be a 'possession for ever', nor would he be disposed in a serious history to give space to a speech that had rhetorical merit only. The spoken word was, moreover, by his own admission an elusive quarry; and convention forbade Athenian politicians to read from a prepared text. Finally, the remarkable stylistic homogeneity of the speeches proves that, even if any original speeches were available to him, he cast their content in his own words. On the other hand there is no reason to doubt Thucydides's word when he says that he has tried to preserve the truth, both as to substance and as to form of argument. We can confidently assume that in cases where well-chosen arguments were known to have been used, these were reproduced in his version. It is also quite credible that individual phrases, especially those with a memorable or gnomic quality, like some of those in Pericles's Funeral Speech, are preserved intact. There is also no good reason to doubt whether any of Thucydides's speeches, with the exception of the Melian Dialogue, had an historical counterpart. The case may perhaps best be stated thus: Thucydides adhered to truth in substance where it was known to him and did not conflict with his artistic demands; in style he sought uniformity above all, but admitted individual utterances when these had special merit.

The thirty political speeches in Thucydides's history are too varied in character and content to allow any useful sub-classification. Some contain arguments that were appropriate to individual situations and reflected the mental atmosphere prevalent at a particular time; others expound more general theories of moral and political philosophy, in keeping with the author's conception of the educative purpose of history. Characterization of the speaker is never the historian's primary purpose, so that, when he assigns opinions to a speaker which are a reflection of that speaker's character, he is doing no more than meeting the demands of historicity. The political speeches are a storehouse of opinions, not necessarily all those of the historian, on a range of topics germane to the war, and contain the quintessence of the rational element in his history.

Most of the speeches are presented in pairs stating opposite points of view, an arrangement which satisfied the literary tastes of the day no less than historical reality, though the antithetical mode of expression was also a characteristic of the Greek language; but the sophists also made it a central feature of their teaching, and Thucydides adapts the resources of the language and his own training to his special purpose. In the first pair the Corcyreans urge the Athenians to accept their offered alliance,[39] the Corinthians to reject it.[40] Both speeches obey the canons of contemporary deliberative oratory in their employment of the themes of justice and expediency. The Corcyreans lay the greater stress upon the latter, arguing that the proposed alliance would produce an invincible combined fleet. They also talk dangerously about the use of such a fleet in the coming great war. Their reference to the justice of the alliance which they anticipate as their opponents' line of argument is fleeting and hollow: they merely assure the Athenians that their acceptance would not contravene the letter of any treaty. The Corinthians rely exclusively upon justice, accusing the Corcyreans of irresponsibility. Their tone is one of righteous remonstration as they urge upon the Athenians what they consider to be the only just course, not to interfere between colony and mother-city, a course which they themselves faithfully followed in the recent quarrel between Athens and her 'colony' Samos. Finally, they point out that in practice it is impossible to distinguish between justice and expediency since 'advantage accrues mostly from actions involving the smallest degree of injustice'.

This pair of speeches is an interesting example of the adaptation of arguments inherent in a political situation to current modes of thought and literary practice. Equally interesting is the relative authority accorded to the two sides in the debate. The reader of these speeches receives the strong impression that the Corinthians have the better case, and that the Athenians, in accepting the Corcyrean alliance, precipitated the war. Thucydides explains their reasoning: they had come to regard war as a certainty, and preferred to have Corcyra as an ally than as an enemy. In this mental condition questions of justice did not come into consideration, so that the Corinthian mode of argument appears to have taken no account of the Athenian mood at the time. And yet arguments based on justice were the strongest that the Corinthians had, and therefore fulfil Thucydides's criterion of 'what should have been said'; moreover, such arguments *ought* to have convinced the Athenians, if they had been in a normal frame of mind. These speeches illustrate how the success of various forms of argument will depend to some extent on the predisposition of the audience, but that in practice, particularly in international negotiations, such predispositions are difficult to predict. In the event the Athenians took two days to decide on their course of action, from which fact it must be deduced that the arguments used by the two sides made an almost equal impression and were the best available to each.

Another pair of speeches deals with a quite different situation along similar lines. When Mitylene revolted in 428 the Athenians had to decide how severely the islanders should be punished. In an initial meeting the assembly resolved to slaughter the entire male population and enslave the women and children, but soon afterwards had second thoughts. A second meeting was called, in which Cleon, 'who had previously carried through the decision to slaughter, being the most violent of the citizens and the most influential at that time . . .'[41] made a speech which is a marriage of two unlikely bed-fellows, the themes of power-politics and justice.[42] Echoing an earlier speech of Pericles,[43] but lacking his idealism, he bluntly faces his audience with realities: the Athenian empire is a tyranny, which may be kept in subjection only by force or the threat of force. Any sign of weakness on the part of Athens would lead to a widespread revolt, whereby her own security would be threatened. The Mityleneans have thus in effect brought great danger upon Athens, and have shown ingratitude for special privileges and protection they have enjoyed under Athenian rule. It is therefore just to punish them, as well as expedient. This is all good, old-fashioned ethics. The doctrine that justice consists in doing good to one's friends and harm to one's enemies was widely accepted in Thucydides's day, before it was questioned by Plato. Cleon further defines his position by criticizing his audience for allowing themselves to be seduced by new-fangled intellectual and rhetorical arguments. He tells them that they are too easily won over by the verbal displays of clever speakers, who have complicated a simple issue by introducing irrelevant abstract notions and thus causing them to ignore the sound instinct which they had followed in making their first decision. The Mityleneans have wronged Athens deliberately and at an embarrassing time, and the severest punishment should follow as a matter of course.

Powerful as Cleon's speech is as a rhetorical *tour de force* (it is a conspicuous example of practice ignoring precept), it contains a serious flaw. It seems impossible to reconcile the idea of the Athenian empire being a tyranny with that of the 'just obligation' of the Mityleneans, who somehow find themselves in the ambiguous position of being the subjects of a tyranny and members of an empire enjoying special privileges, who commit *hybris*, a crime traditionally associated with men in positions of power rather than their subjects. Cleon might reasonably have enlarged upon the argument that, if a tyrant allows his subjects to enjoy too much prosperity, they will seek more at his expense, by concluding that the only secure tyranny is one in which the subjects are kept in abject slavery. But there would then be no room for his justice-motif: which proves what a precarious partnership he has tried to maintain.

Nevertheless Cleon's insistence on justice and obedience to instinct dictates the form of his opponent's reply.[44] Diodotus chooses the only effective alternatives: expediency and intellectualism. The latter presents no special difficulty: in spite of Cleon's performance, Diodotus could be reasonably sure of a favourable response to an appeal to reason, since reason was a part of the spirit of the age. He sets the tone of his speech at the beginning by saying that good counsel is impaired by haste, and is possible only when reason is allowed to prevail over passion. He adds that those who try to suppress argument are aiming at personal power rather than the common good, whereas a good citizen will use good arguments rather than merely try to intimidate his opponents. Having thus changed the whole atmosphere of the debate in a quite dramatic way, Diodotus proceeds to deal with the matter under discussion. This, he claims, is not a question of what, in strict justice, should be done to the Mityleneans, but of what line of action will most benefit Athens '. . . for if I admit that they are fully guilty of injustice, I shall not advise that they be slaughtered for that reason, unless it be expedient'.

There follows a highly interesting discussion of the theory of punishment, in which Diodotus denies the deterrent effect of heavy penalties—a very modern argument—on the psychological grounds, already familiar to us, that men are ever consumed by hopes and desires which, when strong enough, cause them to ignore danger; and such emotions are most powerful in men who are exposed to the extremes of fortune, poverty and wealth, which induce respectively desperation and arrogance. Having made this negative argument against capital punishment, he adduces positive reasons for not resorting to it: that a city under sentence of death will fight to the last, while Athens herself wants an empire from which she can draw revenues, not a collection of depopulated ruins. Next he momentarily attacks Cleon on his own ground by arguing that it may actually be unjust to punish every Mitylenean for what was probably the act of a small faction in their state. He concludes by appealing once more to reason, urging his audience to exact the minimum penalty necessary in the interests of order and security—the execution of the ringleaders—a decision which could be reached without succumbing to the influence of pity, but would equally show a worthy scorn for the indulgence of anger and revenge.

Diodotus carries the day, but since the earlier meeting actually decided on the extreme punishment and a ship has been sent to put it into effect, great haste is needed. A second ship is sent; the crew ply their oars round the clock, and it arrives just in time to prevent the slaughter. Significantly, we are told that the first ship did not travel in haste 'because of the distastefulness of their mission';[45] and we may reasonably assume that the feelings of this crew were shared by the majority of Athenians. Diodotus therefore probably had the more sympathetic audience. Nevertheless his resources, as second speaker, were circumscribed by the first speaker's treatment of the subject. Cleon had set out to dispel reasoned doubts and to persuade the Athenians to trust their more violent emotions: Diodotus therefore had to re-establish reason and at the same time avoid the charge of softness. The concept of 'what should have been said' is thus widened to include not only what the situation in general demanded but also what the first speaker's oration demanded of the second.

The political speeches after the Ten Years' War assume a new character with the *mise-en-scène* of Alcibiades. Personality now becomes a more important factor in politics, and Thucydides's speeches reflect this change. Nicias, the conservative opponent of the young, talented but arrogant kinsman of Pericles, is allowed to make a personal attack on Alcibiades in the following words:[46]

> And if someone has been chosen to command, and is pleased at the fact—a man concerned only with selfish ends, and moreover rather young to hold a command—because he wishes to be admired for the horses he will provide and to gain prestige from his command through this expenditure, do not provide him with the means of gaining private glory by endangering the city.

Up to this point the political speeches have explored a wide range of topics and situations, but have remained impersonal, relying on the rational and rhetorical elements inherent in each political circumstance. Even Cleon, whose reputation for violence might lead us to assume that he possessed a strong armoury of personal abuse, does not so indulge himself in Thucydides's pages, but argues along the lines of contemporary rhetoric. In what way does Alcibiades differ from Pericles's other political successors, and so transform the political scene? The historian pauses to explain before reporting Alcibiades's reply to Nicias.[47] He says that Alcibiades enjoyed a strong popular following, which he exploited in the pursuit of his extraordinary desire for command and conquest: for not only Sicily, but even Carthage came within the scope of his ambitions. His real abilities were, however, offset by faults which were peculiarly unfortunate for an Athenian who sought eminence in public life: he was personally extravagant and licentious. This combination spelt danger to Athenian minds, which turned to fears of tyranny. Such a man, it was thought, would not scruple to subvert established law for personal power. Consequently, the Athenians never felt they could trust Alcibiades for long, and were unable to make full use of his undoubted talents.

Alcibiades's reply[48] confirms our predisposition to make him the centre of the controversy rather than one side of it. In an egotistical tone, he speaks of his own claims to power, arguing that an individual's actions can bring fame to the whole city, as his own Olympic successes have done to Athens. Turning to the prospects of the expedition, he speaks slightingly of the likely opposition, and recalls the heyday of the empire, when the Athenians engaged the Persians and their Greek enemies at one and the same time. Athens cannot hope to retain her empire unless she takes active measures to expand it, on the principle that attack is the best form of defence. Alcibiades is not like the older Pericles of 431, who laid down Athens's war policy as one of attrition, but harks back to his kinsman's more enterprising days, when under his leadership she fought simultaneously on sea and land against the most powerful opposition, both Greek and barbarian, and yet retained her empire. He represents the modern spirit of youth, but invites the Athenians to take as a corrective to his enthusiasm the advice of some of her older citizens, such as Nicias, 'if he seems fortunate', (in other words 'Nicias is a religious man: therefore some of you may think that he has the support of the gods; for which reason his counsel may be valuable, if for no other'.)[49] By so damning his chief opponent with faint praise he reveals himself as the supreme individualist. The contrast with Nicias is not so much one of conflicting personalities as that of a single, romantic, restless spirit challenging the conservative element in the present leadership. The speeches of Nicias and Alcibiades are thus seen to illuminate the political scene and to explain the extraordinary mood of euphoria which caused the Athenians to undertake the Sicilian expedition. Alcibiades possessed both the personal magnetism and the judgment to lead such an expedition to a successful conclusion; but he also attracted opposition through his egotism, a characteristic which injected a new intensity into political rivalry and hence dictated the course of the war.

Yet another purpose is to be seen in the speeches of the Corinthians, the Athenians and the Spartan king Archidamus in the course of the negotiations leading to the outbreak of the war. These speeches combine ethology and practical politics. The Corinthians describe the Athenian character for the benefit of the Spartans:[50] they are innovating, restless, interfering and inventive, compared with the traditional slowness and conservatism of the Spartans, who must now act out of character, if only temporarily, in order to meet the Athenian danger. The Athenians warn the Spartans of their own strength and resources, and underline the contrast between the traditional and the modern by pronouncing for the first time the dictum that, in political matters, might is right.[51] Archidamus gives a soldier's speech confirming the logistic part of the Athenian argument, and emphasizing the hazards of war against a sea-power.[52] Negotiations continue, and the Spartan ephor Sthenelaidas reintroduces the theme of justice.[53] He reminds the Spartans that they are the leaders of a Peloponnesian alliance, and reasserts the argument that the only question to be considered is that of whether the Athenians are morally in the wrong. 'Decide on a course worthy of Sparta,' he says; 'decide on war.'

After the Spartans decide to go to war, there remain strategic matters to be considered, and Thucydides uses speeches for this purpose also. The Corinthians advise the Spartans to exploit the Peloponnesian advantage in man-power by mounting vigorous land campaigns against Athens.[54] Athenian strategy is outlined by Pericles:[55] the enemy, though numerous, are ill-equipped for protracted campaigns, which require capital outlay and a unified command; more specifically, they are weak in naval power and indifferent at siege operations, so that Athens possesses not only adequate defence against investment by land, but also an effective means of counter-attack in the form of 'commando' raids on the coast of the Peloponnese. This strategy will be effective so long as it is employed wholly and consistently. Since the war has been forced on Athens by the Spartans, the Athenians will have the limited objective of compelling the latter to admit the impossibility of their task. This objective must be pursued with the maximum of economy, by undertaking no rash enterprises and not seeking to enlarge the empire. Pericles followed this policy to the end of his life, reaffirming it even after the disaster of the plague, the severity of which Thucydides ascribes to the overcrowding of the city necessitated by his defensive policy.

Finally we may turn to the most famous of all Thucydides's speeches. In his celebrated Funeral Speech, Thucydides portrays the *Zeitgeist* of the Periclean Age through the mouth of its architect. The numbers of dead were few, and the battle small; but these were the first casualties of the war, and this was the moment for the man responsible for the war to convince his fellow-citizens that the empire which they were defending was worth fighting for and, if necessary, dying for. The case for the Athenian Empire is argued on both a material and a spiritual level, but the two are cleverly linked. The material prosperity, which Athens has acquired by making herself the centre of Aegean trade, is regarded as a means of achieving a fuller life, which Athens is quite prepared to share with any outsiders who wish to enjoy her culture and the benefits of her democratic institutions. Athenian leadership over most of the Greek world, though achieved by physical means, is justified by her superiority in the arts of civilization: she is the 'school of Hellas'[56] (perhaps an original Periclean apophthegm) because freedom and equality have enabled her citizens to exploit their individual talents in public as well as private life, thus creating an inexhaustible source of wisdom and experience in all departments of civic life. The speech has run more than half its course before the eulogy of the dead begins; and one of the themes of this eulogy is, appropriately enough, the superior importance of the city over the individual. The greatness of Athens has been achieved by sacrifice of individual lives, and only so may be maintained. Immortality is impossible for an individual except in the form of renown for his contribution to a great cause; but such renown is enviable indeed: '. . . for heroes have the whole world for their tomb; and in lands far from their own, where the column with its epitaph declares it, there is enshrined in every breast a record unwritten with no tablet to preserve it, except that of the heart.'[57] Men who die for their country are uniquely fortunate in having chosen the most glorious form of death from the innumerable array which fortune provides; and this fact should be a considerable comfort to their relatives.

After reading the Funeral Speech we can scarcely doubt that Pericles at least fervently believed in the Athenian Empire, and possessed the persuasive powers to win over his fellow-citizens. We may also deduce that he had a reserve of confidence from the fact that he does not need to resort to active condolence, but sternly bids the bereaved to shoulder their burden. But the speech is addressed solely to an Athenian audience, and serves the immediate purpose of raising Athenian morale at a critical time: it is not a justification of Athenian imperialism to the contemporary world, or to posterity. In these two respects it fulfils Thucydides's criterion of 'what should have been said', since it gives the reasons why Athens refused to give up her empire, and shows the strength of her resolution. It is also necessary to show by what oratorical powers Pericles was able to dominate Athenian minds, and it is to this practical requirement that we owe the rhetorical excellence of the speech.

The Funeral Oration is, in a sense, a call to battle, and therefore provides a suitable link between the political speeches and the other main group of speeches—those made by commanders to their men before combat. All Thucydides's battle-speeches reflect his interest in morale; but he allows his generals to show different degrees of sensitivity towards the feelings of their men on each occasion. Their anxiety is likely to be greater when confronting a new enemy: therefore in such cases they must be reassured. Before a battle against the barbaric Illyrians, the Spartan Brasidas assures his men that barbarian gestures and noises are devoid of real menace, and that the enemy will not fight in regular order, but will break up in face of a coherent assault.[58] Later, when the Athenians land in Sicily, the nature of the opposition is also unknown: but Nicias's speech to his troops is one of cautious optimism.[59] The expedition is a powerful force of picked men which has already intimidated the Sicilians; but the apparent superiority of the invading force must be weighed against its isolation and the fact that the Sicilians will be fighting in their native country. There is probably a degree of character portrayal here; but it is also likely that the troops were in high spirits which, if anything, needed damping a little. A more difficult task is faced by the general whose men have suffered defeat. In these cases Thucydides resorts to more stereotyped arguments, for instance their fortune must have been unfavourable, and will now restore the balance; if inexperience has been the cause of defeat, as with the Peloponnesian fleet in the early battles, the men will be assured that their courage will compensate for it; and if the victorious enemy was also less experienced, the commander will remind them of past victories over him. These speeches end on a stirring note, alluding to the importance and the glory of victory. In a third type of hortatory speech, that in which the commander is addressing a successful force, there is more scope for reasoned discussion of the tactical and psychological implications of the advantage. In the first specimen of this type,[60] the Athenian admiral Phormio says that the enemy's anxiety will be increased by the mere fact that a much smaller force of Athenian ships is prepared to join battle with a much larger fleet of the enemy. He then enumerates the tactical advantages which they enjoy as a result of their superior seamanship, and concludes by urging them to hold their ranks and remain quiet in order to hear the special orders by which their manoeuvres will be conducted. The speech of Gylippus before the great battle in Syracuse[61] harbour is on similar lines: the Syracusans enjoy the psychological advantage of having been the first to defeat the Athenians on sea, and have successfully imitated Athenian methods, whereas the Athenians are resorting in desperation to the old discredited Peloponnesian method of crowding their decks with hoplites.

Two features are common to the majority of Thucydides's battle-speeches: the speaker subsequently leads his men to victory, having outlined the actual course taken by the battle. As a class, these speeches have further characteristics which weaken their claim to authenticity. In the first place the eve of a battle is a time of great mental stress for all those involved; and it is as unlikely that a commander will be capable of uttering closely-reasoned arguments as that one of his audience will be capable of recording them. The problem of reconciling intellectual and artistic satisfaction with realism is here seen in an extreme form, and the fact that the latter is sacrificed to the former tells us something important about Thucydides.

In summarizing the conclusions on the nature and purpose of speeches in Thucydides, it may be said that they are artistic compositions written in a uniform style apart from certain small concessions made to the character of the speaker in a few cases; that they contain the substance of what was said when this was known to the historian, and when the speaker used the best arguments available; but in all cases, the original material was adapted and expanded in order to include topics and forms of argument that were in current use among his intended audience, the Athenian intelligentsia. Their purpose was primarily intellectual, secondarily dramatic, the latter element being catered for more conspicuously in such passages of vivid narrative as have been examined. Thucydides was the first writer to put into rhetorical form the motives and the rational processes from which spring major political decisions.

All historians are faced with the problem of the importance of individuals in the shaping of events. In Herodotus men reveal their general qualities by their actions and their words, but few characters are clearly and distinctively drawn. In view of his interest in psychology, one might expect from Thucydides a more detailed, analytical approach to characterization; and to a certain extent this expectation is realized. He devotes a long and brilliant chapter to Pericles,[62] whose achievement is summarized in the following words:

> As long as he led the city in peacetime, he conducted her affairs with moderation and protected her from harm; and under his guidance she grew great. And when the war came, he again showed correct judgment of her power.

Thucydides goes on to say that subsequent events confirmed Pericles's clairvoyance and mastery of all aspects of statecraft: after his death his policies were reversed with disastrous results, and none of his successors was able to achieve the degree of personal ascendancy over the Athenian people that had made the constitution under Pericles 'democracy in theory, but in practice the rule of the first citizen'. No politician could wish for a warmer encomium: Thucydides evidently admired Pericles intensely; but the portrait that emerges even from this, the most detailed discussion he gives of an individual, is very far from being biographical in the fullest sense. We are told nothing of Pericles's family background, early education and political career, because Thucydides is interested not in the development of his personality, but only in its effect in its matured form during a particular period of his life. Again, and commendably, Thucydides does not deign to regale us with the many scandalous stories that were told about his private life. In both these extreme cases the same criterion of relevance is applied: only those aspects of a man's character that may have affected his public policy, and hence the fortunes of his city, are revealed. A possible exception to this rule is to be noticed in the case of Antiphon, for whom the historian writes a glowing epitaph on his first appearance in the narrative.[63] There is good reason to believe that personal ties existed between these two men: it has even been suggested that

Thucydides studied rhetoric under Antiphon, who is known to have been a teacher and exponent of forensic oratory. But the disparity between his apparent achievement and the praise he receives may equally well be explained by the nature of his political activities. Thucydides says that he never appeared before the Assembly, nor in any public contest if he could avoid it, being under popular suspicion on account of his oratorical virtuosity; instead he placed his talents at the disposal of his friends, and was responsible for the secret preparations which led to the establishment of the oligarchy of the Four Hundred in 411 B.C.

The only other politician for whom Thucydides expresses unreserved admiration is Themistocles, who emerges from his account as a statesman of real foresight and imagination, in addition to possessing the popular Odyssean cunning we observe in Herodotus.[64] He and Pausanias, the Spartan victor of Plataea, are the only non-contemporary figures of whom we are given a clear account; and the portrayal of the violent and tyrannical behaviour of the latter[65] serves to underline the virtues of Themistocles. Thucydides is more reticent in dealing with his contemporaries, except Cleon, whom he dislikes. After introducing him as 'the most violent of the citizens',[66] he pursues him relentlessly with disparagement at every turn of his career: Cleon boasts that he could succeed in the assault on Pylos where experienced generals have failed, but tries to withdraw when challenged to make good his claim.[67] On being forced to assume the command, he completes the campaign according to his promise, 'mad though this was'.[68] We are further told that in appointing him, the Athenians had envisaged two alternatives, both beneficial: either the campaign would be successfully concluded, or they would be rid of Cleon.[69] Later, when he is campaigning against Brasidas in the Chersonese, he relies more on luck than judgment and dies ingloriously.[70] He receives a most unflattering obituary, being accused of wishing to prolong the war in order that his nefarious activities (unspecified) should remain secret.[71] Brasidas is much more sympathetically treated, though a Spartan: in a chapter devoted to his character and policy, we are told that he combined vigour in action with diplomatic skill, which he used in order to win the trust and goodwill of Athens's allies in the north. His moderation was a lasting source of strength to Sparta in her later dealings with the subjects of Athens; and his career exposes the vulnerability of the Athenian empire and their misjudgment in continuing the war after their victory at Pylos.

Another individual with a special part to play was Alcibiades. Significantly, the first thing we read about him is his illustrious ancestry, on the strength of which he regarded political eminence as his birthright.[72] This claim, which he openly asserted, and his personal extravagance, gave rise to suspicions that he was aiming at tyranny and made him an easy victim of opponents less able and no more high-minded than himself. In this portrayal Thucydides may appear to abandon his normal practice of revealing only his subject's political *persona*: but Alcibiades is an excellent example of the effect of a man's private life upon his public image. Conclusions were drawn from his domestic behaviour, which he took no trouble to conceal because of his overweening pride and love of self-display.

The first appearance of Nicias is an equally good guide to his subsequent role, and suggests that Thucydides may have worded his early references to his characters with special care. We are told that he desired to stop the war in 421, '. . . in order to keep the city's good fortune intact . . . wishing to leave a memory of himself as one who never let the city come to harm'.[73] This is the underlying motivation of Nicias, a kind of introverted patriotism, based upon anxiety for his own good name. This he believed could be best preserved by the adoption of a conservative policy; and even when this was rejected by his countrymen in the case of the Sicilian expedition, he remained true to it, and did his best to ensure that the enterprise was properly provided for. As a general he was able to draw upon a wealth of experience and possessed the kind of foresight that is second nature to the pessimist. In the popular mind he was looked upon in exactly the opposite way to Alcibiades, and more as one would expect a conventional oligarch to be regarded: having a great deal to lose himself, both materially and in terms of reputation, he could be relied on not to risk anything. Athens had more than her share of leaders with drive and initiative: what she needed was a man whom she could trust to act with circumspection. In the event his fear of ill-repute was his and the city's undoing, causing him fatally to delay the return of the expedition from Sicily. The

Athenians forgot that caution is a negative virtue. Thucydides gives him an epitaph that has been variously interpreted, but which may contain more sympathy than irony: he pronounces Nicias 'the least deserving among the Greeks of my time to suffer such a degree of misfortune, since he practised every conventional virtue'.[74]

Of the large number of men who found themselves in positions of authority during the war, only a small number were called upon to make decisions that profoundly affected its course. It is with these men only that Thucydides is concerned; and his interest in them is further restricted to their political activities. Again, in considering their characters he does not raise ethical questions but only observes instances where a reputation for probity (as in the case of Nicias) or laxity (as in the case of Alcibiades) has affected the course of an important career. The avoidance of gratuitous moral judgment is most clearly seen in the case of Themistocles, against whom there was a strong hostile tradition; but it is observable in his treatment of all his leading characters. His conception of 'virtue' is confined to the political field, and hence applies solely to a man's capacity to serve his state. Perfection in political virtue is impossible, but the nearest approach to it is found in the person of Pericles, each of whose successors possessed some, but not all of his qualities. Cleon had his fervent belief in the Empire, but lacked his idealism and his unshakeable authority (Thucydides does not allow us to appreciate his real strength, his grasp of financial matters). Alcibiades was perhaps a better general than Pericles and rivalled his kinsman in popularity, but was unstable and unconventional, and therefore an easy target for slander. Nicias yielded nothing to Pericles in the respect he enjoyed as a soldier and an honest statesman, but he lacked all flair and imagination. Antiphon, it may be surmised, because of his preference for clandestine political machinations, must be judged a statesman of limited resource, who needed a particular situation in which to operate successfully. Thus, as the historian himself says, Pericles's unique powers are best seen through the careers of lesser men.

It has been observed that the one constant and determining factor in human affairs is man's own nature, either operating through individuals or manifesting itself in social trends.

We have also seen that Thucydides's approach to this anthropocentric world is predominantly scientific and analytical.
This being so, religion and supernatural agency might be
expected to have little or no place in his history. It is nevertheless
desirable to examine his treatment of these matters, since it will
be found both to qualify and to confirm the present picture of his
general attitude. Whether or not Thucydides believed in the
existence of gods it is impossible to say with certainty; we can,
however, define his attitude to prayer, the inefficacy of which he
states on a number of occasions. As for oracles, he draws attention
to their ambiguity, which he no doubt regarded as deliberate,
and on one occasion takes the trouble to show that an oracle
conveyed no more than any intelligent observer might have
deduced from the situation.[75] His attitude to superstition also
appears at first sight to be unambiguous: he shows dismay at
Nicias's decision to delay the departure of the Athenian fleet
from Sicily on account of an eclipse of the moon, saying that he
was 'too addicted to divination and such things';[76] and when
describing a battle that took place shortly afterwards, he says
that the Athenians thought that the thunder and heavy rain
which accompanied the fighting were 'intended to contribute
towards their destruction', having already said that such weather
'normally occurs in the autumn season'.[77] It is his practice to
mention current beliefs on individual instances of alleged divine
activity, but if a rational explanation of the phenomenon is
available, he prefers it, and sometimes explicitly rejects the
supernatural one. And yet there is some room for uncertainty
as to his precise position. In an introductory chapter[78] he says
that an exceptional number of natural disasters occurred in the
course of the war; and in spite of the possibility that this reference is merely an example of Thucydides's practice of keeping
his readers informed of popular views, it must be pointed out that
his interest is usually restricted to those opinions which affected
the course of events. There is therefore still room for the
possibility that Thucydides was not an atheist, but believed in
supernatural powers who were able, when they chose, to influence
the course of human affairs, but did not do so in response to
human prayers; or again, he may equally well have believed
that the gods existed as a superior race with elemental
powers, but took no active part in man's world, and merely

commented on the more extreme examples of his wickedness and folly.

On a practical level, Thucydides certainly valued religion as a social force which constrains men to adhere to moral codes, without which civilization cannot subsist. Failure in religious observance is among the symptoms enumerated when the moral disintegration caused by the war, and on a smaller scale by the plague at Athens, is being described. But in observing this we once more find ourselves faced with ambiguity: Thucydides did not believe that men could influence the gods through prayer, but thought it useful to society that they should think they could, because morality is founded upon the belief that wrongdoers will be punished even when no human agency can detect their sin. To this proposition may be added another external influence to which Thucydides attaches importance—the imponderable element, Chance. The chief characteristic of this power, which can upset all human calculations, is its impartiality. It should therefore function as a restraining influence upon those who enjoy prosperity, causing them to treat those less fortunate than themselves with moderation, in the realization that a stroke of Chance could easily reverse their positions. This is its chief importance: otherwise it should be ignored, for the very reason that it is unpredictable; and it should not be blamed for misfortune when human error is the real cause. Indeed, nothing that has been said about superhuman powers should be allowed to obscure the paramount importance of human calculation and judgment in Thucydides's interpretation of events. However, in emphasizing the importance of rationalism there is some danger of making his attitude to religion and morality appear unduly shallow, and even cynical. In fact Thucydides reacts to cases of extreme cruelty with the same horror as any normally decent person would express; while his deep concern for the sufferings which men inflict upon one another is reflected in the choice of words in the famous excursus on sedition in Book III, in which we read that revolution is 'savage', 'war is a violent preceptor', and 'audacity' is one of the most prized virtues in these troubled times.

To summarize the achievement of Thucydides is a difficult task, because, like his contemporaries the dramatists, he brought his chosen form of literature to a point of perfection never subsequently exceeded. His achievement consists primarily in his reconciliation of the rival claims which were already being made upon history by literature and science: by steering a middle course between the Scylla of colourless chronography and the Charybdis of sensationalist romanticism, he struck the ideal balance and left his successors with the unenviable task of measuring up to his standard. The scientific elements of his history are perhaps the more obvious: they are seen in his attitude to factual material, the choice of which is strictly limited by his self-imposed standards of truth and relevance. The part played by aetiology and diagnosis is an aspect of the same essentially scientific outlook, as is his decision to make a single, palpable phenomenon the subject of these studies—the unchanging nature of man, which operates in an observable physical environment. The literary qualities of his history are less easily defined. We have seen how, in choosing to include speeches, Thucydides was making a conscious choice between mere chronicle-writing and history with literary pretensions. But the speeches are also made to satisfy his scientific demands, containing as they do most of the reasoned arguments and analysis of motives, opinions and psychological pressures that lead to decisions and actions. More pervasive, and more purely artistic, is the style of both speeches and narrative. In any book intended for non-specialists as well as for those acquainted with the Greek language, it is clearly impossible to do justice to this part of the subject; but it will suffice to say that Thucydides observed the distinction between literary and non-literary language more thoroughly than almost any of his contemporaries, and wrote in a characteristically artificial style in which he strove constantly to express complex thoughts in a few words, and cultivated variety even when expressing parallel thoughts. The demands which he thus made on his readers were intellectual rather than emotional: he plainly intended that only those readers who were prepared to exercise their mental powers should derive any edification from his work; but the means by which this purpose was achieved were purely artistic.

It has been further suggested that artistic motives are to be seen behind the arrangement of events. Surely it is no accident that the Funeral Speech, that proud eulogy of Athenian achievement, is followed directly by the horrors of the plague? Surely we are expected to draw certain conclusions from the juxtaposition of the Mytilenean episode, in which Athenian humanity finally prevailed, and the slaughter by the Spartans of the survivors of the siege of Plataea? Again, does not the historian draw a clear contrast between the character of Brasidas and that of Cleon? Imaginative commentators have multiplied instances of the use of arrangements like these to create an effect.[79] But in no case is it possible to demonstrate that fact or chronology have been distorted in order to give point to an antithesis. The artistry of Thucydides is the more remarkable for the fact that he does no more than underline the operation of forces inherent in the events themselves, without dramatic over-emphasis and without falsification.

CHAPTER 3

Xenophon

LYSANDER SAILED into the Piraeus in May 404 B.C. The terms of surrender to which the Athenians had agreed were less severe than they might have expected: indeed, Sparta alone, for mixed reasons of sentiment and self-interest, had stood between her and the total annihilation urged by the other members of the Peloponnesian alliance. But in the event the conditions of peace imposed by Sparta gave birth to internal forces that were more destructive of human life than the war had been. The democracy was dissolved, and political power was vested in thirty men of oligarchic sympathies. The replacement of democracies by oligarchies was universal in the Spartan programme for the reorganization of the Greek world; but in every city where there was a change of constitution the new regime needed moral, and in some cases physical support. Both these were provided by the Spartans, who installed garrisons of their own troops; but they made their maintenance the responsibility of the new governments. At Athens, as elsewhere, the oligarchs were both unable and unwilling to meet this expense from their private funds, and found a short-term solution of the problem in the murder of the wealthiest citizens and the confiscation of their property. But these murders lost the Thirty Tyrants, as they had come to be called, the little support they had, and resuscitated the dormant forces of democracy. There was a counter-revolution in which the Thirty were overthrown after a short but bloody war, and democracy was restored. The Spartans, through the same lack of resources that prevented them from maintaining their own garrisons, and also because of divided opinion among their leaders, took no effective steps to reassert their authority. Elsewhere Sparta played the role of 'liberator of Greece' with no greater success, and lost her wartime allies Thebes, Corinth and Megara in the process. Disillusioned by her oppressiveness and indecision, the Greeks were

66

nevertheless in no position to challenge her leadership seriously for some ten years; and that decade was one of the turning points of Greek history.

No ancient writer was more intimately involved in the important events of these years than Xenophon, the son of Gryllus. The deme of Ercheia, where he was born, was a rural district about ten miles to the north-east of Athens. The interest which he shows in certain of his writings in agriculture and horses enables us to assume with some confidence that his father was an upper-class landowner. But the annual Spartan raids on the Attic countryside which were a feature of the first years of the war may well have rendered Gryllus's tenure of his property precarious: at any rate, in the earliest story we have of Xenophon he is living in Athens.[1] It describes his first encounter with Socrates. The old philosopher met the handsome youth in a narrow passage, and stretched out his staff to bar his way. He then inquired where every kind of commodity could be obtained, and upon receiving an answer to each of his questions, finally asked: 'And where do men acquire virtue?' Xenophon was puzzled, so Socrates said: 'Then follow me and learn;' and in this way Xenophon became a pupil of Socrates.

The reminiscences (*Memorabilia*) which Xenophon later wrote of the teachings of Socrates are probably a mixture of those parts which he could understand, those parts which he himself judged to be useful, and the accounts written by other authors of whom he approved. To claim, as many scholars do, that Xenophon's Socrates is merely the mouthpiece for his own theories is to beg the question: to what extent were these theories themselves derived from the teachings of the master, however imperfectly understood? Moreover, the case against the authenticity of Xenophon's Socrates is ill-served by comparing him with that of Plato: for even if it is admitted, as it must be, that Plato was closer to Socrates than Xenophon was, and better-equipped mentally to understand him, there is a strong likelihood that the extraordinary intellectual powers and literary talents that he displays in his dialogues have resulted in an even more distorted picture. Nevertheless, in Xenophon's *Memorabilia* we find a mild, humane, uncontroversial and decidedly prosaic preceptor who, in the light of events, baffles comprehension. How, we are led to ask, could such a man have aroused popular hostility, and eventually have become a martyr to the misunderstanding of his fellow-citizens? The teachings attributed to him by Xenophon are concerned mainly with man's cultivation of self-discipline as a necessary preparation for useful service to the community, and as such can only be deemed beneficial, or at worst harmless. Yet the result of his trial shows that he made enemies among the aristocracy, two of whose members were his accusers, and among the common people, by a majority of whom he was condemned to death.

We must therefore conclude that the *Memorabilia*, apart from the section that deals with the charges made at his trial, contains only the more exoteric parts of his teaching. We may further surmise that Xenophon was excluded, probably by both inclination and capacity, from membership of the inner circle of Socratics to which Plato belonged. The story of his induction into the Socratic coterie implies that he did not of his own accord seek membership. There is another story which throws corroborative light upon this impression of his relationship with Socrates. He tells us himself[2] of a letter that he received in the year 402, when he was about twenty-five years old, from a Boeotian friend of the family named Proxenus, who had virtually severed his connections with his homeland in order to take up a permanent position on the staff of the young Persian prince Cyrus, who was satrap of north-west Asia Minor. In his letter Proxenus described his life in glowing terms, and promised Xenophon a similar position of trust and intimacy with Cyrus if he should decide to join him. It was a big decision; and Xenophon sought the advice of Socrates as to whether he should go. Socrates, foreseeing the possibility that his countrymen might view with disfavour the association of one of their number with a man who had so recently done great harm to the city, advised him to consult the Delphic oracle. This Xenophon did, but somewhat disingenuously: he inquired of the prophet not whether he should go, but to what gods he should sacrifice in order to ensure a successful mission and a safe return. Evidently the moral influence of Socrates upon Xenophon had not been great enough to curb his taste for adventure; nor had certain of his teachings apparently made any impression. Socrates advocated obedience to the state and respect for its will: Xenophon proposed to associate with one of the worst enemies of Athens. Socrates concerned himself with problems of right and wrong, and had sought an answer to Xenophon's question along moral lines: should Xenophon go? Xenophon approached the matter in a completely different spirit, avoiding the moral issue and considering only the practical question of success. If we further consider why Proxenus's invitation should have seemed so attractive to Xenophon, the rift between them widens further. Xenophon undoubtedly hoped to enrich himself in the course of his adventures, whereas his master was proverbially indifferent to worldly wealth: and when later he was established on a country estate at Scillus, he lived in a considerable degree of physical comfort, and in his famous descriptions of the estate itself and other places he saw on his travels, he shows a keen interest in the rural scene, which Socrates found so alien and irrelevant.

In spite of these fundamental differences of outlook, the names of Socrates and Xenophon remained closely linked in later tradition. Especially relevant is the opinion of Cicero, who was fully aware of the volume of Xenophon's historical writing, but nevertheless preferred to number him among the philosophers. Herein perhaps lies the key to the character of Socrates's influence upon Xenophon: his teachings induced, even in his less receptive pupils, a philosophical attitude of mind, causing them to seek a theoretical basis for investigation and to discover ideal forms of the active elements in their chosen study. In Xenophon's historical writings, the *Anabasis* and the *Hellenica*, the latter aspect of his influence is pervasive; but to dilate on this theme would be to anticipate the main discussion of this chapter.

The other early influences upon Xenophon are less easy to isolate, and the efforts of scholars to do so have met with little positive success. Allusions to lines from Homer, Hesiod, Theognis, Epicharmus, Pindar and the tragic poets have been found or inferred in his writings; but these prove only that he was reasonably well-read, attended dramatic performances, and possessed a moderately retentive memory. The influence of the sophists is, however, another matter. The name of one important sophist, Prodicus of Ceos, who is said to have identified the good with the useful, has been linked by tradition with that of Xenophon, the story being that Xenophon attended the lectures given by Prodicus at Thebes after he had been captured by the Boeotians while on active service.[3] If this is true, we must believe either that the Boeotians treated their prisoners of war with great liberality, or that Xenophon received special treatment because of his connection with the family of Proxenus. Neither of these possibilities seems very likely; but the doctrine ascribed to Prodicus is prominent in Xenophon's writings, and appears to have suited his cast of mind. Indeed, his interest in the practical problems of life and their solution gave him natural affinities with the sophistic movement, whether he studied their teachings actively or not. To this general observation may be added a particular case: Xenophon's style shows a working acquaintance with the rules of contemporary rhetoric, one of the aspects of sophistic teaching; but his employment of rhetorical forms of expression is mainly confined to set speeches, leaving the main body of his narrative a model of simplicity, clarity and naturalness that won universal praise as such from the later critics of antiquity.

Far from spending all his youthful years in conclave with Socrates and other teachers, Xenophon probably played an active part in the later campaigns of the war, perhaps from 406 until the end. Direct evidence of his military service is lacking, unless the Prodicus story be accepted as such; but his early appearances in the *Anabasis* give the impression of a man young in years but completely at home on the battlefield. Moreover, Athens needed all her young men for the final struggle, so that Xenophon is unlikely to have escaped his obligations even if he had wished to do so; and as surrender was followed by humiliation, internal upheaval and final reconciliation, we may look to the vividness and detail of his narrative of these events in the second book of the *Hellenica* for evidence, albeit latent and supposititious, of his presence and participation. In particular, his account of the military operations that culminated in the overthrow of the Thirty contains the kind of exact information that could only have been supplied by one who was present.[4] This does not, of course, rule out the possibility that the information was supplied to Xenophon by someone else; but in view of what has already been said about Xenophon, there is no strong reason to doubt that he participated in these operations, perhaps supporting the democrats in the later stages after becoming disgusted at the excesses of the oligarchs.

A further deduction may be made from the graphic quality

of this part of the *Hellenica*: that he wrote it while his impressions were still fresh, and that the first two books of the *Hellenica* were therefore written before he joined Cyrus and Proxenus. The case for assigning this part of the *Hellenica* to the years 403 and 402 can be further supported by comparing the author's attitude to certain individuals who appear in both the *Anabasis* and the *Hellenica*. It is true that such differences might be the result of the different purposes of the two works—that the *Anabasis* openly purported to be autobiographical, whereas in this section of the *Hellenica* Xenophon was trying to be objective and impersonal, like Thucydides. But one of these examples of dual portraiture seems, at least to the present writer, to override this distinction: that of Cyrus himself. In the *Hellenica* he makes a most unpromising debut, by detaining some Athenian ambassadors for three years, contrary to international convention;[5] and subsequently the historian does nothing to correct this initial impression of him. In the *Anabasis*, by contrast, Cyrus is the model ruler, who won the *trust* of his subjects through his complete probity. The admiration that Xenophon conceived for Cyrus during his brief but close association with him must have made objectivity, let alone the admission of cardinal faults, impossible in a work written after the expedition.

Thus Xenophon may have begun his long career as a writer before the great adventure that he immortalized with his pen. But his impatience for action and desire to make good the losses in wealth that his family must have sustained at the hands of the Thirty or the democrats, or simply from the expenses of the war, was at this time greater than his interest in history or his respect for the advice of Socrates. In accepting Proxenus's invitation, however, he was to find very much more adventure than he could have expected; for, in common with all the other mercenaries who took service under Cyrus (except the Spartan Clearchus, who was appointed commander of the Greek contingent), Xenophon knew nothing of the real purpose of the proposed expedition at its outset, but understood that it was to be directed against some dissident hill-tribes in a remote region of Cyrus's satrapy. In fact, Cyrus was planning nothing less than the seizure of the throne of Persia from his elder brother, the king Artaxerxes. Such an enterprise could have no chance of success if Cyrus employed the Asiatic forces available to him, for these were similar in quality and inferior in numbers to those of the king. He therefore used the influence he had acquired in Greece during the war through his friendship with Lysander in order to raise a force of Greek hoplites, whose fighting qualities were known from past experience to be superior to those of the lightly-armed Asiatics. He had little difficulty in raising, through his agents and friends, the numbers he required, since the war had left a surplus of trained soldiers, and he offered good pay and the prospect of rich booty. Five armies were assembled in the first instance, in order that the size of the whole should not arouse suspicion at an early stage. Finally they all came together at Sardis, whence they set out eastward in March of the year 401. Xenophon must have made daily notes of distances, terrain and occurrences *en route*, so detailed and self-consistent is his narrative. The *Anabasis*, or 'March Up-Country', is therefore a condensed diary, embellished by further reminiscences of what was thought and said, and later when quarrels arose involving the author, by the arguments with which he defended himself at the time, and which he wanted to be accepted by a wider public.

Doubts and fears as to the real purpose of the expedition preyed more and more upon the minds of the Greeks, and matters came to a head when a hundred men were lost in a skirmish as the army was approaching Tarsus through mountainous country. On arrival at the city, the men flatly refused to march any farther. Clearchus, whose qualities as a leader and a disciplinarian had already proved invaluable, had to resort to diplomacy after force nearly cost him his life. He made two subtle and conciliatory speeches, in which he pledged himself to remain with his fellow-countrymen, most of whom were Peloponnesians like himself; but he also pointed out that refusal to march would mean that they were no longer in Cyrus's service, and would cease to draw their pay. This argument, supported by a promise of a fifty per cent rise, had the desired effect: astute leadership and a common hope of gain had silenced the objectors, and no more questions were asked until the army reached the banks of the Euphrates, when Cyrus revealed his plan openly for the first time. The latter part of the journey across Northern Syria into the Arabian Desert must have been taxing in terms of physical endurance, but the fascination of that strange land inspired Xenophon, whose short but vivid description[6] shows a countryman's interest in the teeming wild life, which was the more easily observed because of the flatness and treelessness of the place ('like the sea'—to a Greek, no known land could have seemed comparable). Some of the animals, like the bustards which, like partridges, could only fly short distances, provided a welcome variation in the soldiers' diet; others, like the agile and elusive gazelles, ostriches and wild asses were less obliging, but provided some sport instead.

Once across the Euphrates, and with full knowledge of its destination, the army became an immediate and formidable threat to the throne of the king, who, though forewarned of Cyrus's intentions, had taken no steps to protect his kingdom. But now what had seemed to him impossible had been achieved: an army that included ten thousand seasoned Greek hoplites had penetrated to the heart of his empire. His measures to meet it were hurried and makeshift; but he had vast resources of man-power and equipment on which he could draw at short notice, so that the army which ultimately took the field against Cyrus outnumbered his own by at least three to one. Xenophon gives a memorable description of the approach of the king's huge host.[7] First a huge darkening cloud of dust appeared on the horizon; then helmets and armour could be discerned flashing in the sunlight; and finally the enemy's dispositions could be plainly distinguished: the cavalry with their white panoply, Persian infantry with their wicker shields, and Egyptians with their full-length shields of wood; and in front of these chariots with scythes bound to their wheels.

The two sides drew up in battle-order on a plain near the village of Cunaxa, some fifty miles to the north-west of Babylon. The king's numerical superiority was so great that his right wing extended far outside the left wing of the Cyreans, so that there was danger from the outset of an outflanking movement. Artaxerxes himself, after the fashion of Persian monarchs, stationed himself at the centre-rear of his army behind six thousand picked troops. When battle was joined, Cyrus concentrated the full fury of his assault upon the enemy centre, which retired sufficiently to expose the king to his view; where-upon Cyrus, bent upon personally administering the *coup-de-grâce*, hurled himself into the royal bodyguard, and managed to inflict a flesh-wound on Artaxerxes before being overcome and slain. Meanwhile Clearchus on the right had won a complete and costless victory. But the death of Cyrus deprived the expedition of its purpose, so that the Greeks found themselves at one with the king in one strong desire: that they should return to Greece at the earliest opportunity. He furnished them with guides and provisions to help them on their way, and their journey might have been uneventful had not the treacherous and vengeful satrap Tissaphernes plotted their destruction. He lured the five Greek generals into his tent under the pretence of a parley, and murdered them and all their attendants save one, who managed to return to his companions, 'holding his intestines in his hands', and gasp out the terrible news.[8]

Aimless, isolated and leaderless, the Ten Thousand seemed certain to be swallowed up and forgotten in this vast, hostile land. The murder of the generals is the critical point in Xenophon's story, and underlines the greatest single lesson that he learnt from his experience: the importance of good leadership. His interest in this problem prompted him to examine the qualities of the dead generals, and of Cyrus himself, in detail by means of pen-portraits, the first of their kind in classical literature. Unlike the brief notices in Thucydides, these portraits begin at the point in each man's life where training crystallized into ambition. Cyrus, born to rule, had the moral and physical education suited to a future king, and excelled in both aspects. As satrap of Lydia he earned the trust of his subjects, and never abused it. The secret of his success was the example of his own blameless life and the generosity with which he rewarded those who served him.[9] He seems to have represented the ideal as conceived by Xenophon at the time of writing: the Greek generals possess some of his qualities in different degrees, but serve mainly to illustrate his perfection by showing the consequences of failure to achieve the right blend. Clearchus was motivated by a love of adventure and war, and his qualities as a leader developed from this. He was a harsh disciplinarian, believing that an army should fear its general more than the enemy. In crises he was an ideal leader, because the soldiers somehow saw in his fearsome mien a defence against the enemy, and looked upon him as a protective father-figure. But with the passing of danger their tolerance of his severity flagged, and they looked for a gentler master.[10] Clearchus did not, like Cyrus, have a vocational attitude to leadership but regarded it as a means of satisfying his love of war.

Proxenus was a friend of Xenophon; but intimacy does not necessarily lead to greater understanding and Xenophon is somewhat vague as to his purpose in life. He 'wished to become a man capable of great deeds', and to this end he became a pupil of Gorgias of Leontini. The fact that Gorgias is chiefly remembered as a teacher of rhetoric suggests that Proxenus's original intention may have been to make his mark in a political rather than military environment. But Xenophon tells us no more about his early career, and goes on to describe how he saw in his friendship with Cyrus a possible passport to fame, power and wealth; but he loyally hastens to add that Proxenus wished to have none of these things except by honourable means. Indeed, his essentially noble nature made him insufficiently harsh to deal with the more unruly of those under his command. He thus lacked the qualities that Clearchus possessed in excess, and compensated for this deficiency by his greater humanity.[11]

Xenophon's picture of Menon is wholly defamatory because of private enmity. He is credited with no interest in ruling for its own sake, but solely as a means of acquiring wealth. Material greed was his abiding vice, and he abused his position and the confidence of his friends in order to glut his avarice. Xenophon strikes a characteristically moral note at the end: Menon did not die a quick death along with the other captured generals, but perished 'like a criminal' after a year of abuse and degradation.[12]

Each of these portraits begins with the question of motivation; and in each case the man's reason for seeking leadership affects his performance as a leader. In fact, the most successful leader is the one in whom no independent motive can be discerned, but for whom leadership is a natural, atavistic function—Cyrus, who was destined from birth to be a ruler and educated accordingly. He was the only leader in this group with a full understanding of the balance between privilege and duty that is essential to the effective exercise of command. Xenophon idealistically tells us nothing of his methods of dealing with the disturbances that arose in his satrapy: we are asked to assume that such problems never arose because he never made enemies among his own people. Clearchus and Proxenus, by contrast, have disciplinary troubles arising from their own weaknesses, which in turn are the consequence of their secondary interest in the problems of leadership. The portrait of Menon underlines the dependence of good leadership upon moral qualities. None of Xenophon's subsequent leader-figures (excepting himself) is a commoner: after considering Cyrus he decided that the ideal leader must be destined from birth and trained from earliest childhood, in order that the qualities essential to his vocation should have become an integral part of his character by the time he is called upon to exercise his power.

The predicament in which the Greeks now found themselves demanded the emergence of new and untried talents for command. In Xenophon's story the man of the moment is the author himself; but his account has been questioned by some of the more sceptical commentators, who refer to the version of the expedition preserved by Diodorus Siculus, and the allusion to it in Isocrates which does not corroborate his claim of having provided initiative and support for flagging morale at the critical time. The explanation of this discrepancy is not difficult to find. Diodorus was a compiler, writing some four hundred years later, who did not compare rival versions, but used the one that happened to be available or written on a scale that suited his overall scheme, in this case that of Ephorus: Xenophon's *Anabasis* was either not available or was too detailed, and would have had to be summarized, a wearisome task for a man who was proposing to include the whole of the inhabited world in his purview. Isocrates was chiefly interested in the achievement of the Ten Thousand in marching *into* the king's domain and defeating him in battle a few miles from his metropolis; whereas Xenophon was, on his own admission,[13] 'neither a general nor a captain nor even an ordinary soldier' until he came forward to offer his services after the murder of the generals. Nor did he then become supreme commander, but himself advised that this office be conferred upon a Spartan, Cheirisophus, and only later allowed himself to be elected. And finally, a rival version, by Sophaenetus of Stymphalus, was also current when Ephorus wrote. It is therefore not surprising that Xenophon's name does not occur in all the later versions.

After introducing himself at the beginning of Book III, Xenophon proceeds to give a deeper and richer self-portrait than any of those he draws of others. A careful examination of the feelings and opinions that he reveals as the story unfolds will provide a sound basis on which to form an understanding of his qualities as a historian. The dream which he says he had on the night after the murder of the generals, and his interpretation of it, make a good starting-point. He dreamt that a thunderbolt struck his father's house, which became engulfed in flame. Though frightened by this vision, he considered it coolly for a while, and observed that it had involved a great light from Zeus, which could make it a good omen. This interpretation tells us two important things about Xenophon: that he was pious and optimistic, two interdependent characteristics which colour his attitude to all questions. Believing that the gods took an intense and individual interest in the actions of men, he personally took care to consult them at every turn in his life, and was therefore confident that they would not desert him in his present plight. This optimism was now to prove invaluable, for it gave him the will to seek a way out and to inspire his comrades to share his hopes for the future. He also assures them that the enemy himself has forfeited divine favour by breaking his word, a most useful argument for his immediate purpose of reviving morale, but also one that he uses extensively elsewhere in the *Anabasis* and the *Hellenica*, and is fundamental to his whole conception of historical action. Equally characteristic is his allusion to the practical advantage that may now be taken of the enemy's folly: with the truce broken, the Greeks may acquire supplies by force where previously these had to be bought.

Having thus won the confidence of the officers in Proxenus's contingent, to which he was attached, he assembled the remaining officers from the rest of the army. In the speech addressed to them he impresses upon them their duty to serve their men, and links this concept with the oligarchic principle in general: 'In peacetime,' he says, 'you had more property and more political power than they; now, in war you ought to be braver than the common man and to plan and toil on his behalf wherever the occasion demands.'[14] He then urges them to choose new generals as soon as possible, since '. . . without rulers nothing fine or good can be done, and this is especially so in military matters. Discipline ensures safety, while lack of it has often brought destruction'. This discipline is achieved through the example given by those who are superior both in counsel and in physical courage, who are accepted and obeyed only when they are seen to possess these qualities. Later, when speaking to the troops, he urges them to cooperate with their officers in the enforcement of discipline, so that the army might have 'not one, but ten thousand Clearchuses'. This last speech is a skilful piece of hortatory oratory, but the speech to the officers, adumbrating as it does a parallel between the officer class in the army and the oligarchy in the city-state, contains the essence of Xenophon's political thought.

In truly oligarchic fashion, the officers choose successors to the dead generals from among their numbers, and assemble the army in order to inform it of their decision to ignore the king's demand that they should lay down their arms, and to strike northwards towards the Black Sea. In another long speech he adds further colour to his self-portrait.[15] One of his audience sneezes, thus confirming his faith in divine tutelage. This reference is not intended to be funny, for the Greeks genuinely believed a sneeze to be propitious; but in much of the rest of this speech, in which he outlines the army's advantages and minimizes its weaknesses, he shows a welcome sense of humour. The army is deficient in cavalry, a weakness that later has to be remedied in order to provide some form of mobile protection for the rear, the most vulnerable part of an army in retreat: but for the present Xenophon merely scoffs '. . . nobody has ever died in battle through being kicked or bitten by a horse . . .'[16] there is only one advantage which cavalry has over infantry, and that is that they have a safer means of retreat'.[17] The speech raises further points of interest. He compares the undoubted military superiority of Greek over barbarian with the attraction of the easy life in the king's domain: death in battle is less to be feared than demoralization through the influence of luxury. There was a danger that, like the Lotus-Eaters, the Greeks '. . . enjoying the company of these fine big Persian women, might forget their way home'.[18] But that is not all. He goes on to say that their first duty is to return home and tell their countrymen of the wealth and vulnerability of the Persian empire.[19] This is probably the first allusion to the possibility of a Greek conquest and occupation of Persia, and is therefore a highly prophetic anticipation of the course of Greek history.

Xenophon was assigned to command the rear, and thus bore the main responsibility for the safety of the retreating army.

Progress was slow and arduous, and the army's lack of cavalry initially proved to be a serious weakness against the hit-and-run 'Parthian' tactics of Tissaphernes's mounted archers. Xenophon therefore organized a scratch force of cavalry and one of slingers, and inflicted heavy casualties on a surprised enemy. The fighting in the mountains of Kardouchia (Kurdistan) was conducted with the same intelligent improvisation and adaptation of basic tactical principles to new conditions: here forward reconnaissance followed by the expulsion of the enemy from all high ground in the army's line of march ensured it a safe passage through the many ravines which the local tribesmen had intended to hold against them. But the most rigorous test of Xenophon's powers of leadership came from the weather, when the army was travelling through the Armenian mountains. Hunger, frostbite and snow-blindness so demoralized some of the men that they refused to go on, and would have died when only a few miles short of a village where food and shelter awaited them, if Xenophon and his men had not forced them to their feet. Xenophon had already encountered this peculiar test of leadership, when it was not a matter of making men fight well, but of persuading them of the necessity of simple action. The first occasion had been when snow had fallen upon the sleeping army during the night. Xenophon describes the incident in the following manner:[20]

> While they were spending the night there, there was a tremendous fall of snow which covered the men and their arms as they lay; and the snow imprisoned the baggage animals also. And there was a general reluctance to get up, because the snow that had fallen on them as they lay and had not slipped off was warm. But when Xenophon brought himself to get up without his clothes on and to split wood, soon someone else got up and took over from him. And after that others got up and lit fires and rubbed themselves down with ointment.

Here, as elsewhere, we are not concerned with the truth of Xenophon's account (though there is no good reason to doubt it), but with his conception of the qualities which leaders ought to show at critical times. Here there are two—physical endurance and personal example. Both may be paralleled elsewhere in the *Anabasis*, but the former is the more important for a general understanding of Xenophon. It helps to account for his admiration of Spartan institutions, and was also a quality attributed to Socrates by the Cynics and Stoics, who claimed to be his true descendants. Combined with self-control, its active counterpart, it is the prime Socratic ingredient of ideal leadership as personified by Agesilaus and Jason of Pherae in the *Hellenica*.

The climax of the northward march came on the fifth day after leaving the friendly city of Gymnias. As the van of the army reached the crest of a mountain called Theces, a cry arose which Xenophon, ever vigilant in the rear, at first interpreted as a signal of an enemy attack. But as the cry passed swiftly through the ranks it became discernible as one word, a word charged with emotion: '*Thalassa! Thalassa!*' To Greeks who had been land-locked for nearly a year, their first sight of the sea was an over-whelming experience. As many as could rushed to the summit: there were tears, much embracing and mutual congratulation.[21]

It was decided to make the rest of the homeward journey by sea, 'resting stretched out on deck, like Odysseus', as one tired infantryman put it.[22] But ships proved scarce, and the army's progress along the coast was by no means easy. In the course of this part of the march a matter arose that illustrates the effect that the whole experience had had on Xenophon. He had been impressed by the orderly and civilized manner in which the army had conducted itself in response to the leadership of himself and his fellow-officers, and had no doubt come to enjoy his own share of authority and popularity. With these thoughts in mind he formed the idea of founding a Panhellenic city on a favoured site near the coast. Unfortunately the plan was divulged by a confidant before he could present it openly to the army, giving rise to the absurd accusation that Xenophon had intended to 'trick' the army into remaining in Asia. This notion of 'deceiving the People' frequently arose as an accusation made in the demo-cratic assemblies against leaders whose policies had misfired, 'as if,' as Thucydides says, 'the assembly had not itself ratified the policy.'[23] But Xenophon had not yet proposed anything; and in a witty, well-argued speech,[24] he asks the men to think for themselves, and to reflect that his accusers were placing a very low value upon their intelligence if they thought them unable to distinguish between north, south, east and west and were thus unable to tell which way he was leading them. The charge was quickly dropped; and not long afterwards the army offered him the supreme command. He describes his reaction to this offer honestly and realistically:[25] 'He reflected that if he accepted the command, his own fame would be greater among his friends and his name would become better known at Athens; while he might also be the cause of some good to the army.' Such considerations inclined him towards acceptance; but, realizing that this could equally lead to disaster, he made his usual oracular consultation, and adopted the god's advice to refuse the command. He had become more scrupulous in his attitude to oracles, and perhaps more devoutly religious, since that first recorded occasion.

The army divided into three parts, only to reunite after a short time. Ships were still not forthcoming, and some of the cities through which they passed were unfriendly; while others, like Sinope and Heraclea, were only too pleased to supply food and money in order to be rid of them. Eventually they were forced to take service under the Thracian prince Seuthes, after the Spartan harmost of Byzantium, Aristarchus, acting under Persian influence, had refused to accommodate them. Seuthes at first provided well for the army in return for its services, through which he overcame some of his most troublesome enemies and received some useful lessons in campaigning from Xenophon. But relations became strained when he fell into arrears of pay, and assumed a personal character when Xenophon himself pressed strongly for his soldiers' dues. He gave Seuthes a long lecture on the obligations of kingship (the quality that had distinguished Cyrus);[26] and Seuthes, suitably impressed, paid up. Xenophon reminds us of the 'apologetic' purpose of the latter part of his story when he affirms that he personally received hardly any of this money, and proves his point by recalling that he had to sell his horse, of which he was very fond.[27]

Returning with a remnant of the Ten Thousand to Asia Minor, he made, with the consent of Zeus, a lucrative raid upon the estate of a wealthy Persian named Asidates, and received the pick of the booty, thus ending the campaign 'at least in the position to do someone else a good turn'.[28] He then handed the army over to Thibron, the Spartan general who was about to make war on Persia. This was in March 399. It was probably soon after this that he heard that he had been banished by his fellow-citizens. Of the two reasons that the authorities give for his exile, friendship with Cyrus and 'laconism' (friendship with Sparta), the former seems the more likely. But either or both of these might have been excuses for excluding an absent oligarch,

who, like Critias, the hated leader of the Thirty, and the detested
Alcibiades, had been an associate of the recently condemned
Socrates. Xenophon may thus have been the victim of an
intensifying left-wing campaign that happened to coincide with
his return to the Greek world.

For most of our information concerning the remainder of his
life we are at the mercy of second- and third-hand sources like
the biographers Plutarch and Diogenes Laertius. His marriage
to Philesia probably belongs to the years immediately following
his exile. They had two sons, Gryllus and Diodorus, the former
of whom died fighting bravely in the Athenian cavalry at the
Battle of Mantinea in 362. But their early years were spent under
the Spartan discipline, while their father continued to serve under
Spartan commanders—first Thibron, then Dercylidas, and
finally the king Agesilaus. He remained in close touch with his
Spartan friends for some thirty years, initially because he shared
their desire to make war upon the Persians, whom he had found
to be treacherous and cowardly enemies. Subsequently he became
personally attached to king Agesilaus, and accompanied him on
his campaigns. In 394 came a moment of decision. Agesilaus
was recalled to Greece, where an alliance of Greek cities, including Athens and Thebes, was mobilizing against Sparta. Xenophon
had to ask himself where his allegiance lay: with his friends or
with his city? If, as seems likely, he was already under sentence
of exile, he had little choice, unless he should choose to stand
aloof from the war altogether. In the event he probably chose to
fight beside his friends, and was thus ranged on the Spartan
side in the battle of Coronea, which ended in an ill-defined
victory for Agesilaus.

During the four or five years of their acquaintance, the
personality of Agesilaus impressed itself upon Xenophon's mind,
and gradually overshadowed his dimming memory of Cyrus.
Slowly the new ideal leader emerged, possessing all the qualities
that Xenophon considered necessary: military knowledge and
practical skill in its employment, attention to discipline leavened
by humanity, resilient personal courage, and providence. These
qualities are already familiar: but Agesilaus possessed a further
quality which Xenophon had, since his earlier experiences, come
to regard as indispensable in a man whose actions affect the lives
of others—piety. Agesilaus was scrupulous in religious observance;

but his piety is also seen in his dealings with other men. He invariably honoured treaties and agreements (all of which were formally contracted in the name of the gods), and baffled dishonest opponents, like the satrap Tissaphernes, by his very reliability. An extension of this notion of piety was a particular sense of duty, by which he saw his kingly power only as an instrument of a higher order (which it was, since the Spartan kings were, in all essentials, 'constitutional monarchs', who could be deposed and even executed if they acted in defiance of the law). Xenophon was fully aware of the debt he owed to Spartan law for his picture of an ideal monarch: he not only wrote an encomium of Agesilaus, one of the earliest of its kind, soon after his death in 360, but also wrote a treatise on the Spartan Constitution.

Xenophon was granted an estate at Scillus, near Elis, by the Spartan government, perhaps on the recommendation of Agesilaus. For the next twenty years he had time to think and time to write. Every four years visitors to the Olympic festival travelled along the road that bordered his estate, and no doubt strangers as well as old acquaintances were welcomed to share his board in exchange for news of the outside world. The rest of his time was spent organizing his estate in harmonious company with his wife and his staff of servants, and, in the time-honoured tradition of retired generals, writing his memoirs. The whole of the *Anabasis* probably belongs to this period, whether it was written in two parts, as most authorities now believe, or not. The *Spartan Constitution*, except the final chapter, which is a later addition, was also probably written at Scillus, as were his treatises on *Estate Management*, in which he advocates a degree of freedom and authority for the wife of the châtelain that is remarkably liberal for fourth-century Greece; and that on *Equitation*, which is his most professionally accomplished technical treatise. Over half of the *Hellenica* was also probably completed, at least in an early draft, before he left Scillus.

His expulsion came not long after the Spartan defeat at the battle of Leuctra in 371. A few years later, when relations between Sparta and Athens had improved, the Athenians recalled him from exile; but whether he returned to Athens, and if so for how long, remains obscure. We know that his sons fought at Mantinea, and the treatise on *Revenues* was written for the edification of Athenian men of state. The remaining Socratic works, the

Memorabilia, *Symposium* and *Apology*, which were probably completed during this period, also have a peculiarly Athenian relevance. Nevertheless there is a tradition, which cannot be altogether discounted, that he made Corinth his home. The most satisfactory solution, in the absence of direct evidence, is therefore that he lived in both places, in Corinth between the time of his expulsion from Scillus until his recall, and at Athens from that time (perhaps 367–365) until his death. Wherever he was, this final period saw no diminution of his literary output, for during it he completed the *Hellenica* and wrote the *Agesilaus*, in which he incorporated several passages from the longer history. He also wrote a short dialogue on tyranny called the *Hiero*, his most polished literary composition; a tract on the duties of a cavalry officer called the *Hipparchicus*, perhaps written for the instruction of his sons; and the *Cyropaedia*, a romantic story with a didactic purpose describing the education and reign of Cyrus the Elder, the founder of the Persian Empire. This, his longest work, is less significant for its intrinsic merits than for its place in the history of literature as an influence in the re-establishment of romance as an element of historiography. It contains a distillation of all Xenophon's ideas, but since it is far from being history it can have no place in the present discussion.

The date of Xenophon's death is uncertain, but most commentators assume that he continued to write to the end, and that therefore he died not long after the publication of his latest work, the *Revenues*, which was probably 355 or 354. Perhaps they are right; but one authority, though admittedly isolated and of no great weight, includes him in its list of nonagenarians,[29] so that if our original date for his birth is correct, the possibility must not be ruled out that he lived until about 337.

Xenophon wielded the pen for much longer than the sword; but over the whole period of his literary activity there was one work which occupied him, either continuously or intermittently. This was the *Hellenica*, a history of Greece from 411 to 362 B.C. It is upon his performance in the seven books which comprise this work that he must be finally judged as a historian. It will be more than usually appropriate to begin our examination at the beginning and to observe how Xenophon himself embarks on his narrative. He says 'after these events . . .', and describes the Athenian and Spartan naval manoeuvres that followed upon the events described by Thucydides at the end of his unfinished eighth book. Thus, in a purely literal sense, Xenophon is Thucydides's continuator. But this fact, together with the explicit statements of certain ancient authorities that he completed Thucydides's unfinished history of the Peloponnesian War, has given rise to much conjecture as to the exact relationship between the two historians. Was Xenophon chosen by Thucydides to complete his work, and provided by him with the basic material, or did he chance upon a draft left by his dead predecessor? Or did he admire Thucydides from a distance and decide to complete his work to the best of his ability without access to his original notes? Or again, did he merely choose the point where Thucydides left off to begin an account that was independent both in substance and in spirit of that of the older author? In the absence of any contemporary statement connecting the two, the *Hellenica* itself is the sole source of evidence of Xenophon's relationship with Thucydides. But its value as such depends to some extent upon an assumption that is wholly unwarranted: that Xenophon, in trying to emulate Thucydides, enjoyed a certain degree of success; or conversely, that if he failed to measure up to Thucydides's high standards, it is to be assumed that he did not try. It would be difficult to find two men whose literary talents and intellectual qualities were so different. Xenophon wrote simply, naturally and with great facility, like a literary counterpart of the French composer Saint-Saens, who admitted that he 'produced music as an apple-tree produces apples'. Thucydides's prose shows every sign of effort and self-torture: no ancient work better fits the Ciceronian description of 'smelling of the lamp'. But in conjunction with this inherent unlikelihood that Xenophon could have succeeded in any serious attempt to model his history upon that of Thucydides, we have to consider whether, in spite of his shortcomings, he might not have *thought* that he succeeded. There is ample evidence that Xenophon's self-critical faculty was as small as his literary facility was great; but the following features of the *Hellenica* suggest that Xenophon imitated Thucydidean method as faithfully as his ability and peculiar talents would allow.

In the first place, Xenophon follows Thucydidean seasonal chronology for a time, though this turns out to be temporary, and breaks down after a few years. He also adheres to the principle of impersonal objectivity for the duration of the Peloponnesian War, though we know from his other works that this is out of character. Again, there is no difficulty in detecting the Athenian identity of the author, as events are described mainly from an Athenian viewpoint. Xenophon also appears to share Thucydides's political views, disliking demagogues and the excesses of the mob and favouring a moderate oligarchy. But, in respect of coverage and interpretation of events Xenophon's account of the last eight years of the war, which occupies the first book and nearly half of the second (which together amount to less than a single book of Thucydides), is conspicuously un-Thucydidean. To mention only the most obvious deficiencies, Xenophon gives little indication of the continuing effect of party rivalry at Athens upon the course of the war: he pays scant attention to the personality and policy of Cleophon the lyremaker, the heir of Cleon's *Machtpolitik*, which Thucydides had examined so carefully; and he does not mention the Spartan overtures for peace after the battles of Cyzicus and Arginusae, which were rejected on the advice of that politician. In fact, a general absence of interest in the political situation is the most important departure from Thucydidean method. But on the level of technical competence also these books fall far short of their model. In particular, cross-references are often obscure or completely absent, so that we are introduced to previously unknown characters (in addition to those mentioned by Thucydides, whom we are plainly expected to know) without any explanation of their provenance or function. In addition to these faults of omission, several episodes are included that are both trivial in themselves and have no subsequent effect on the war, so that it becomes increasingly evident that Xenophon has entirely different editorial criteria from Thucydides, even allowing for the real possibility that he was careless in his methods. It is therefore better to abandon the comparison of Xenophon with Thucydides, and to consider whether any pattern exists in Xenophon's choice of material.

Certain generalizations are possible. Events of themselves, except climactic moments like the fall of Athens, do not move Xenophon: when he is narrating routine occurrences he can be soporifically dull. Given certain stimuli, however, his interest is aroused and his narrative is transformed. The chief of these

stimuli is personality. The first example of this is the appearance
and operations of Alcibiades, whose leadership and understanding
of the main strategic problems of the war enable him to turn
events in Athens's favour. The effect of his personality is illustrated in an extended description of his return from exile, which
occurs in the midst of a narrative in which all other actions have
been described with the utmost brevity. Xenophon tells us how
the Athenians thronged to the harbour 'in wonder, wishing to see
Alcibiades, and saying that he was the best of the citizens'.[30] To
Xenophon, the danger of possessing such a personality is not
purely political as in Thucydides—that men thought he was
aiming at tyranny; but personal with political consequences—that
it made others jealous and caused them to seek to overthrow him.
This uncomplicated interest in personality is further illustrated
by the space accorded Hermocrates, the Syracusan commander
who played a negligible part as commander of the Syracusan
ships sent to the aid of the Peloponnesians. Xenophon gives a
detailed account of the reaction of his men to the news that the
Syracusan government had passed a sentence of exile upon him
and his fellow-commanders:[31] the men wish to have no other
leaders, and the officers insist on obedience to the orders of the
government; and the episode ends with an appreciation of
Hermocrates's enlightened leadership. The Spartan admiral
Callicratidas likewise makes a comparatively brief appearance,
but is given two short speeches in which to present his character
and opinions.[32] He is at once the ideal patriot, devoid of personal
ambition and happy to serve his country in any capacity required
of him, and a Panhellenist, who spurns Persian gold and appears
to favour a *rapprochement* with Sparta's enemies in order to
enable Greece to present a united front against the despised
barbarian.

Whereas unimportant men like Callicratidas and Hermocrates
are thus clearly characterized, Lysander, the chief architect of
the Spartan victory, remains comparatively colourless throughout
apart from the impression of shrewdness and opportunism we
receive from his first interview with Cyrus, in which he waits
until the young satrap has become mellowed with food and wine
before asking him to supply extra pay for his marines.[33] Xenophon
admired generous, chivalrous and heroic qualities more than
those of diplomacy and subterfuge, however useful the latter

might be; but a careful examination of Xenophon's treatment of Lysander reveals a gradual improvement after the initial comparison with Callicratidas, which is decidedly unfavourable to Lysander. Later, in the campaigns preceding the final battle of Aegospotami, the historian conceals some of Lysander's mistakes and gives a full account of his successes. But neither he nor Cyrus, of whom Xenophon's portrait in the *Hellenica* is on the whole unfavourable, appears to have struck Xenophon as an interesting personality at the time of writing.

A further aspect of Xenophon's interest in personality is his presentation of strategic or political situations through the eyes of protagonists, but without composing formal speeches. The situation is rather presented as a brief dramatic scene. Thus, instead of simply saying that Athens was impregnable so long as she could withstand a siege and continue to import provisions, he portrays the Spartan king Agis looking out from his fortress at Decelea and powerlessly surveying a continuous stream of merchantmen with bulging holds making full sail for the Piraeus.[34] This graphic demonstration causes him to recommend the seizure of Byzantium as a preparatory step to the strangulation of the Athenian corn life-line. This scene is probably unhistorical, since Agis must already have known the cause of Athenian strength; but as a means of impressing the strategic realities upon the reader it is undoubtedly effective. Later, on a less dramatic level, we read that Cyrus refused to consider an Athenian request for aid, in spite of the intercession of Tissaphernes, who used an argument *suggested to him by Alcibiades*, that Persian policy should aim to maintain all the Greek cities in a state of equal weakness, and not allow any single one to grow powerful.[35] But no Persian satrap needed a Greek to tell him that; nevertheless, when represented as coming from Alcibiades the argument gains in force, if only as a sardonic commentary on the great Hellenic dilemma by the one Greek who fully understood it. It is Alcibiades too who summarizes the Athenian weakness in the epitome of a speech before the battle of Cyzicus: 'We are without money: the enemy has a plentiful supply from the king.'[36] The underlying reasons for thus presenting the determining factors in the war are probably two in number. The first reason has already been implied: that the proper conduct of a state's affairs depends upon a balanced mixture of qualities in its leaders—courage, providence and loyalty—so that it is an essential part of a historian's business to show these qualities in operation. The second reason is primarily artistic: the presentation of events in the context of human observation and calculation has an obvious appeal to a human audience. Xenophon extends this principle to scenes in which mass reaction may be portrayed, as that in which the Athenians hear the news of the defeat at Aegospotami,[37] and later when the Long Walls are demolished to the accompaniment of flutes.[38]

But the most extended expressions of Xenophon's feeling for a dramatic situation are the full-length speeches. The relative infrequency of these in the *Hellenica* compared with Thucydides is due to Xenophon's narrower conception of their function. The first, by Euryptolemus on behalf of the Ten Generals who were being tried for abandoning the crews of some of the ships sunk at the battle of Arginusae,[39] serves to dramatize the illegality of the charge and the fact that the generals had only come to face it through their own reluctance to place blame upon their accusers, who were the real culprits. The speech is thus a forensic oration designed to meet the needs of the particular case, and not to point to any general conclusions or even to throw light on the political nature of the trial. Broader issues are, however, raised in the two speeches that form the central tableau of the story of the rise and fall of the Thirty Tyrants. The speech in which Critias accuses Theramenes of undermining the authority of the Thirty[40] is a defence of oligarchy, and of bloody revolution as a means of establishing it; while that of Theramenes[41] is a defence of the moderate line, both in policy and in its implementation. But both speeches are at the same time specially adapted to the particular situation: both include personal attacks on the opponent's political record, Critias in particular seeking to make the issue personal by claiming that Theramenes is guilty of betraying his friends (a striking depiction of the oligarchic mentality, but also an effective tactical argument when it is remembered that he was speaking before the Boule [Senate], which contained a majority of those friends). Theramenes, though generally more objective, nevertheless begins by referring to past inconsistencies in Critias's political postures. Most of Xenophon's political speeches have a closer affinity with the *ad hoc* political harangues of minor Attic orators like Andocides and Aeschines, than with Thucydides's highly-wrought expositions of permanent political truths.

In view of the interest that he shows in personalities and dramatic situations, it is remarkable that Xenophon succeeds in remaining objective throughout most of his narrative of the war and the oligarchic revolution. There are two places, however, where his reserve breaks down and reveals characteristics which later assume considerable importance. The first is his account of popular reaction to the news of Aegospotami. Thucydides may here be profitably re-introduced for purposes of comparison, since in his description of the arrival of the news of the disaster in Sicily at the beginning of Book VIII he is interpreting the feelings of the same Athenian people in similar circumstances. His narrative runs as follows:

> When the news was brought to Athens, for a long time they disbelieved it, even though it was stated plainly and unanimously by survivors from the disaster itself; and they did not then believe its full extent. But when they realised it, they turned in resentment upon the politicians who had encouraged them in their enthusiasm for the expedition, as if they had not themselves voted for it, and were angry also with the prophets and soothsayers, and with all those whose divinations had given them the hope of conquering Sicily. Great consternation and fear now obsessed them, and they felt surrounded by troubles.

The emotions attributed to the Athenians by Thucydides are mainly the 'public' ones of fear, chagrin and anger with their leaders for misguiding them. In Xenophon these same Athenians are credited with possessing consciences: they not only grieve for their dead relatives and fear for themselves, but are kept awake at night by the feeling that the fate they are about to suffer is a deserved punishment. Two factors are involved here. One is the panhellenic ideal: it is no accident that this passage is preceded by one in which Philocles, an Athenian general who has been captured by Lysander, is executed by him for cutting the right hands off some captured Corinthians. The other is the broad and ancient concept, so prominent in Herodotus, of the nexus of crime and punishment. Commentators who have been shocked by Xenophon's lack of sympathy for the plight of his fellow-citizens have failed to appreciate Xenophon's individuality in combining old-fashioned morality with a forward-looking attitude to inter-state relations.

The other passage is the famous death scene of Theramenes, one of the most dramatic moments in the whole of ancient historiography. Theramenes has won the verbal battle with Critias, but the latter, seeing his own security threatened if Theramenes is allowed to escape, falls back on force and has him arrested.[42]

> When Critias had said this, Satyrus dragged Theramenes from the altar, and his attendants assisted him. Theramenes, as was natural, called upon gods and men to witness what was happening. But the senators remained silent, seeing that the men stationed at the railing were of a similar character to Satyrus, and armed with knives, and that the area in front of the senate-house was full of guards. So they led the man away through the market-place, protesting at his sufferings in a very loud voice. One of the things he is reported to have said is this: when Satyrus told him that if he did not keep quiet he would rue it, he demanded: 'And shall I not rue it if I keep quiet?' And when, on being compelled to face death, he drank the hemlock, they said that he splashed the last drops out, as in the game called *kottabos*, and said: 'This to the fair Critias.' Now I am not unaware that these sayings are unworthy of record; but I consider it admirable in the man that, with death so close at hand, neither his composure nor his sense of humour deserted him.

This is the first of many judgments that Xenophon makes in the first person. It has been evoked by the ethopoeic quality of Theramenes's utterance, and he makes this his excuse, somewhat apologetically, for recording it. The apology is itself of some interest, and seems to imply the author's recognition of certain standards—which can only be Thucydidean standards—of relevance and suitability for historical material. But here is a situation he cannot resist: what has attracted him is Theramenes's *courage*, for it is only with the aid of such a quality that he could have kept both his sense of humour and his composure in the face of death. No subsequent character is portrayed under such conditions: Theramenes's is the only utterance of 'famous last words' in the *Hellenica*.

So far we have only discussed the first two books of the *Hellenica*. The remaining five cover a further forty years of Greek history, and conclude with the Battle of Mantinea in 362.

In passing from Book II to Book III the reader soon becomes conscious of two important changes. The first is a new orientation: Sparta is now the centre of interest. The second is a more subjective treatment of the historical personalities. The former is explained satisfactorily, at least for the first fifteen years or so, by the fact that Sparta dominates Greek affairs during these years. But even in his account of her actions he shows a lively interest in her national character and institutions over and above the strict requirements of history as previously conceived by him. Moreover, certain important events and developments are omitted or underplayed because they occur outside the immediate sphere of Spartan activity. Thus the exploits of the Athenian admiral Conon that led to the important battle of Cnidus are omitted, and the battle itself is presented as a piece of bad news reported to the Spartan king Agesilaus.[43] Later, the events surrounding the King's Peace are given from a markedly Spartan point of view, with Sparta negotiating from a better bargaining position than her enemies (a different picture to that given by Diodorus); and in the sequel, the Spartans are styled 'champions of the King's Peace',[44] but we are told nothing of the dismay expressed by other Greek cities at the abandonment of most of Ionia to Persian rule. (Where is Xenophon's Panhellenism now?) But perhaps the most glaring omission to the modern reader is that of the formation of the Second Athenian Confederacy which, for all its weaknesses, endured as the last federalizing force in Greece until the onset of Macedonian power. Its existence is first recognized in the *Hellenica* as a *fait accompli* at a time when it was already experiencing the financial difficulties that were later to prove its undoing.[45]

But not all omissions and misrepresentations can be attributed to bias in favour of Sparta. Even his account of their destruction of Mantinea, which the rest of the Greek world at the time condemned as a barbarous act, admits of an alternative interpretation. When he says that the division of the old city into four villages freed the Mantineans of the 'troublesome demagogues'[46] it is surely the oligarch rather than the pro-Spartan that speaks. Much less disputably devoid of specifically Spartan bias is the omission of a reference to the foundation of the Arcadian city of Megalopolis in 368, which is one of several important events that have no special connection with Sparta, either for good or ill.

And finally we must refer to a passage which flatly relegates Sparta to a secondary place in Xenophon's allegiance: [46(a)]

> One could quote many examples from Greek and barbarian history of how the gods do not ignore deeds of impiety and injustice. And now I shall refer to the present instance: the Spartans, who had sworn to respect the autonomy of the cities, seized the Theban acropolis, were punished by receiving their first defeat ever at the hands of the men they had wronged; and as for the citizens who admitted them to the acropolis, wishing to enslave the city to the Spartans and themselves to rule as tyrants, a mere seven of the exiles were sufficient to put an end to their rule.

Here Spartan action in seizing the Cadmea is openly criticized, and in language which points to standards of conduct which no friendship will condone. The Spartans commit impiety; the gods punish them, using the wronged men as their instrument. This is not merely an isolated criticism: the Spartans lose a large measure of the historian's favour after this episode. It is, moreover, a situation that has certain elements of tragic drama. The above passage is preceded by a summary of the political situation, which finds Sparta supreme over her enemies and in firm unanimity with her friends. Then, like a tragic hero, she oversteps herself, commits *hybris*, and is pursued by the inevitable *nemesis*. This old-fashioned moral-religious interpretation of events is found throughout the last five books of the *Hellenica*: all men and all nations are judged according to its canons, and none can escape censure when he transgresses them.

When we come to consider the second characteristic of these last five books, the treatment of historical personalities, the two chief changes to be noticed from the earlier books are once again the moral-religious tendency, and the intrusion of the author's opinions stated in the first person. Both these are to be found in his treatment of the career of Agesilaus, which dominates these books to an extent altogether disproportionate to its historical importance. The quality of this king that Xenophon is most concerned to display is his piety, and it is to this above all that we are asked to believe that he owed his success. But Xenophon was initially attracted to Agesilaus for two more practical reasons: because the king's self-appointed mission, the destruction of the Persian empire, was one which appealed strongly to him; and because he was a man invested with military command, who

afforded Xenophon a unique opportunity of studying the practical
problems of leadership. Either in the normal course of friendship,
or in gratitude for his kindness and hospitality, Xenophon
formed an idealized picture of the king's qualities, and pauses
at many points in his narrative in order to illustrate them from
his words and actions. One passage from many will suffice as an
example of this procedure. Xenophon has just described a full-
scale review of the army which Agesilaus held at Ephesus, and
goes on:[47]

> It made the whole of the city in which it was being staged into a
> worthy spectacle: the whole of the market-place was full of all kinds
> of horses and arms for sale, and the smiths and craftsmen and workers
> in bronze and leather and the painters were all making arms for war,
> so that one might actually think the city was a military workshop.
> The sight was one to warm the heart: first Agesilaus, then the other
> soldiers wearing crowns retiring from their military exercises and
> dedicating their crowns to Artemis. For where men show their
> respect for the gods, practise the arts of war, and exercise themselves
> in obedience to commands, surely that place is full of fair hopes for
> the future!

In such passages as this (and there are many in the last five
books), we are no longer concerned with history, but with
biography, encomium and, in the loosest possible sense, philosophy. Xenophon is using his own reminiscences of Agesilaus to
propagate his views on the ideal aims and occupations of man.
Other characters are treated in the same way, though all on a
smaller scale, and most of them are represented as inferior to
Agesilaus in some important respect. First there are his predecessors in the Asiatic command: Thibron, who illustrates the
old Staff-College dictum that 'there are no bad soldiers, only
bad officers'; and Dercyllidas, who avoids all Thibron's mistakes,
wins over the Asiatic Greeks and holds the satraps at bay in
preparation for the arrival of his greater successor, Agesilaus. Of
the two satraps, Tissaphernes is devious and deceitful, but falls
into error when dealing with Agesilaus because he assumes that
others are like himself; while Pharnabazus is honest, but rightly
complains that the behaviour of his colleagues has harmed his
reputation.[48] Most other leaders who receive praise are pale
imitations of Agesilaus: Iphicrates the Athenian encourages the
competitive spirit in his men, and makes elaborate security

arrangements for the protection of his camps at night,[49] but is also censured for over-confidence.[50] Phoebidas, Sphodrias and Epaminondas all share the dangerous desire for glory which distinguished the able commoner from the kingly figure of Agesilaus, who was born into fame and could therefore aim at loftier things. Jason of Pherae, however, is described in terms which bear comparison with Agesilaus.[51] His neighbour Poly-damas of Pharsalus, himself no mean leader, describes him as a man of great energy, whose power rests not upon numbers of fighting men, but their quality, which he has fostered by making a military career attractive and choosing the best of the many who wish to serve with him. His success lies in his own self-sufficiency (he is a truly 'Socratic' general) and his grasp of the principle of reward for service: this he follows in the short term, by allowing ample rest to his men after immediate objectives have been achieved, and in the long term by gratuities, care during illness, and even the payment of burial expenses. As a type of intelligent, enlightened and vigorous barbarian Jason bears certain points of resemblance to Philip II of Macedon, in so far as we are able to form a picture of that monarch by reading between the lines of the mainly hostile tradition. He is different from Agesilaus in that he exercises absolute civil as well as military power, and is therefore in a better position to create a class of military élite with special privileges. He also fully understood the most profitable rôle in Greek politics for an influential outsider, as well as his geographical advantages. He is a formidable and prophetic figure, and could easily be a disguised portrait of Philip, whose activities fall outside the scope of the *Hellenica*, but who could nevertheless have been well-known to Xenophon and admired by him at the time of writing of the sixth book.

Concentration upon biographical and moralistic topics has undoubtedly destroyed the balance of these books and deprived us of valuable historical material. But, just as in the discussion of the effect of his Spartan orientation it was found that certain omissions could not be thus accounted for, so when we consider the most glaring example of the underestimation of an individual, we are faced with the same difficulty. Epaminondas, the Theban leader, was probably the most gifted Greek of his generation, both as a general and as a politician; but Xenophon mentions him for the first time when he is nearing the end of his career.[52] His critics simply say that this is because he hated the Thebans and wished to minimize their achievements. But his notices of Epaminondas, when they appear, are far from disparaging. He praises his generalship and makes him talk good sense. What is surely missing is not goodwill, but knowledge. This is probably true of a great deal of what is missing from the *Hellenica*. His descriptions of the great battles of Leuctra and Mantinea, which have justly been criticized for their meagreness and lack of self-consistency, are conspicuous examples of the same deficiency: for there was nothing Xenophon liked better than the opportunity of describing a battle, and when provided with first-hand knowledge he was fully capable of doing justice to the occasion. Thus two factors prevented him from fully covering events, the one editorial and the other circumstantial. In two important passages he admits a degree of subjectivity in the choice of his material. The first follows a sentence in which he describes the popularity of Teleutias, the brother of Agesilaus, which his soldiers showed by applauding him as he retired from an annual command. Xenophon continues:[53] 'I realize that this episode contains no significant expenditure or hazard or ingenious device, but, by Heaven, it seems to me to be a worthy subject for a man to ponder—by what actions Teleutias so disposed his men towards him: for this is an achievement far more noteworthy in a man than what he spends and the risks he takes.' Later, in order to explain his decision to include a description of the siege of the small city of Phlius, he says: 'Whenever the big cities do anything distinguished, all the historians record it; but it seems to me that when a small city has performed many great deeds, these deserve to be publicized even more.'[54] He then goes on to say that Phlius remained loyal to Sparta after most of her other, stronger allies had deserted her; and he describes how they repelled the besieging Argives.

As statements of the criteria for the choice of historical material, these passages deserve close attention. Conventional history contains accounts of expenditure (in other words records of numbers of troops, ships and equipment), 'hazard' (the political and strategic problems inherent in each situation), and the 'devices' (the manner in which the latter were negotiated). It is also concerned primarily with the policies and actions of major powers. Xenophon proposes to include actions which illustrate the noblest human qualities, and thus affirms a belief in the direct and positive moral lesson to be learnt from history by the study of virtue in action. This is essentially a departure from the view of Thucydides, whose purpose was certainly no less educational, but who looked upon the events he describes as having a cautionary value, illustrating how human weaknesses can become the instruments of mass destruction in a political environment. There is also a difference in the writer's standpoint: in Thucydides, 'war is a violent teacher', and events are allowed to imply their own moral; in Xenophon, the writer himself is the teacher, carefully selecting his subject-matter in order to illustrate the virtues of kingship and leadership, without which human society cannot prosper.

In a third passage, in which he explains the method of narration he proposes to adopt, he says '. . . and of the actions themselves I shall describe those that are noteworthy, and shall pass over those that are not worth mentioning'.[55] This passage, which precedes the two above, offers no criteria of selection, and therefore bears only one reasonable interpretation. It is Xenophon's way of admitting that his account is far from complete, by characteristically rationalizing his lack of full intelligence of events.

In view of these manifestations of a progressively diminishing regard for the principles of historiography as laid down by Thucydides, we should not leave Xenophon before considering whether any vestiges remain in the last five books of Thucydidean influence. Firstly, events are assigned to years and seasons down to the year 376 (towards the end of Book V), though this procedure becomes more and more haphazard, and is abandoned altogether after that year. More interesting are the several formal speeches, made in a strictly political context, that Xenophon has composed in a spirit that is recognizably Thucydidean. They differ, as in the earlier books, by being more narrowly conceived and suited to the special circumstances, but vary more in style and scale, ranging from such brief utterances as that of Pharnabazus to Agesilaus at their first interview[56] to the two florid orations of Procles of Phlius.[57] They probably catch the spirit of contemporary politics more authentically than those of Thucydides, containing as they do such recurrent motifs as the recollection of past connections and services, historical precedents, and religious considerations introduced in the framework of the triple themes of justice, expediency and possibility. One of a group of three ambassadorial speeches throws further light on the diplomatic scene.[58] The speaker, the Athenian Autocles, who is, moreover, described as a 'very skilful speaker', begins his speech to the Spartans, with whom his city is negotiating an alliance against Thebes, by saying that frankness is the only sound basis for negotiation between cities. He then goes on bluntly to accuse the Spartans of breaking their covenant to guard the autonomy of Greek cities, 'appearing to prefer tyrannies to proper constitutions'. The following Athenian speaker, the famous orator Callistratus, adopts a somewhat more conciliatory tone, but is not afraid to mention the Spartan error in occupying the Cadmea. There is little reason to doubt that these speeches are an authentic reproduction of the general tone in which Greek politicians of the fourth century habitually addressed one another, even if they did not actually adopt it on this occasion. Knowing this, we are in a better position to understand why Greek cities had difficulty in maintaining friendly relations.

What else can be learned from the *Hellenica* of the political problems of the age? He shows full realization of the necessity to preserve individual autonomy. Athens, Sparta and Thebes each in turn comes to grief because of her imperial ambitions. The hopeless impasse to which the whole Greek world came at Mantinea, which itself decided nothing but left Greece in the same state of confusion as before, was the result of yet another effort by a Greek city to set itself above its neighbours. Lycomedes the Arcadian was here the man responsible, because he caused his fellow-Arcadians to 'swell with pride'.[59] Earlier Xenophon has described with simple clarity the position of *Zugzwang* at which the leading Greek cities had arrived before turning in humiliating desperation to the Persian king for a solution of their problems.[60] But, like Thucydides, he can offer no solution. It is tempting, in view of his interest in leadership and his dislike of the Persians, to read into his history the advocation, along lines more directly followed by his contemporary Isocrates, of a panhellenic expedition; the more so, since no writer was better able to vouch for its prospects of success. But Xenophon remains true to

Thucydides and his ideals in this at least: his *Hellenica* is in no sense a work of political propaganda.

From an original intention to write an objective and factual account of the history of Greece, Xenophon came to realize, over the period of some fifty years in which he was engaged on its composition, that his literary talents and philosophical interests equipped him ill for the task. The somewhat abrupt change in style, mood, bias and scope which is noticeable at the beginning of Book III probably signifies the lapse of some years, and perhaps the intervention of the mind-broadening experience of the *Anabasis* between these two parts. It is also possible that the last five books are not all at an equal stage of completion, but that the author had written certain of the parts concerning Agesilaus as memoirs, after the manner of the *Anabasis*, and had inserted them in the *Hellenica* before he had had the time to revise and adapt them. But amid all these more or less likely conjectures, the *Hellenica* can be viewed as an entity, in every part of which are to be found traces of Xenophon's original intentions, and, more important for our purpose of tracing the development of ancient historiography, the many innovations which reflect the political, philosophical and literary ideas that were current in the first half of the fourth century. The various conflicts are portrayed: imperialism against autonomy, private and public obligations, panhellenism and nationalism, and over all the explicit statement of a lesson to be learnt from the idealized portraits of the individual men who shaped events. It is to the presentation of such themes as these that Xenophon's talents are best suited; and these themes become a permanent part of ancient historiography.

CHAPTER 4

Polybius and his Predecessors

XENOPHON IS the only fourth-century historian whose work has survived in a sufficient quantity for analysis. In considering his contemporaries and the following generation of historians it is pointless to devote much time to what, in many cases, can be little more than a catalogue of names. Certain members of this catalogue have been credited by different scholars with the authorship of a famous fragment of Greek history called the *Hellenica Oxyrhynchia* (so named from the ancient Egyptian town of Oxyrhynchus, where it was discovered at the turn of the century along with a large quantity of other valuable papyri). The fragment is a detailed narrative of the years 396–395 B.C. Of the various nominees for authorship the most likely, in order of precedence, appear to be Cratippus, Daimachus of Plataea, Ephorus of Cyme and Theopompus of Chios, though the first two owe their position to our comparative ignorance of them and their work, through which we are deprived of refutatory evidence. The fragment itself, ironically enough, has brought more pain than joy to historians, who have deplored the caprice of fate that left us Xenophon's *Hellenica* instead of the work of this unknown historian, whom they pronounce to be more scientific in his methods and a better judge of causation. The little that we do have on which to form an opinion does not arouse the same enthusiasm for its literary merits, and it has little to contribute to our knowledge of the development of historiography. It is more profitable, therefore, to return to the catalogue, and to select from it those names that have enjoyed most renown in the later tradition.

Of the four already named, Cratippus and Theopompus were, like Xenophon, continuators of Thucydides. Methodologically, they probably represented the opposite extremes suggested by their illustrious predecessor: Cratippus being a conscientious, accurate and impartial narrator of facts, who, we are told, disapproved of the inclusion of speeches; while Theopompus, who possessed quite considerable literary gifts, embellished his narrative with a maximum (some would say an excess) of rhetorical devices. This tendency may have been due as much to his training as to his natural gifts, for he was a pupil of the Athenian rhetorician and educationist Isocrates, who, with the best intentions, taught the power of the spoken and written word as a major influence in politics. Unfortunately, in demonstrating this power he was forced to admit its ambivalence: 'Words,' he said, 'enable us to tell the same story in many different ways, to make great things appear humble and to invest humble things with grandeur.'[1] The danger of exploiting this power when writing history is obvious; and from our limited knowledge of Theopompus it seems that he succumbed to it, though in an individual way. Most of the fragments of his writings are concerned with the bad moral effects of various forms of luxury, self-indulgence and licence upon peoples and upon persons in high places; and there is every reason to believe that he used his talents and training to shock and exaggerate in order to force home his moral lesson. But the two main works of Theopompus, the *Hellenica*, a history of Greece from 411 to 394 in twelve books, and his *magnum opus*, the *Philippica* in fifty-eight books, must, from their very size, have contained much more than a succession of polemics. The latter, to judge from its name, may be related to the Isocratean concept of a Greek world unified under Macedonian leadership, a broad theme which seems to imply its author's freedom from local partisanship. Moreover, those surviving fragments of the work which are not concerned with moral censure reveal, in their ensemble, a wide but by no means uncritical interest in most of the studies which were considered proper for a historian to pursue in his day—geography, ethnology, mythology and political psychology. But in the latter study he had one serious limitation: a negative approach. He does not appear to be sufficiently well-informed on military matters to provide parallel instruction or edification in that field. Nevertheless, in an age that was notoriously more interested in style than in content, he became a very popular writer.

Ephorus of Cyme was also a pupil of Isocrates, but the political aspect of his master's teaching that chiefly influenced him was the superiority of Greeks over barbarians. As in the case of

Theopompus, tradition has supplied us with few biographical details; but the few known facts about Ephorus point to a life-span covering the first three-quarters of the fourth century. His major work was a history of the Greek world, embracing a period of some 750 years down to the invasion of Asia by Alexander. He had finished twenty-seven of the intended thirty books when he died, and the work was completed and published by his son Demophilus.

Most of our conclusions about Ephorus's *Greek History* depend upon the well-founded assumption that Diodorus Siculus used it as his main source for the years which it covers. From Diodorus's derivative version, the greater part of which is extant, we gather that Ephorus attached less significance than Theopompus to the career of Philip of Macedon, that he was pro-Athenian and anti-Spartan, and impartial towards Thebes. This suggests that he did not follow and accept the teachings of Isocrates through the whole gamut of their changes: for Isocrates, from originally claiming the leadership of the Greek world for Athens, later became disillusioned with his city's failure to stake her claim to it, and turned his attention to Philip, abandoning hope for ever of a coalition of Greek states and turning for salvation to the strong leadership of an able and ambitious individual. Ephorus drew more upon the purely rhetorical side of Isocrates's teaching than upon its political aspects. Sharing the current view of history as a source of moral edification, he used the rhetorical powers he had acquired in order to glorify virtue and exaggerate vice. But even in this he was more moderate than Theopompus, if we are to believe the comparison of the two attributed to Isocrates, who is supposed to have said that Theopompus needed the rein, Ephorus the spur. As to his reliability both as a transmitter of information obtained from earlier sources and as a chronicler of contemporary events, it can be asserted with some confidence that he was honest, if not always discriminating, in his handling of the often conflicting traditions. The resultant narrative was sober and sometimes rather colourless, lacking in biographical interest, but with a mild moral flavour; while his lack of first-hand knowledge of military and naval matters rendered most of his battle-narratives uninformative. Nevertheless, the very lack of a strongly personal flavour, whether in praise or censure, won the trust of later historians, because it seemed to accord better with the laudable aims of universal history than the petty tirades of Theopompus. Consequently Ephorus probably enjoyed the widest circulation among both serious and casual readers of any Greek historian since Herodotus.

Another important figure in the development of ancient historiography was undoubtedly Timaeus, who came from Tauromenium in Sicily. His long life-span, which stretched over ninety years from the middle of the fourth century, enabled him to witness not only the immediate revolutionary effects of the career of Alexander the Great, but its later consequences in the vicissitudes of the Hellenistic monarchies and the leagues of city-states which superseded the independent local polities of the classical period. The word 'Hellenistic' implied cosmopolitanism within the Greek world, the submerging of local city-state differences and the acceptance of the name 'Greek' as a sufficient designation of national identity. This idea of the unification of the Greek world was achieved by Alexander in his lifetime, but after his death his successors (Diadochi) divided his empire into three kingdoms, which subsequently splintered even further. Nevertheless a form of unity was achieved, but by cultural instead of political means. A common dialect was developed, through the incredible industry of scholars and creative writers working in the great new libraries at Alexandria and Pergamum. By means of this *lingua franca* (called the *Koiné*, an example of which is the Greek of the New Testament), communication was possible on all levels throughout the Greek world.

In the broadest sense of the word, Timaeus was perhaps not truly Hellenistic. As a Sicilian, he set out to make Sicily the centre of his interest, and so to push Athens, Sparta and their factious neighbours to the back of the historical stage, which they had occupied for so long. His main work was a *History* in thirty-eight books, dealing primarily with Sicily, but also covering outstanding events in Libya and Italy. Thus the Romans and Etruscans came within his scope, and he may have originated the idea that Rome and Carthage were founded at the same time. His interest in Sicily was thus by no means narrow and parochial: indeed, the circumstances of his life ensured that this should not be so. His father Andromachus was tyrant of Tauromenium, but was expelled, together with his family, when his city was taken over by Agathocles, tyrant of Syracuse.

Timaeus went to Athens, where he lived for forty years, perhaps between 329 and 289 B.C. There he completed his education and began his literary career, but later probably returned to Sicily and died there.

That Timaeus was an important historian is to be deduced from the attitude of his younger successor Polybius. On the one hand, he starts his own history where Timaeus leaves off, and does not attempt to supplement the older historian's narrative; and on the other hand, he devotes most of his twelfth book to a detailed criticism of Timaeus's methods. When divested of their petulance and rancour, which may well be the result of jealousy, Polybius's criticisms yield some important facts about Timaeus. The most important of these is his adoption of the Olympiad as his unit of chronology, a practice which was followed by many of his successors who might otherwise have abandoned chronology as a hopeless task. The Olympiad, a period of four years marked by the celebration of the famous games, was a popular and easily distinguishable unit whose use would be acceptable throughout the Mediterranean world. In tracing history back to the first Olympiad, traditionally assigned to the year 776 B.C., Timaeus found himself confronted with a prehistoric age, and with a need to clarify his attitude to the mythological material with which he had to deal. He appears to have taken his stand on the side of respect and rationalization rather than contempt and rejection. Unfortunately in the nature of things many of his explanations could be no more than tentative conjectures, and they occasionally resulted in absurdity; and he further made himself a fair target for criticism by his own violent reproof of others. At the hands of Polybius he was especially vulnerable to the charge of bookishness, which that historian in his self-satisfied way condemns as a poor substitute for firsthand experience of politics and war. Living at Athens and writing a history of Sicily, Timaeus must certainly have spent much of his time browsing in libraries (as Polybius accuses him of doing). But the result of this was a very broad range of interests which produced a work of considerable general cultural value, and one which satisfied a growing demand from an increasingly literate public.

In terms of historical circumstance, the original Hellenistic historians were the historians of Alexander's conquests. The most important of these are those who accompanied him on his expedition, Aristobulus, Ptolemy, Callisthenes, Nearchus, and Onesicritus. Unfortunately the work of none of these survives, but indirect evidence suggests that none of these men, except possibly Nearchus, was able to avoid emphasizing one angle or another of the career of the most controversial figure in ancient history. There can at least be little doubt that Alexander's exploits, which gave birth to legends in lands as far-flung as Arabia and China, gave a tremendous stimulus to a new branch of history pioneered by Xenophon in his *Cyropaedia*—the historical romance; and there is good reason to believe that his contemporaries were no more capable of being sober and factual about Alexander than later generations.

Turning finally to Polybius, we are emphatically back in the world of reality; or so he never tires of telling us, for no extant historian devotes as much space to explaining to his readers his methods and intentions, and assuring them of his special qualifications for his task, which is to tell the truth simply and to interpret it correctly. Since in Polybius's case the circumstances of his life are especially relevant to an assessment of these qualifications, it is useful to give the known facts before further considering his claim. The son of Lycortas, an eminent citizen of Megalopolis in Arcadia, who also held high office (probably the presidency) in the Achaean League, Polybius was reared in an environment dominated by politics and public affairs, and, such being the way of the Greek world, by war, either actual or threatened. He seems to have shown an early interest in the latter: after an education in which the emphasis was probably upon practical rather than purely literary or academic matters (in his *History* he likes to quote from Homer and the Attic tragedians, but this is a tendency found only too often in writers with little depth of knowledge, who wish to create the opposite impression), he wrote a treatise on *Tactics*, which was probably the fruit of actual experience in the field. In 182 B.C., when he was still a comparative youngster, he was chosen to carry to burial the ashes of Philopoemen, the greatest of his countrymen. A year later he was selected as one of the League's three ambassadors to visit Ptolemy V Epiphanes of Egypt, but the embassy was called off. Then, in 170–169 he was appointed to one of the senior offices of the League, that of Cavalry Commander.

The years of Polybius's infancy saw the final exchanges of the Second Punic War, which culminated in the battle of Zama in 202 B.C., when Scipio Africanus defeated Hannibal, elephants and all, and established beyond further doubt Rome's supremacy in the Mediterranean World. By the time Polybius reached manhood, Rome was inextricably involved in Greek affairs. Like his father, Polybius probably upheld, nominally at least, the principle of Achaean independence; but he must have come to realize, at an early stage of his career, the necessity of avoiding friction with Rome. But the Romans, who had originally interfered in Greek affairs solely in order to quell the ambitions of the Hellenistic monarchs Philip V and Perseus of Macedon, and Antiochus of Syria, also became involved in the politics of the Achaean and Aetolian leagues. Finding themselves out of their depth in the cross-currents of Greek political intrigue, the Romans, mistaking honest neutrality for veiled hostility, resorted to the mailed fist, which had served them well in the past, as the most effective substitute for an imaginative foreign policy. After they had defeated Perseus at the Battle of Pydna in 168 B.C., they accused the Achaeans of not showing their colours clearly enough. A thousand eminent Achaeans were deported to Rome, ostensibly to stand trial and answer for the wrongs done by their people; but the real purpose of this cruel Roman measure was to have hostages against future disaffection.

Most of the Achaeans lived out their lives in obscurity, scattered among the country towns of Italy; none seems to have stood trial, and many died before any returned home. But for Polybius internment brought far greater fame than he could, in this age, have achieved in his native land. He seems to have satisfied his captors that he was not one of those responsible for fomenting anti-Roman feeling in Greece, so that they allowed him the same freedom of movement as any other foreign *persona grata*. He chose to remain in Rome where, with time on his hands, he could draw on some at least of the very rich literary and documentary sources which the city was acquiring in a quantity that increased with her conquests. But it is doubtful whether he could have enjoyed prolonged residence in the capital if he had not succeeded in striking up a friendship with a young member of a famous family, Scipio Aemilianus, the son of Aemilius Paullus, victor of Pydna. Polybius tells how the young

Scipio approached him in a library in order to discuss the contents of certain volumes, and how out of this chance meeting, there grew a relationship so intimate as to be comparable with the *rapport* that exists between father and son.[2] When Scipio found himself at the head of Rome's armies, his Achaean tutor, now his adviser and friend, was always at his side, tendering counsel and adding to his own understanding of Rome's military power. He witnessed Scipio's Spanish campaigns and was present at the destruction of Carthage in 146 B.C.; and when, in the same year, it was the turn of Greece finally to lose her independence, he went there soon after the destruction of Corinth in order to help his countrymen to secure as favourable a settlement as possible. Far from being reviled as a traitor, he earned their permanent gratitude, which many cities expressed by erecting statues of him. In addition to these 'tours of duty' in company with Scipio, he made journeys which were purely exploratory, including sea voyages through the Pillars of Hercules (Straits of Gibraltar) when he sailed along the coasts of Portugal and Africa. More significantly, he followed the route taken by Hannibal over the Alps some seventy years earlier.

These travels provided vital material for his great work, the *Histories*, which he had probably begun as a History of Achaea before his exile, but which he now conceived, in the light of events, on a much larger scale and with a different centre of gravity. Assured in her political supremacy, Rome was also beginning to rival Athens as a cultural centre, though prominent men there were turning to Greek literature as a source of models and theories. Scipio himself embraced the new Hellenism whole-heartedly, and gathered about him a circle of men who shared his desire for knowledge or were able to satisfy it. Polybius became one of the central figures of this circle; but the traffic of ideas that their many discussions produced was two-way, and gave him an understanding of Roman politics and the Roman national character such as he could hardly have acquired by any other means, so that his debt to the Scipionic Circle was probably as great as his contribution. He certainly seems to have thrived in its stimulating atmosphere; for, though little is known about his later life, there is no reason to reject the tradition that he lived to the age of eighty-two, when he died as the result of a fall from a horse while hunting.

Political and military experience, hours of study, extensive travel and discussion with his intellectual peers qualified Polybius uniquely for his task, which he conceived on a characteristically Hellenistic scale: the *Histories* comprised forty books, of which Books I to V have survived more or less intact, while fragments of the remainder amount to about one-fifth of the original work—sufficient to enable us to form an idea of its scope and plan. The most remarkable and original thing about Polybius's *Histories* is that their Greek author has made Rome his focal point, and further claims that he is writing genuine universal history. Ephorus's concept of universal history was inspired by the Isocratic ideal of pan-hellenism and was a product of national pride; and even Timaeus, in advancing the claims of his native Sicily, was writing about a civilization which was predominantly Greek. Polybius proposed to show that this Greek self-centredness was not only unrealistic in his own time, but should be abandoned for ever. Furthermore, from the accomplished fact of Roman mastery he had drawn certain conclusions, which he believed might benefit those who took the trouble to study them. He states his purpose thus:[3]

> The one aim and object, then, of all that I have undertaken is to show how, when and why all the known parts of the world fell under the dominion of Rome.

with which passage may be compared another, written in a more rhetorical vein, at the beginning of the first book:[4]

> ... Can anyone be so indifferent or idle as not to care by what means, and under what kind of constitution, almost the whole of the inhabited world was conquered and brought under the dominion of the single city of Rome, and that too within a period of not quite fifty-three years?

Thus Polybius's theme is a recent political phenomenon, the rise of Rome, which he intends to expound by the dual means of narrating events and explaining their significance where possible. At first sight the above passages do not appear to break new ground: Thucydides and Herodotus both claimed to investigate causes. But Polybius is different in that the subject he has chosen is characterized by evolutionary growth to a point of indisputable supremacy. He is thus able to offer the perfect lesson—that of success—whereas his greatest predecessors can only tell of frustrated ambitions and human folly. Thus the confidence with which Polybius states his didactic purpose was not merely a device to overcome the hostility of his countrymen, for whom his *Histories*, written in difficult Greek, were primarily intended: it was based on the firm conviction that he was witnessing the establishment of the most permanent empire ever seen in his world; which says something for his prophetic powers.

Polybius describes his conception of history as 'pragmatic', by which he means that the factual material should consist primarily of events which directly affect the political situation, and their interpretation should likewise be concerned primarily with political implications. This rules out everything that is merely marvellous, terrifying, or amusing: history is to be a serious subject, if it is to provide instruction for men of state, as he intends it should. In order to meet this requirement the historian must possess special knowledge and experience in politics and war, together with a capacity for exhaustive inquiry and critical research, not only into documents and other second-hand evidence, but through autopsy of places and the cross-questioning of witnesses. In what class of men is this rare combination of qualities likely to be found? In one only: among men of action, like himself, who have played a personal part in public life; and who are therefore able after the event, through their experience, to ask the right questions of witnesses and to 'read between the lines' of their answers.

In adopting this extreme view of the purpose of history and the qualifications necessary in a historian, Polybius was openly challenging prevalent attitudes. By his time history had undergone all the literary influences that could affect its development: epic, tragedy, rhetoric, the Hippocratic writings and, most recently through the stimulus of Alexander's exploits, romance. Polybius was in the position to review its progress under these influences, and in the hands of many writers whose credentials he might more safely challenge than those of the venerable triad of Herodotus, Thucydides and Xenophon. The zeal with which he exposes the faults of these historians may seem excessive both in tone and in scope—he devotes the whole of Book XII to a detailed criticism of Timaeus, and incidentally manages to include some harsh judgments of Ephorus and Theopompus—but his strictures bring to light admirably the problems faced by the historians of his day. Of these the most important had already been recognized by Thucydides: the physical difficulty of obtaining accurate information. Like his great predecessor, Polybius accepted the restriction of time in the interests of truth, and refused to attempt to reconstruct the distant past in the absence of reliable verbal and documentary evidence. The temptation to relax Thucydides's standards was greater than ever before: the most popular historians of his day were true children of their age, preferring the silence and comfort of libraries, where they found history in many different guises, to the din of the assembly or the battlefield. Polybius makes two specific criticisms of this remote antiquarian approach. Most important, he claims that lack of practical experience deprives a man of the basis for sound judgment, a weakness which will affect both his handling of his sources and his commentary upon the action. Secondly, because of his remoteness both in time and in spirit, he will be unable to arouse the interest and enthusiasm of his readers through his description of the events themselves, but will be forced to resort to artificial devices which will distort the truth. The forms which this distortion takes are again two in number, corresponding with the two literary genres that were exerting most influence upon history in his day: rhetoric and tragic drama. The former he sees as the worst enemy of his ideal of history, which he defines in order to show its incompatibility with all forms of free composition:[5]

> The special province of history is, first, to ascertain what the actual words used were; and secondly, to learn why it was that a particular policy or argument failed or succeeded. For a bare statement of an occurrence is interesting indeed, but not instructive: but when this is supplemented by a statement of cause, the study of history becomes fruitful. For it is by applying analogies to our own circumstances that we get the means and basis for calculating the future; and for learning from the past when to act with caution, and when with greater boldness, in the present. The historian therefore who omits the words actually used, as well as a statement of the determining circumstances, and gives us instead conjectures and mere rhetorical exercises, destroys the special use of history.

In this fundamentally important passage Polybius clearly defines the limits within which the historian may be allowed to exercise his imagination: he may seek to explain causes (for which task he will need the special qualifications observed above), but he must not exploit historical situations, or fill gaps in his knowledge of them, by free literary composition. Since this passage has a bearing upon both Polybius's attitude to causes and to his attitude to the inclusion of live speech, it will be discussed further at a later stage. For the present it is necessary to consider that other supposed enemy of good history, tragic drama. As before, Polybius selects a particular culprit, this time Phylarchus of Athens, who wrote a history of Greece covering the years between 272 and 220 B.C. The specific charge against Phylarchus and his kind is that they attempt to arouse their readers' emotions rather than stimulate their reason; and Polybius further argues that absence of the rational element can even diminish the emotional impact, since without a clear knowledge of the causes of catastrophes we cannot feel the measure of indignation or pity that they deserve. A full knowledge of the facts is essential for emotional as well as intellectual satisfaction. We are almost made to feel that a good tragedian must first be a good historian and to forget for the moment that Greek tragedy was primarily concerned with portraying the collective human condition, and used mainly mythological material for the very reason that the establishment of detailed fact was irrelevant to its purpose. Polybius's claim seems especially bold and original in view of the long-standing kinship that had existed between history and tragedy, which is to be traced to their common dependence upon the epic tradition for their original material. There is, moreover, some evidence of a growing tendency in Polybius's time to identify the purpose of history and tragedy, since both were seen to describe human sufferings and to draw moral conclusions from them. But his objection is not so much to purpose as to method: theatrical and emotive writing inhibits the reader's rational processes and deprives him of the full benefit of the lesson he is supposed to be learning. We may further doubt the strength of Polybius's hostility to 'tragic history' (which might, in spite of its histrionic postures, nevertheless contain the truth in substance), from the fact that he does not attack its earliest avowed exponent, Duris of Samos, who was probably Phylarchus's model. It is even possible that his attack on Phylarchus is not entirely impersonal: Phylarchus supports the cause of the Spartan king Cleomenes III against Polybius's favourite Aratus. It would therefore be unwise to pursue Polybius's criticism of 'tragic history' too far.

If truth is all-important, then bias must be uncompromisingly condemned. In spite of the above example of Polybius's own bias, he says some hard things about other historians on this score. But he makes one important concession: that historians may through patriotism treat the actions of their own countries sympathetically, provided that they do not distort the facts. He took full advantage of this concession in his account of Achaean affairs, but also kept his main purpose firmly in view. In a noble passage, he states his position with impressive gravity:[6]

> I am aware that some may be found, regarding it as their first duty to cast a veil over the errors of the Greeks, to accuse us of writing in a spirit of malevolence. But for myself, I conceive that with right-minded persons a man will never be regarded as a true friend who shrinks from and is afraid of plain speech, nor indeed as a good citizen who abandons the truth because of the offence he will give to certain persons at the time. But a writer of public history above all deserves no indulgence whatever, who regards anything of superior importance to truth. For in proportion as written history reaches larger numbers, and survives for longer time, than words spoken to suit an occasion, both the writer ought to be still more particular about truth, and his readers ought to admit his authority only so far as he adheres to this principle. At the actual hour of danger it is only right that Greeks should help Greeks in every possible way, by protecting them, veiling their errors or deprecating the wrath of the sovereign people—and this I genuinely did for my part at the actual time: but it is also right, in regard to the record of events to be transmitted to posterity, to leave them unmixed with any falsehood: so that readers should not be merely gratified for the moment by a pleasant tale, but should receive in their souls a lesson which will prevent a repetition of similar errors in the future.

This passage, in which echoes of Thucydides are combined with a reminder of Polybius's fuller involvement in the events of his day than his predecessor, is a fitting point at which to turn from precept to practice, and to begin the examination of the positive qualities of his history.

The study of causes is central to Polybius's didactic purpose, and is therefore a suitable starting-point. Polybius conceived of three kinds of cause: the original or real cause, which may be either a genuine feeling or grievance, or the result of a cold and cynical calculation of advantage; the pretext or advertised cause, chosen by leaders after action has been decided upon in order to justify it to the rest of the world; and the first act itself. Applying this scheme to the expedition of Alexander, he says[7] that the original cause is the example of earlier defeats of Persia, the return of the Ten Thousand under Xenophon (Polybius appears to have been one of those who accepted Xenophon's version) and the campaigns of Agesilaus, all of which had exposed the weaknesses of the Persian empire. These defeats caused Philip to view the conquest of Persia as a real possibility, from which he might obtain great prestige and material rewards. He therefore looked around for a pretext, and found a ready-made one in the Isocratean theme of vengeance upon Persia for the wrongs done to Greece by Darius, Xerxes and Mardonius. Alexander merely inherited his ambition, and his crossing into Asia was the first act of the war, not its cause.

The original cause is the product of a number of mental operations. First a situation is analysed, and a judgment formed as to possible means of exploiting it. Then individual disposition comes into play: to take the above example, Philip's decision depends upon the fact that he is of an ambitious disposition. The plans and calculations that follow his original appraisal of the situation are consequent upon his ambition. Thus reason operates within a wholly personal framework, and the importance of the individual leader, whether he be king, general or politician, is paramount in Polybius's scheme of causation. It is also characteristic of the Hellenistic outlook, which reflects the domination of the Greek world by absolute monarchs. Throughout his history he frequently describes an individual as 'the originator' of an important action; but the most famous example of the importance of individuals occurs in his discussion of the Second Punic War, for which he makes the Carthaginian general Hamilcar Barca responsible. Personally undefeated at the end of the First Punic War, Hamilcar accepted the terms of peace imposed on his country only as a temporary arrangement. Later, after the Romans had taken advantage of Carthaginian weakness by seizing Sardinia and imposing a further indemnity, Hamilcar was able to persuade his countrymen to subscribe to his private desire for revenge, and obtained their full support in his seizure of southern Spain, from which Hannibal subsequently set out on his famous march over the Alps.

Such was the importance of personality in Polybius's opinion that it is no surprise to find him devoting whole chapters to character-sketches of famous men. In all of these he aims at a balanced estimate of virtues and faults: indeed, he takes particular pleasure in drawing attention to the coexistence of opposite qualities in the same man, as in the case of Aratus, whom he judges to be an able and resourceful strategist, who however lacked physical courage at the moment of combat. Such is human nature; but in a man who makes his mark upon history, positive virtues must necessarily preponderate. Polybius criticizes the libellous portrait of Philip II of Theopompus on the grounds that a man who spent so much of his time in drunkenness and debauchery could never have been successful as a king and a conqueror.[8] Such portraiture, because it is designed to amuse rather than to edify, is open to the charge, very serious in Polybius's view, that it does not attempt to explain the facts of history. But to form a fair estimate of a man in public life is no easy task, for leaders and politicians are often forced by circumstance and interest of state to act contrary to their true natures. Tyrants, like Agathocles in Sicily, often begin their rule harshly, but once their power has been firmly established they may become mild and humane. The case of Hannibal is one of the most difficult of all, because not only did he undergo the most exacting labours, in the course of which he was forced to commit acts of extreme cruelty in order to survive, but also his position of command was not as absolute as that of a tyrant, so that he was subject to the influences of his immediate subordinates, with whom he was in daily personal contact. Polybius therefore records the popular opinions of Hannibal's main faults—that the Carthaginians thought him avaricious, and the Romans cruel—and expatiates on his undisputed prowess as a general.[9] But even here the picture is two-sided: beside his masterly control of the army in the field must be placed his handling of an overall strategic problem with which most conquerors are faced at some time in their careers: which of his enemies should he attack first? Hannibal, like Hitler in 1941, made the wrong choice. Scipio Africanus, by contrast, never makes mistakes. Polybius's portrait of his patron's ancestor is wholly laudatory, and its chief interest lies in its revelation of the qualities that Polybius most admired. He regards as both derogatory and untrue the idea that

Scipio succeeded through heaven-sent good fortune, and asserts that he made his own way through the exercise of reason and calculation.[10] Similarly, he earned popularity not through any divine aid but by showing himself to be generous, courteous and wise. All his military campaigns were characterized by a happy blending of careful circumspection, exploitation of the element of surprise, and courage in action.

Perhaps the most interesting of Polybius's pen-portraits is that of the Achaean statesman and soldier Philopoemen, who had been a formative influence upon his own career, and was also the subject of one of Polybius's early works. He makes two important points in his introduction. Why, he asks, did so many historians record such dry information as the founding of cities, and pass over in silence the characteristics and aims of the men who founded them?[11] Two essential objects of history are to be achieved by examining character: its educational purpose is met by the provision of models for imitation; and the interests of truth are preserved, since it is undeniable that human character plays a major role in the shaping of events. The other point he raises is the distinction he feels he must make between his earlier work on Philopoemen, which was a panegyric, and the present portrait, which is part of a history.[12] The latter must be absolutely un-committed to extremes of either praise or blame, but must base its judgments upon an impartial interpretation of the facts. Polybius then proceeds, in his account of Philopoemen's work, to illustrate his qualities purely through a detailed description of his reforms of the Achaean cavalry, ungarnished by personal comment. Thus in his hands the biographical sketch is restored to respect-ability as a legitimate, and indeed necessary, component of serious history; and most of his successors followed his lead.

Still on the subject of causes, we turn from the general to the particular, and recall Polybius's stated purpose, to explain the rise of Rome '. . . by what means and *under what constitution* almost the whole of the inhabited world was conquered and brought under the dominion of the single city of Rome . . .' Polybius believed that Rome's secret of success lay in the stability and flexibility of her political and military institutions, and devoted the whole of his sixth book to a description of them. The discussion of constitutions in Greek literature dates from the last half of the fifth century, and later both Plato and Aristotle concerned themselves with the problem of the ideal state. But their whole approach was different from that of Polybius. They were concerned primarily with an imaginative construction of a community in which the highest human cultural and ethical aspirations might be realized; Polybius, true to his pragmatic purpose, was interested in the state's capacity for subsistence, resilience and survival. He sets this tone by saying that the state owed its origin to the weakness of the individual man, who, like other animals, needed communion with his fellows as a defence against the hostile forces of nature.[13] (In Plato and Aristotle man is sharply distinguished from other animals in having a soul, and his instinct to live in communities is attributed to a desire to live a fuller life.) Polybius then describes the different forms of government that developed in these primitive communities. The earliest was kingship, which arose through the physical strength and courage of individuals. Once established as monarch, the chosen man would be looked to as the fountain-head of law and justice, and would be honoured and protected if he carried out his duties well. If the monarchy brought prosperity the people would wish it to continue, and on the death of the king appointed one of his sons in the natural belief that he would be like his father. But hereditary power is different from power that has been earned by merit: it engenders an empty arrogance, which can turn a king into a tyrant. When this happens, the people, resenting his high-handedness and self-indulgence, find new leaders and cast him out. For a time these new leaders, chosen because they are the most eminent of the citizens by reason of their wealth, act in concert for the common good; but after a time they too come to regard government as a means of personal gain rather than as an altruistic duty. Their rule degenerates from aristocracy to oligarchy, and they are in turn discredited. No longer trustful of individuals, the people invest the sovereign power in an assembly of themselves, and the state becomes a democracy. But democracy is not immune from corruption: richer citizens use their money to bribe their way into office, and the more eloquent or vociferous exercise an influence disproportionate to their worth; and so democracy degenerates, through a conflict of private interests, into mob-rule, and chaos reigns until a single strong man can re-establish order and begin the whole cycle anew. Such is the erratic progress of a state under the simple constitutions of monarchy, aristocracy and democracy: each degenerates into its evil counterpart, tyranny, oligarchy and ochlocracy respectively (the latter term perhaps being the invention of Polybius). No state can achieve organic growth if subjected to continuous upheavals of this kind, and yet their occurrence seems to be a manifestation of a law of nature. Stability must therefore be artificially imposed; and the prescription for this is the mixed constitution. The Spartan reformer Lycurgus realized that simple constitutions are unstable, and devised a constitution for his city which contained each of the three elements, the power of each being held in check by the others so that none should predominate. Because of this artificially stabilized constitution Sparta subsequently enjoyed virtual freedom from internal strife.

The Roman constitution, in which the element of kingship is the consulship, that of aristocracy the senate, and that of democracy the popular assembly, was evolved over a number of years as the result of recurrent pressures from within and without. It is obviously outside the scope of the present study to discuss Polybius's account of the Roman constitution in detail: in fact, our only concern is to discover his reasons for praising it above all others. His chief interest in Rome is in her success as a conquering nation. We are therefore obliged to accept his reasoning when he says that the Roman constitution must have been better than that of Sparta because the Romans made the greater and more permanent conquests. But, it may be objected, success in conquest depends more upon military efficiency than upon political stability. Polybius's description aims to demonstrate that the two are interdependent. He follows his account of the several powers and duties of the consuls, the senate and the people with an authoritative analysis of the elements of the Roman army, its rules, its personnel, its equipment and its standard manoeuvres and dispositions.[14] The crucial link between these two accounts is, however, neither political nor military in the purely technical sense, but psychological: in both fields of activity virtue is rewarded and vice punished. In the army brave men receive crowns and other decorations, while cowards suffer cudgelling (the *fustuarium*) or, in the case of mass dereliction of duty, the execution of every tenth man (*decimatio*).[15] In the civilian sphere there is greater scope for the creation of a system and an environment in which every citizen feels that the state depends upon his efforts and will reward them handsomely. Polybius follows a chapter in which he ascribes the military superiority of Rome over Carthage to her employment of her own citizens in her army instead of mercenaries, with one describing the Roman methods of recognizing distinguished service to the state.[16] The reason for this juxtaposition may not at first appear obvious: but the knowledge that his services, both civil and military, would receive recognition by ennoblement or public praise, even posthumously conferred, must have been a powerful spur to the citizen-soldier, and must in large measure have accounted both for his individual fighting qualities and for the almost inexhaustible supply of his kind on which the city could draw. Polybius was impressed as much by Rome's capacity to survive disasters and win through as by her talent for conquest; and his view of Rome's early achievements became the prevalent one in the later tradition.

The great enigma of Polybius's history is the presence along-side an unending quest for reasons and causes, and a faith in the power of the mind to discover and explain, an equally pervasive concern with the interference of an incalculable and capricious force in human affairs, which he called *Tyche* (Chance or Fortune). Leaving aside his use of formulae like 'Chance dictated that . . .' when he means no more than 'it happened that . . .', there are many cases in which Chance seems to play an independent and decisive rôle. From an examination of all the instances, apart from those of a formulaic character, of the operation of Chance, it is possible to discern two distinct kinds. Firstly, when human calculation is confounded by a sudden, unpredictable disaster, like an earthquake that buries thousands beneath the rubble of their own homes, a freak storm that destroys crops as they are about to be gathered, a plague that decimates a crowded city, or a drought that parches and debilitates all living things, the cause is unknown, and yet some superhuman power seems to have been at work; so Polybius calls it 'Chance'. In the second case, men themselves sometimes behave unexpectedly, either greatly exceeding or falling far below their own or normal human standards of performance or behaviour; so that similarly, when no rational cause can be discovered for their aberration, 'Chance' must once again be held responsible. The part played by Chance in the latter case is sometimes fundamental, as with Rome herself, whose conquests may be rationally explained only after the special qualities of her people have been understood; and these qualities are the gift of pure Chance. Nobody was more aware than Polybius himself of the dangers of ascribing too much to Chance. 'Those things,' he says, 'of which it is possible to find the origin and cause of its occurrence, I do not think we should ascribe to the gods';[17] and these include some phenomena which might at first sight appear to be the legitimate province of Chance. He instances the low birthrate in contemporary Greece, for which he blames the selfishness and greed which has become endemic among his countrymen, and says: 'On this subject there is no need to ask the gods how we are to be relieved from such a curse: for anyone in the world will tell you that it is by men themselves, if possible, changing their objects of ambition; or, if that cannot be done, by passing laws for the preservation of infants.'[18] The power to change such things and to avert such disasters is in human hands, and men should not blame the gods when their own folly is responsible.

By representing the rise of Rome as the result of a national character conferred upon her people by Chance, Polybius makes that power central to his theme, and appears thereby to detract from the educational value of his history. But to teach his readers the power of Chance is itself an educational aim, which, if realized, will fortify them morally against its worst effects. They will learn that, though they may conduct their affairs with all due regard for the problems involved, they may still come to grief, as have many men more gifted and more exalted than themselves. They will learn also that, though success may attend their efforts, its duration may be short, and in almost all cases, prosperity will ultimately come to an end. A study of the undeserved misfortunes of others provides two important lessons: it teaches us not to exult in success, nor to use it immoderately; and it teaches us to bear our own calamities with philosophical calm, in the knowledge that our misfortune is merely a part of the common human experience.

The earlier examination of Polybius's historiographical principles, and his criticisms of those of his predecessors who unwittingly ignored them, lead one to expect penetration, impartiality and an unemotional presentation of the facts. It may be said at once that in the vast majority of cases this is what we get. It is seldom necessary to correct his conclusions on the main issues: only in a few cases where he is personally involved does his judgment sometimes waver. For example, on a national level he shows a strong prejudice against the Aetolian League and the Aetolians, whom he calls selfish, greedy and unjust; to his own Achaean League, however, he devotes a long section which tends to the conclusion that it was honourable in its aims and largely successful in its dealings. In the most important case, however, that of the Romans themselves, his judgment is balanced and full: we read variously of their resolution and resilience in adversity and their physical bravery, which counterbalanced the superior generalship of the Carthaginian Hamilcar; but we also read of their fear of the Gauls, whose appearance in north Italy in 225 B.C. reminded them of the great Gallic invasion of 390–386,[19] in which they had been almost extirpated from their ancestral city. There was panic also when the news of the disaster at Cannae reached Rome, but 'the peculiar excellence of their constitution and their capacity for good counsel enabled them not only to recover Italy, but also to defeat the Carthaginians and within a short time to obtain dominion over the whole of the inhabited world'.[20] A somewhat idealized picture, to be sure, but one in which virtues and faults both play a part.

As to Roman policies, he expresses disapproval of their seizure of Sardinia, but persistently upholds the view that the Roman conquest of the East was not the result of a deliberate policy of imperialism, but happened through a lack of courage and good faith on the part of the Greeks and their other Aegean neighbours. And as a final example, nothing could be more admirably penetrating than his summary of Carthaginian weakness:[21]

> Three things must be noticed in regard to the Carthaginians. First, among them the means of life of private persons are supplied by the produce of the land; secondly, all public expenses for war materials and stores are discharged from the tribute paid by the people of Libya; and thirdly, it is their regular custom to carry on war by means of mercenary troops.

The same preoccupation with fairness and truthfulness is to be found in his employment of live speech. Here his standards are more exacting than those of Thucydides. Speeches 'summarize events and provide continuity';[22] and again: 'The historian should not aim at producing speeches which *might* have been delivered . . .'[23] but his function is above all to record with fidelity what was actually said or done, however ordinary it may be.' The spoken word is firmly bound to the factual material, which it should elucidate and rationalize. In a third passage, however, he says:[24]

I do not think that it befits statesmen to be ready with argument and exposition on every subject of debate without distinction: they should rather employ those suited to the particular occasion. Similarly, it is not the business of the historian to practise his skill and show off his ability to his readers, but rather to devote his best efforts to discovering and recording what was actually said, and even of this only the most important and effective parts.

This passage contains definite indications that Polybius recognized the problem that had exercised the mind of Thucydides in regard to speeches. Indeed, he clarifies it further: the speeches which were actually made might not, for two well-defined reasons, have been worth recording verbatim. The speaker may have resorted to the only too common expedient of reeling off a series of rhetorical commonplaces; or he may simply have failed to speak to the point. We are once again back to the problem of reconciling 'what was called for' (in other words the ideal speech, which would be of real use to the historian's audience of budding statesmen) and 'what was actually said'. Polybius comes a little nearer to its solution, at least theoretically, by claiming the historian's right to select from the actual speeches only what was essential. Thus to him speeches were in no sense intended to dramatize, since he was quite prepared to deprive them of all artistic form in order to realize their narrow purpose and no more. In practice, many of them are presented in reported, not live speech.

The majority of Polybius's Roman speeches are made by men who are connected in some way with the family of his patron Scipio Aemilianus. Two of these, that of P. Scipio to his troops before the battle of the Ticinus,[25] and that of Scipio Africanus,[26] together with the two speeches of Hannibal with which they are paired, are replete with the familiar sentiments common to

battle-speeches down the ages. Not perhaps a damning observation in itself: but it has also been shown that Scipio was taken
by surprise at Ticinus, and did not expect a battle, while in his
speech before Zama, Africanus tells his men that they are about
to fight for dominion over the whole world, surely a startling
anticipation of the future course of history. The Scipionic
speeches are a special case, and reflect his interest in the family
which he believed to have done most to place Rome in her
exalted position. But there remains a possibility that Polybius's
versions of these speeches are derived from originals preserved
either by his historical sources or in the family archives.

The remaining speeches may with greater confidence be
regarded as genuine, at least as to their general content, in
accordance with his stated principles of selection. The recurrence
of certain metaphors, similes and other sentiments in them is no
proof of their spuriousness, since many of these can be traced to
a common ancestry in earlier literature, which was the common
property of each and every subsequent speaker. It must be
remembered that Polybius, through his wide travels and his
privileged position in Rome, and also because he lived in an age
in which all kinds of writing, literary and documentary, were
preserved with diligent and scholarly care, was in a far better
position than Thucydides to obtain exact information as to what
was said when he was not himself present. In certain cases it is
evident that he had access to more detailed information than he
felt it necessary to divulge; and in such cases it is interesting to
see what he records. From the conference of Philip V and the
Greeks at Naupactus in 217 he reports only the speech of one
Agelaus, a native of that city.[27] The reason for the choice is that
that speaker expresses two views which came to be widely held
in Greece: that whether Rome or Carthage won the present war,
the victor would not rest content with her conquest; and that this
menacing 'cloud in the west' could only be held by the combined
resolution of the whole of Greece, including Macedon. Two later
speeches likewise serve to enucleate the main political and moral
issues of the time—those delivered by Chlaeneas of Aetolia and
Lyciscus of Acarnania at a conference held at Sparta in 211 B.C.[28]
The first of these recites the historical reasons why the Greeks
should not place their trust in Macedonian leadership and why
the proposal of an alliance with Rome against Philip V should be

attractive to them. Lyciscus states the opposite case, praising the work of Philip II in the Sacred War of 357–346, and his plans to conquer the hated Persians, which were realized by Alexander. The length allotted to Lyciscus probably reflects the direction in which Polybius's sympathies lay—against the Aetolians—but the two sides of the controversy, which was central to the problem of Greek unity, are fairly given. His speeches, and his summaries of speeches, contain few of the general ideas that we find in Thucydides's discourses, but instead a great abundance of relevant facts, proofs and precedents. They contain a lively presentation of contemporary realities, and play a vital part in the historian's central purpose of explaining causes.

It remains to consider the purely literary qualities of the *Histories*. By now we should know what to expect, having seen how Polybius tried to rescue history from adulterating influences. On the credit side, one need not feel deprived at the complete absence of sensationalism—no histrionics, no painting of gruesome scenes of carnage: for instead we have a competent, clear and technically knowledgeable account of battles and stratagems, and a precise description of the psychological reactions of the participants in each situation. In the matter of style itself, it is completely wrong to suppose that Polybius was negligent or ignorant of the basic rules. It is well known, for example, that he scrupulously follows the accepted practice of avoiding hiatus, or the clashing of vowels at the beginnings and ends of words. Studies of his word-order and vocabulary reveal further evidence of care in composition and effort to achieve precision. He is also by no means averse from the infusion of a little colour by means of similes, of which he is remarkably fond. But against this must be set his almost complete failure to master periodic structure. This would not be a fault in an author who wrote in a consistently simple style; but Polybius is not such an author. His sentences are longer, and contain more subordinate clauses than, for example, those of Xenophon or Diodorus Siculus. But there is little attempt to arrange these clauses elegantly, or to provide variety of kind; on top of which he has a penchant for the 'articular infinitive', by which the infinitive is made to do the work of a finite verb, thus depriving the clause of the element of action. Furthermore, in spite of the care he shows in his descriptions, which is reflected in the high frequency of adverbs and adverbial phrases, his choice of nouns often shows the influence not of literary language but of contemporary 'officialese', the *Kanzleisprache* of the Hellenistic court bureaucrats. This often led to a negation of the precision which he sought, and was one of the reasons why some of the more purist critics, like the Atticist Dionysius of Halicarnassus, found him unreadable. His concern to avoid the faults of his predecessors caused him to overtax his limited literary talents, and to fall back upon devices which, in his hands at least, could not be integrated into a style suited to the writing of history.

But it would be grossly unfair to leave Polybius on a note of censure. As a highly intelligent observer and participant in an age of momentous change, a Greek who assumed the task of informing his fellow-countrymen that Rome was henceforth to be their mistress, he possessed most of the qualifications of a great historian: impartiality, a sense of educative purpose, and the faculty of perceiving essential and 'epoch-making' elements. He was also a reformer of the genre, recalling Thucydidean standards and adding the contemporary ingredients of individualism and an overt didacticism which admits personal judgments on a wide range of questions, rational and moral. And finally, all historians of the Punic Wars and the second century agree that our knowledge of these years without Polybius's guidance would be crepuscular in the extreme.

CHAPTER 5

Sallust and his Forerunners

THE FIRST five hundred years of Rome's history were a
stern struggle for survival. When she started life (traditionally in the year 753 B.C.) as a small, unexceptional
Italian city occupying a strategic position on the south bank of the
river Tiber, her chances of establishing an independent enclave,
between the powerful Etruscan cities to the north and the Greek
colonial cities to the south, must have seemed slight. But a more
permanent danger was inherent in the geography of Italy itself,
which was subject to intermittent incursions by roving tribes from
central and northern Europe, and which, being a peninsula,
could provide means of ingress but not of transit, and was
therefore peculiarly sensitive to external pressures. Early Rome,
unlike her wealthier neighbours, did not depend upon maritime
trade for her prosperity, but upon the soil of Italy. She could not
therefore retire behind her walls and rely on her merchantmen,
as Athens did in the Peloponnesian War, but had to contest each
and every challenge to her territorial sovereignty. This she did
successfully by adapting her constitutional machinery to the
needs of military organization: citizens assembled on the Field of
Mars, the war-god, summoned by a trumpet-blast, both for
political meetings and in order to serve the city under arms, which
they were frequently required to do at short notice. The *legio*
('levy'), in spite of its apparently casual and amateur character
(which later writers liked to exaggerate), proved equal to the
demands made upon it in the early years, and encouraged Rome's
neighbours to seek defensive alliances with her. Almost im-
perceptibly, she became the leader of a league of Latin cities. In
some cases alliance was preceded by conquest, the result of an
enlightened Roman preference for partnership over servitude;
while in others it arose from a desire for protection, readily
satisfied by a city which, organized to the limit of her resources
with a Spartan military efficiency, could not hope to hold out in
isolation indefinitely.

Whether deliberately sought or accidentally acquired, leadership brought involvement and responsibility. The early history of Rome is a story of successive wars. After composing her differences with the Latin cities, she combined with them against the Sabines, the Aequi and the Volsci, in a series of wars which occupied most of the fifth century. In 405 B.C. the Romans dealt a severe blow to Etruscan power by the capture of Veii, but fifteen years later themselves suffered a crippling setback at the hands of the Gauls, who occupied most of the city and failed to scale the Capitol only through the vigilance of the sacred geese. Disease, not Roman arms, finally induced them to come to terms and retire; and the rest of Italy drew a conclusion which the Romans spent the rest of the century in refuting. Most of her allies, thinking she was no longer a major power, repudiated her leadership. But if Rome's small resources of manpower were no match for the numberless Gallic hordes, her superior organization gave her an advantage over her neighbours which was enhanced by their inability to combine against her. She reimposed her alliance individually upon each Latin city, allowing them their independence in return for military service. The new confederacy was tested to the utmost in the three Samnite Wars which were waged between 343 and 290 B.C., and which established Rome as the undisputed mistress of Central Italy.

Embroilment with the wider Mediterranean world was now only a matter of time; but the process was accelerated by Rome's failure to define her sphere of interest. She allowed herself to become involved in a dispute with Tarentum (modern Taranto), then a powerful but remote city, which hired the war-hungry king Pyrrhus and his mercenary army and subjected Rome to her first military ordeal against professional opposition. Rome emerged with credit, if not with glory, having enjoyed the advantage of superior numbers through the firm allegiance of her allies. Her status as a major power was signalized in 273 B.C. by the diplomatic initiative of Ptolemy II of Egypt who, by proposing a treaty of friendship, implied an admission of parity between the wealthiest of the Hellenistic monarchies and the leader of a new Italian confederacy. But not every Mediterranean power reacted to the rise of Rome in such a sanguine spirit. Her willingness to take up the cudgels against distant enemies and to follow disputes to their conclusions alarmed the Carthaginians, who were maintaining a precarious hold on parts of Sicily. On leaving that island for the last time, Pyrrhus was said to have observed: 'What a cockpit we are leaving for the Romans and the Carthaginians to fight in!' That fight lasted intermittently for the rest of the third century. Being rich in material resources but poor in manpower, the Carthaginians made wide use of mercenary troops. They were surprisingly defeated on sea, where their greater experience should have given them the advantage. On land they generally had the better commanders, but lack of determination or a unified plan on the part of their home government often caused them acute embarrassment. Nevertheless, with generals like Hamilcar Barca and his son Hannibal, they were able to inflict defeats which would have broken the will of lesser states, especially as the most severe of these happened in allied territory, giving the victors good cause to hope for widespread desertion from the Roman standard. But the disasters of Trasimene and Cannae, far from concluding the war, served only to protract it: the Romans declined henceforth to meet Hannibal in a pitched battle until they had regained their strength and learned the strategic lessons of their defeats; and their allies, with few exceptions, remained loyal. Finally, after reinforcements had failed to reach him, Hannibal sailed back to Africa to defend his homeland, and at the Battle of Zama was defeated in 202 B.C. by the Roman general who had learnt most from him, Scipio Africanus.

With the eclipse of Carthage as a major power, the centre of contention shifted eastwards, where autocratic power allied to insatiable ambition was about to plunge the whole of the Greek world into the melting-pot. Most of the Asiatic empire of Alexander the Great had disintegrated soon after his death, and the remainder, consisting of Greece, Asia Minor, Syria, Palestine and much of Egypt, was divided among three royal houses descended from his most able captains, Antigonus, Seleucus and Ptolemy. These three dynasts and their descendants lived in uneasy contiguity for the best part of a century, until a critical moment in the history of Ptolemaic Egypt, the accession of the boy-king Ptolemy V, coincided with the reigns of Philip V in Macedon and the Seleucid Antiochus III, who carried out Asiatic conquests as far east as India. In 202 B.C. these two expansionist monarchs entered into a brigand's agreement to divide Ptolemy's overseas territories between them. These included several outposts in the Aegean; and it was Philip's naval activities that led to Roman intervention. In 201, Rhodes and Pergamum, two peaceful and prosperous maritime states, finding themselves unable to cope with Philip on their own, sought Roman aid, recalling that Philip had made an alliance with Hannibal soon after Cannae, and hoping that Roman resentment against him might be rekindled to some practical effect. But statesmanship demanded more reasons than mere resentment for Rome's first commitment to an active overseas alliance, especially at a time when she was still reeling from Hannibal's last blows. Initially the war-weary populace voted against renewed hostilities; but an influential section of the nobility was in favour of intervention, and its method of working its will upon the sovereign assembly is an interesting illustration of the degree of sophistication attained in Roman politics by this time. It differentiated motive from argument: to the people a blunt manner and a simple proposition was the best approach, so the consul Sulpicius argued that Philip V's insatiable ambition would bring him to Italy if he were not stopped beforehand; and the people agreed that it would be better, given the choice, to fight the war on foreign rather than Italian soil. But the motives actuating Rome's leading men were varied, some narrower than the national interest, others transcending it. The former, involving the contending ambitions of the patrician families and their efforts to win support, are of minor concern. The latter, comprehended in the single word, *Philhellenism*, are of abiding importance to this study.

Roman admiration for Greek civilization was born in the early days of the Republic, and was already strong when a board of ten senators visited Greece in 452 B.C. in order to study the laws of Solon. That was a time of internal conflict and disturbance, and the spirit of compromise through which Rome's statesmen extricated her from her troubles may well have received its first promptings from the example of the famous Athenian lawgiver. Later, as she matured and came into more direct contact with the Greek world, she found that it had much more to offer. The earliest Latin literature dates from the years following the end of the First Punic War (241 B.C.) when a number of poets of real distinction began to adapt Greek literary forms and metres to the Latin language. Naevius and Ennius each produced Roman epic and drama, and found a sympathetic audience among an increasingly leisured and opulent nobility. The Roman debt to Greece, which with the growth of the native Latin genius later became a matter of more evenly-matched controversy, was at this time still acutely felt by these aristocratic patrons, many of whom learned Greek and visited the Greek centres of culture—Athens, the first 'university city', Rhodes, with its rhetorical school founded by Aeschines, the opponent of Demosthenes; Pergamum and Alexandria, with their great libraries and resident grammarians and scholars. Therefore, when they saw this civilized world threatened by Philip and Antiochus, whom they regarded as rude outsiders, many enlightened Romans felt an obligation to interfere. The Greeks had stood for freedom, defended it, and thrived under it: it was now the duty of all those who had benefited from their example to guarantee that freedom in perpetuity.

Philip was defeated in a closely-fought battle at Cynoscephalae in 197 B.C., and the 'freedom of Greece' was proclaimed at Corinth the following year. There is no compelling reason to believe either that the philhellenic sentiments of Flamininus, the general who assumed the dual role of victor and herald of liberation, were in any way insincere, or that they were not shared by some of his most influential peers. Moreover, those who attributed Rome's interference in Greek affairs to diplomacy rather than sentiment, must find considerable cause for embarrassment in the sequel. For although the enthusiasm which all Greeks present had shown for Flamininus's Corinthian proclamation seemed universal at the time, the Aetolian League took it as an affront, and guaranteed their support to Antiochus if he should decide to occupy Greece. A second Roman army, a second campaign, and a second victory, this time at a famous battle-site, Thermopylae (191 B.C.), did little to further the cause of good Graeco-Roman relations, and achieved no lasting settlement. And the Romans continued, through the inhibiting influence of philhellenism and the lack of a definite political or strategic plan in Greece, to pursue an erratic and ambiguous course. It has already been seen how this ended. The Greeks, for their part, had once more revealed themselves as a people by whom unity, if it was to be attained at all, must be attained at the expense of liberty by imposition from without.

But in the cultural field the rôles of conqueror and conquered were reversed, and remained so for many years. In the words of the poet Horace:[1]

> Graecia capta ferum victorem cepit et artes
> Intulit agresti Latio.

('Captive Greece overcame her uncouth conqueror, and introduced the arts into rustic Latium.') Historiography, a late arrival on the Roman cultural scene as upon that of Greece, was less obviously dependent upon Greek models than Roman oratory, drama and epic. Indeed, the study of history was not without purely Roman antecedents. The priestly college of the *pontifices* kept records from the earliest times not only of treaties and other events which had a bearing upon the city's religious observances, but also, on a day-to-day basis, of any important happenings, whether of secular or divine significance. Records of a more personal and biographical kind were kept in the private houses of those families whose members had played an active part in public life. The present generation had a strong interest in publicizing the exploits of their ancestors, for it was upon these that their prospect of a successful political career initially depended. From the earliest days of the Republic, high office was the jealously-guarded privilege of those men who could boast a family history of service to the state. The busts of their ancestors, subscribed with laudatory accounts of their deeds (mostly warlike), which most illustrious families displayed in the forecourts of their houses, served a purpose which was much more practical, and therefore more characteristically Roman, than the mere expression of idle and insensate pride. And as pressure upon the 'Magic Circle' of senatorial families grew from the swelling ranks of able commoners who sought to break their oligarchy, they found ever more compelling reasons to appeal to a wider public.

Here, then, were conditions favourable to historiography: the long-established tradition of official record-keeping, the personal interest of men of weight in the publication of accounts of the past which would put the exploits of their ancestors in a favourable light; and, at the close of the third century, the stimulus and guidance of Hellenistic models, the most influential of which laid stress upon the practical utility of history and the importance of individuals, two qualities which might be expected to guarantee both public circulation and aristocratic patronage. History thus began its career at Rome with a well-defined set of precedents and aims, and these may be discerned, in spite of its fragmentary character, in the work of the first Roman historian, Fabius Pictor. A member of a famous and powerful patrician family, and a distant relative and contemporary of Fabius Maximus, whose policy of defensive attrition during the Second Punic War saved Rome after Cannae, but was later discredited and abandoned, Fabius Pictor was the first of a long line of senators who devoted their few hours of leisure to composing their own versions of events in which they had an interest, whether immediate or remote. Fabius thus wrote within strictly limited terms of reference. He recorded only enough to enable the reader to mark the decisive steps in a series of actions or deliberations. If his account tended towards chauvinism and glorification of the Fabian family, he was in good company— that of the very historian who criticized him for these faults, Polybius; and it seems clear from the testimony of later writers who used him, including honest men like Livy and Cicero, that he extracted from the public records available to him as accurate and self-consistent an account of early history as their fragmentary nature allowed.[2] But perhaps the most interesting fact about Fabius is that, in spite of his patriotism and his family pride, he wrote in Greek. There are three possible explanations for this. The first, which has gained wide acceptance, is that Fabius, like Polybius two generations later, wrote primarily for a Greek public. The second, that he aimed at an educated Mediterranean public including Romans like himself, depends to some extent on the third proposition, that Greek was the only tried language of historiography, and that there were several good precedents for using it in non-Hellenic histories. It might be easier to choose between these explanations if we knew with some precision when he wrote. If he commenced his task as early as the outbreak of the Second Punic War (218 B.C.), as is quite possible, or even after Cannae, a time which would have suited a special purpose, it is difficult to see who his Greek public could have been. But equally we have no fragments with any markedly Greek interest even if it is assumed that he wrote twenty years later, after Rome had become embroiled in Greek affairs. The argument against a primarily Greek orientation of Fabius's history may be concluded, paradoxically, by deduction from his use of the Greek language: how could a Roman hope to find a sympathetic public among style-conscious connoisseurs for a history written indifferently in their native tongue? It therefore seems fair to conclude that Fabius Pictor aimed to provide the civilized Mediterranean world with a plain account of the history of a city whose emergence as a great power was becoming increasingly evident; that he tried to portray the rise of Rome as a phenomenon devoid of imperialistic or acquisitive motives, and guided by the honest counsels of its senior governing body, the Senate, which in turn relied upon its most able members, some of whom happened to be related to the historian.

The tradition of combining service to the state with historiography became firmly established at Rome. Unfortunately most of Fabius's contemporaries who are known to have composed history have left posterity with more information about their lives than their work. L. Cincius Alimentus attained the rank of praetor in 210 B.C. and the dubious distinction of capture by Hannibal. In the next generation, C. Acilius shared the experience of Fabius in having his knowledge of Greek put to practical use: Fabius had been deputed to consult the Delphic oracle, and Acilius acted as interpreter for a visiting Athenian embassy (155 B.C.). Postumius Albinus, who achieved the consulship in 151 B.C., was no doubt voicing the misgivings of all the above-named when he apologized in his introduction for his shaky Greek.

Far more interesting than any of these unsubstantial figures, and a welcome addition to an unavoidably colourless list of precursors and pioneers, is the man who for later generations was the embodiment of every kind of peculiarly Roman excellence, Marcus Porcius Cato. In a state whose aristocratic leaders were increasingly succumbing to foreign influences, Cato was a plebeian who capitalized on national pride. The image he projected of his ancestors and himself was that of sturdy farmers who, like Cincinnatus of old, had loyally exchanged ploughshare for sword in the service of Rome. Not for him the misdirected humanity, the tolerance born of weakness, the necrophilic homage to a defunct greatness which had emasculated Rome's hellenized leaders: not for him indeed, for the opposite line afforded a more promising political platform. It brought him the consulship in 195 B.C. at the early age of forty, at a time when that office was still almost monopolized by a narrow circle of patrician families. Throughout his career he continued to uphold the Roman national identity by seeking to preserve those aspects of her character which had made her great: asceticism, which had in the past been necessary in order to meet the needs of agriculture and war; honesty in both private and public affairs, with its concomitant observance of religious proprieties; and finally the vigorous suppression of all influences that tended to corrupt these qualities.

Cato attacked the prevalent liberalism on a wide front, arguing that it was incompatible with Rome's position of authority. In 184 B.C. he was armed with the most potent weapon of reform in the Roman state, the censorship, and used it to maximum effect. Taking the influx of wealth from the East as the tangible cause of corruption, he imposed a 'luxury tax' on a wide range of imported goods, and further forbade the use of money for purposes of ostentation, such as the erection of statues. He also conducted his attack on the moral level by making full use of the censor's power to remove undesirable members from the Senate. He rid himself of some dangerous opponents by this expedient, including Quinctius, a consular and a member of the hellenizing family of Flamininus, whom he charged with the murder of a noble of the Boii, a tribe of southern Gaul, in a drunken outburst at a banquet, a crime which demonstrated the effects of excess in situations involving honour, diplomacy and responsibility. Tradition attests that he carried his strictures to extremes. Perhaps the best of the many stories told about him is that of the unfortunate senator who lost his seat in the senior chamber because he was seen kissing his wife in the presence of his daughter. One of the favourite subjects for declamation in the later schools of rhetoric was 'Should Cato marry?' Cato's enemies made sure that the pupils had a wealth of colourful material on which to draw.

Like the littoral gesticulations of King Canute, Cato's efforts at moral reform were doomed to failure; negative and repressive, they propounded no logic that seemed cogent at the time for the abandonment of a life which seemed, to most men of intelligence, to be the rich and just reward of conquest. But his generous endowment of talents enabled him to carry his nationalist crusade to greater lengths on another front. He was probably the first Roman to write history in his native tongue. The seven books of his *Origines* traced the history of Rome and her immediate neighbours from their beginnings down to his own day. The surviving fragments of the work are variously informative: some reveal only the interest suggested by the title, dealing with the foundation-legends of the various Italian communities which formed the nucleus of the Roman empire. There is throughout a markedly materialistic tendency, typified by one reference to rich iron and silver mines, and other geographical and biological descriptions which betray their author's interest in business and agriculture. But there is also evidence that his introduction of ancient legends and customs was intended for the edification of his readers; and, as a more personal instrument of propaganda, he incorporated some of his own speeches in his narrative, thus making his history a platform from which to launch his own political views. Apart from being a striking variation of the accepted historical practice of including formal speeches, together with another device this illustrates one of the many inconsistencies which make Cato one of the most intriguing figures of antiquity: for with this blatant self-assertion we have to compare his refusal throughout the *Origines* to refer to any of Rome's generals by name, conferring this honour upon one combatant only—a certain Carthaginian elephant named Surus. Thus may Cato be said to have added to his other achievements the distinction of having anticipated the Marxists in his opposition to the 'cult of personality'; himself, of course, excepted.

The *Origines* were the work of Cato's last twenty years (*c.* 168–149 B.C.). Now a less prominent public figure, he felt less obliged to match precept with practice. Mellowed by success and family life, the man who had condemned usury now lent out portions from a considerable fortune to maritime syndicates. Money-lending is both leisurely and lucrative: and Cato, who was after all human, appears to have yielded to the temptations of that seductive combination, and to have been indiscreet enough to expose himself to charges, gleefully filed by his enemies, under the sumptuary laws which he had himself created. But leisure also meant time for wider reading. It is certain that Cato learnt Greek (though characteristically he is said to have done so rapidly in order to prove that it was an overrated accomplishment). The *Origines* show no signs of anti-Hellenism: indeed the legend which made Aeneas and Ascanius the founders of Rome is accepted, and other Greek influences are admitted into early Roman history. Hellenistic influence is to be found in the title, which may even be a translation: there being a branch of Hellenistic historiography which was concerned with the foundation of cities. The treatment of a wide range of subjects of general cultural interest, not excluding political theory, is in the familiar Hellenistic tradition. Cato's banishment of trivial references to eclipses and famines, which was a Hellenistic feature but also the kind of material which found its way into the writings of those of his Roman predecessors who followed the pontifical *annales* uncritically, is an isolated if welcome gesture of independence. By contrast, his speeches reveal a thorough knowledge of Greek rhetorical theory, and certain fragments of narrative have a distinctly Xenophontine flavour. Xenophon was a very popular author among the Romans: we are told that Scipio Africanus always kept a copy of his *Cyropaedia* to hand, that Caesar and Antony both admired the *Anabasis*, and that Cicero translated the *Oeconomicus* in his youth. His attraction for Cato must have been strong, for the two men shared an abiding interest in agriculture and war. The sentiment expressed by Cato that the leisure activities of men of action should go on record no less than their public lives is to be traced to Xenophon; and Cato, like Xenophon, in his geographical and biographical descriptions draws attention to the material advantages of his subjects—Cato's rivers are 'great and fine' but also 'full of fish', just as Xenophon's aesthetic pleasure in hunting bustards is greatly enhanced by their palatability.

But if the *Origines* are the product of many influences, their novel qualities should not be discounted. The medium in which they were written was the earliest literary Latin prose. It provided a model which might, through changes of taste and temperament, prove uncongenial to later writers; but even those who rejected it must weigh its qualities with care. For Cato's style was a remarkable compromise between long-established, mainly Greek theory, and the practical needs of contemporary Latin. He plainly accepted the Thucydidean view that written prose should be as unlike the spoken language as possible; he shows a fondness for archaisms and further indulged in what appears to have been a Roman penchant (it is found in their comic poets), for coining strange new words, especially diminutives. We may thus leave Cato with the impression of a gifted, colourful historian, with the quality of that peculiarly Roman deity, the two-faced Janus, looking inward to Rome's past glories and outward to a future, in which she must face many new and insidious forces, and decide which to absorb and which to reject.

Singularly few of Cato's immediate successors exerted any discernible influence on the development of Roman historiography: indeed, it is one of the tragedies of the last third of the second century that Rome produced no native witness to her dramatic internal upheaval with the talent or the understanding to elucidate it for posterity. The tradition, such as it is, shows aristocratic bias towards a popular revolution, and is consequently full of misrepresentations. Of the lost Roman histories of the age of the Gracchi, perhaps that of Coelius Antipater should cause most regret, for here at least was a writer who combined a capacity for thorough research with a training and an interest in the artistic presentation of his material. Livy used him widely, no doubt appreciating his command of a degree of stylistic elegance not to be found in any of his contemporaries. Among the next generation, Claudius Quadrigarius and Cornelius Sisenna deserve mention. Claudius was mainly interested in wars, and wrote about them in a racy, colourful style, which attracted later anthologists and so secured the survival of a few fragments. Sisenna was a more serious historian who, in the manner approved by Thucydides, wrote contemporary history, playing the rôle of Clitarchus to Sulla's Alexander. His history of the Social and Civil Wars of 90–82 B.C. shows a wide range of interests, including philosophy (he was an Epicurean), geography and mythology; but most remarkable of all was his apparent attempt to extend the vocabulary of the language beyond all previously conceived bounds. He was perhaps the most startling neologist to claim the serious attention of Latin readers.

With the death of Sulla in 78 B.C. Rome entered upon one of the most turbulent periods of her history. The struggle for power between the old patrician families and the 'new men' started by the Gracchi resolved itself into a contest of individuals for the support of the army. Marius, who initiated this change of emphasis, Sulla, Lepidus and Pompey all started as generals and later became political reformers; constitutional legalities were placed upon the rack of expediency and ambition with dictatorships, successive consulships and extraordinary commands; and over all proceedings hung the threat of force like an incubus, ready to terrorize the weaker spirits into acquiescence. But Romans could not easily be intimidated: indeed, upon some the vicissitudes of the age acted as a stimulus. The political struggle produced the finest Roman oratory, just as Athenian eloquence had found in Demosthenes its finest exponent at a time of comparable crisis. Poetry, too, flourished in the hands of Lucretius and Catullus. As to history, there was an ample number of men of action with literary talent to fulfil the Polybian qualification for a potentially good historian. The most famous of these was none other than Julius Caesar himself.

The *Commentaries* on the Gallic Wars and the Civil War are so familiar as the mother's milk of unweaned Latinists that their unique place in Roman historiography is often overlooked. Their purpose is implied by their name. A *commentarius* was originally a bald account of routine day-to-day occurrences written by soldiers and statesmen in the same spirit of concern for the preservation of records as that which actuated temple and domestic secretarial officials to keep inventories of property and diaries of forthcoming events (which were also called *commentarii*). All such records were kept to compensate for the fallibility of the human memory. This function of an *aide-mémoire* found literary application as soon as conditions were suitable. Two, in particular, were needed: the existence of historians of repute, and that of individuals who could supply the bare facts, and had personal reasons for wanting them published. In the earlier days there were many Roman statesmen who thought themselves capable of giving an attractive and convincing account of their careers, and several of these autobiographical works are known to us by name. But as literary standards rose, we find even a man of Cicero's attainment recognizing historiography as a profession in which he lacked the necessary specialist skills. When he wished the year of his consulship to be immortalized in prose, he did not attempt the work himself, but approached the historian Poseidonius, offering to supply the details in the form of a *commentarius*, which the master would elaborate into history by applying his special techniques.

The fate of Cicero's *Commentarius* is both amusing and instructive. Poseidonius returned it, saying that it was already a literary masterpiece requiring no further embellishment from him. Appreciating neither the praise nor the diplomacy of this rejection, Cicero offered his *Commentarius* to other historians, but received a similar reception each time. Yet, though no Roman can have had a stronger yearning for glory than he, he never published it,[3] but contented himself with referring at every opportunity to his *annus mirabilis* in his speeches. No such qualms restrained Julius Caesar from publishing his *Commentarii*, and we are therefore entitled to question their purpose. Were they really intended merely to provide the material for others to elaborate? Caesar's friend and continuator Hirtius, and Cicero himself, both praise the elegance, simplicity and precision of his style, the very qualities which make the *Commentarii* the ideal introduction to continuous Latin prose. Since then much scholarly work has been done, most of it tending to show that a great deal of thought and care went into their composition. The circumstances under which they were written throw further light on their likely purpose. Caesar, unlike Cicero, had strong political reasons, say in 50 B.C., for publishing an account of his Gallic campaigns which would win him support; and again, in 47 B.C. it was important for him to show how his vanquished enemies had brought an unnecessary war upon the Republic: all of which would have been irrelevant after a lapse of some years while the *Commentarii* were being professionally 'processed' into *historiae*. From the fact that the *Commentarii* were published for immediate consumption with a well-defined political purpose it may be deduced that Caesar considered that their literary form was satisfactory.

But how reliable are they? Ever since Caesar's contemporary Asinius Pollio accused him of inaccuracy, doubts have been expressed as to his veracity. On the broad issue of the strict necessity of conquering Gaul, modern readers may find his insistence upon the need to avenge insults, as well as actual injuries, in the interest of maintaining the dignity of Rome intolerably petty and specious; but it probably seemed perfectly

reasonable to his contemporaries. Again, his practice of intervening in disputes which appeared to be outside his immediate
jurisdiction must be viewed against the very flexible official
Roman attitude to the scope of provincial commands. Even the
extreme example of his transgression of boundaries, his invasion
of Britain, did not excite much adverse comment. After self-
justification we may consider self-advertisement: a long and
mainly successful war was a splendid medium through which to
celebrate his military prowess. There are instances when strict
truth is sacrificed in order to leave his reputation unblemished.
He frequently describes battles as closely-fought, but only
admits defeat in engagements in which his subordinates were in
command. The repulse he sustained at Gergovia in 52 B.C. is an
example of tendentious presentation. Here his troops were badly
mauled in a premature attack on the town's defences. Caesar
blames this setback upon the excessive enthusiasm of his troops,
who are said to have advanced beyond the immediate objective
and been trapped beneath the city walls.[4] There is good reason
for believing that the capture of Gergovia had been Caesar's
original objective at the beginning of this manoeuvre; but even
if he is right in claiming that his troops got out of hand, this is
not a favourable reflection on his generalship.

Distortions and misrepresentations are probably more frequent
in his account of the Civil War, in which he was fighting for his
life, and after which he had the task of convincing his countrymen
of his innocence of original aggression. The first six chapters of
Book I, in which Caesar tells how diplomatic exchanges broke
down in the face of his enemies' determination to encompass his
downfall, contain the greatest concentration of overt or implied
personal judgments. From them we receive the firm impression
that a small oligarchic faction succeeded in persuading Pompey,
against his better judgment, to add his authority to their cause
and so help them to stifle the popular will. In reality, of course,
the political situation was rather more complicated than this,
and had arisen at least in part through Caesar's use of the people's
spokesmen, the tribunes, to promote his own interests. For the
rest, the intransigence of Pompey is exaggerated, the extent of
Caesar's defeat at Dyrrachium (Durazzo) is minimized, and the
mutiny of the ninth legion at Placentia is not mentioned;
but most of all, his personal animosity against the leading

Republicans ever smoulders close to the surface and their motives and actions are made to appear in a poor light.

Yet it is only a careful reading of the three books of the Civil War that reveals this personal bias. To someone approaching it as a simple account of a war written by an eye-witness the overwhelming impression is similar to that conveyed by the seven books of the Gallic War—that the author is primarily a student of military strategy and tactics who has adapted his undoubted literary gifts to the needs of clear and logical exposition. This repudiation of the stylistic devices of which he probably had full command—he was second only to Cicero as an orator—is deliberate. It probably had less to do with the limitations of the form of the *Commentarius* than with his own conception of the style that was best suited to the description of military manoeuvres. Posterity should be grateful for his choice, for he has left us some of the most authoritative accounts of siege operations and battle tactics, and some fine examples of his forethought and improvisation. It is small wonder that of all ancient writers he is the most read by professional soldiers.

The last surviving historian of the Republic resumed the orthodox tradition of Latin historiography. Gaius Sallustius Crispus, known to the later world as Sallust, was a Sabine from Amiternum (near modern Aquila). He was born in 86 B.C. thus coinciding in time and locality with the internecine upheaval of the Social War, which was followed successively by the establishment of Sulla's military dictatorship and an unstable oligarchy. The little we can deduce from his name and from local archaeological evidence suggests that his family were fairly large fish in a small pond, with political sympathies tending towards the popular, plebeian side. We may with greater certainty affirm that he migrated to Rome and began a political career while still a young man. In his own brief reference to his early career[5] he describes how his honest ambition became perverted through contact with the vices of others of less noble disposition but similarly intent on advancement. He goes on to admit that he should have decided at an early stage that political eminence would be no compensation for the loss of his self-respect; but that in the event his desire for glory proved too strong.

The first public office Sallust is known to have held is that of tribune for the year 52 B.C., which confirms his popular sympathies. Two years later he was expelled from the Senate, to which his tribuneship had given him access, on charges of immoral and profligate living. Two stories of his misconduct found their way into the later tradition. The first made him a participant in the mystic rites presided over by one Nigidius Figulus, for which he was twice accused of sacrilege, but acquitted both times. In the second story Sallust figures as the paramour of Sulla's daughter Fausta, the wife of Annius Milo but an accommodating woman. This time he had to pay for his offence, for Milo surprised the engrossed couple *in flagrante delicto*, severely whipped the offending historian, and released him only after he had agreed to pay a considerable sum in compensation. When viewed against the background of systematic denigration to which all public figures were subjected in the late Republic, neither of these stories compels belief. (The latter, in particular, from a political point of view seems too piquant to be true: a supporter of the popular cause and a partisan of Caesar seduces the daughter of the founder of the oligarchic movement, and the wife of a henchman of Pompey, Caesar's most dangerous rival.) But the very existence of such stories is of interest, because they suggest that the victim had attained a position of some political importance. A similar interpretation may be put on his expulsion from the Senate: the censor who secured it being the optimate and anti-Caesarian Appius Claudius Pulcher.

After Caesar had crossed the Rubicon and precipitated the Civil War, Sallust was free to serve his cause more actively. Lacking military experience, he did not at first meet with much success. His first commission was to relieve a force under C. Antonius which was being blockaded by Pompey's ships on the Adriatic island of Curicta. Sallust and a colleague, Minucius Basilus, each commanded a legion; but with the Pompeians enjoying complete command of the sea it was impossible even to take to the water. Caesar could ill afford the losses that resulted from the inevitable surrender of Antonius, and Sallust does not reappear until Caesar was preparing for his departure for the final showdown with the Republicans in Africa. This time he was sent to quell an incipient mutiny of troops who were mustering in Campania, and was fortunate not to be killed along with two colleagues. In the event, it needed Caesar's personal intervention

to quell the mutiny. This particular failure of Sallust was accounted no disgrace, for some of the best generals of the Republic
had been stoned by their own troops. Once in Africa Caesar
seems, with characteristic psychological insight, to have discovered where Sallust's true talents lay—in supply administration. He collected a great store of supplies from the island of
Cercina and transported them to Caesar's headquarters. This is
his only recorded service, but he must have performed many
unspectacular but invaluable administrative duties for Caesar
to have rewarded him with the governorship of Numidia in the
rank of proconsul.

Provincial governors expected enrichment from their office
as a matter of course. Even that most self-consciously scrupulous
of governors, Cicero, returned from Cilicia some £25,000
wealthier, having campaigned for much of his career against the
worst excesses of extortion in the provinces. During the days of
the free Republic, aided by laws created for the purpose, he and
other responsible politicians had been moderately successful in
curbing the avarice of provincial governors; but after Caesar had
become all-powerful it was not safe to invoke any laws. Yet so
manifest was Sallust's guilt that his enemies had the courage to
prefer charges, and he escaped conviction only through the
intercession of his embarrassed patron, which rumour maintained
he had to buy with a considerable portion of his booty. But
Numidia was a rich kingdom, with sumptuously adorned royal
residences and treasuries; so that even after Caesar had exacted
his commission there remained enough for Sallust to build himself a villa and to landscape the famous *Horti Sallustiani* below
the Quirinal, which were later frequented by the emperors Nero,
Vespasian, Nerva and Aurelian.

Well content, in such circumstances, to bid farewell to active
life, Sallust settled down to write history, in which occupation
he was unmolested until the end of his life in 35 B.C. His literary
activities brought him the fame which had eluded him in his
political career. The rhetorician Quintilian compared him
favourably with Thucydides,[6] upon whom he modelled himself.
Tacitus generously called him 'the most illustrious of the Roman
historians',[7] an opinion endorsed by Martial,[8] and Seneca adds a
further note of praise. A modern estimate of Sallust need not be
influenced by his countrymen's expressions of national pride

(mixed, one senses, with relief that here, at last, was a great Roman historian); but such an estimate is also hampered by the loss of most of his largest work, the *Histories*. The surviving fragments of this account of Roman history from the year 78 B.C. are by no means incoherent, but the longest continuous passages consist of four speeches by popular leaders which reveal substantially the same opinions and attitudes as are to be found in the two smaller works which have survived complete.

These two opuscula, the *Catiline* and the *Jugurtha*, are monographs, each dealing with a single episode of Roman history. Each has an extended prologue in which the historian casts his net wide, embracing philosophical, historical and autobiographical topics. Since much common ground is covered, an examination of the prologue of the *Catiline*, with which a general discussion of that monograph will be introduced, will obviate the necessity of a similar discussion when we come to examine the *Jugurtha*.

The opening theme of the *Catiline* is Fame. Man is distinguished from animals through his possession of a mind (*animus*), which governs his actions. This active element in his nature, which he possesses in common with the gods, causes him to try to cross the chief barrier which separates them—mortality. This he cannot do in the physical sense: but if he performs deeds by which posterity will remember him, he will achieve the next best kind of immortality, immortal fame. At this point Sallust abruptly introduces *res militaris*, thus accepting the popular assumption that warfare is the best medium through which man's talents may be exercised. He says that both mental and physical qualities are required for the successful prosecution of a war. They combine to serve man's desire for glory. But war brings conquest, conquest brings domination, and domination breeds avarice, setting a vicious circle in motion which prevents the exercise of the full range of his talents. As with individuals, so with nations. In the case of Rome success in war had produced a change in the national character, resulting in the internal moral and political disruption of the historian's own time.

After a brief explanation of his choice of subject and a character-sketch of Catiline himself, Sallust traces the process of moral decline through the centuries of Roman history. In spite of the brevity and imperfection of this survey, it serves to reflect the great difference between Greek and Roman history, which in turn affected the outlook of the respective historians: whereas the history of Greece is the story of fluctuating fortunes among contending powers, that of Rome is the story of a single power which, from small beginnings, gradually evolved stable institutions and an invincible war machine, with which she conquered the Mediterranean world. Thucydides, viewing a recurring pattern, naturally concluded that human nature did not change; but Sallust, observing the same city still physically intact after seven hundred years, but substantially altered in its moral attitudes, deduced that changing fortunes, if they do not change man's collective nature, at least cause certain of his characteristics to come to the fore and others to fall into the background. Sallust's picture of early Rome is inevitably idealized. The old Romans were zealously patriotic; certain of their neighbours, jealous of their peaceful prosperity, tried to destroy them, but they applied themselves vigorously to self-defence, and won many allies in addition to vanquishing their enemies. At home, they maintained a stable constitution through annual magistracies, by which the human fault of arrogance, which can arise from excessive power, is kept in check. The departure of the kings opened the way to glory for every ambitious citizen, and it was this desire for renown that was the motive force behind Rome's great conquests. At first the material rewards of conquest were not great, so that material greed could find no gratification. But the conquest of Carthage at once removed Rome's last serious rival and opened up unlimited sources of wealth. Avarice now replaced honesty: henceforth everything and everybody could be bought at a price, and money meant power. Honour and glory ceased to have any significance independently of the acquisition of wealth and the enjoyment of luxury, and therefore public office was sought only as a means of enrichment. It was this overwhelming greed that tore the republican constitution apart and alienated Rome's despoiled friends and allies.

Such was the pattern of decline into which fitted Catiline. We can be certain that it was as much the personality and background of this central figure as 'the novelty of the crime and the danger' that caused Sallust to choose the Catilinarian Conspiracy as the subject of his first historical essay. In fact, his choice reflects the moral purpose of the monograph, and warns us not to expect a balanced historical treatment of the episode. Catiline in every way personified the decline. He had great ability, but his talents had been perverted by his environment.[9] He was also of noble birth. This was a vital aspect of Sallust's portrayal, since it was the nobility that experienced the worst excesses of luxury and possessed the greatest power with which to drag the rest of the state down into the slough of idleness and immorality. Catiline hoped to be another Sulla, but was frustrated at every turn. He drew his support from a growing pool of degenerates like himself,[10] contracted huge debts, and multiplied his enemies by a wide range of crimes and outrages. The state of desperation he reached is vividly mirrored by the historian in Catiline's physiognomy:[11]

> His defiled soul, at odds with gods and men, could find repose neither in his waking nor in his sleeping hours, so cruelly did his conscience ravage his overwrought mind. Hence his pallid complexion, his bloodshot eyes, his gait now fast, now slow; in short, there was madness in his face and in his expression.

The vehemence of the historian's language in this description drives home to the reader his preoccupation with moral decline, a problem of his own age to which abler men than Catiline had in fact responded. But at least Catiline was judicious in his choice of a time for rebellion. As Sallust's description of his preparations unfolds, one is impressed by the number and the quality of the support it received: it includes eleven senators, four knights and many men of distinction from the colonial cities. Their grievances against the existing government are genuine enough, and are well expressed by Catiline in the first speech he delivers to his adherents: power and wealth maintained selfishly in the hands of a few men, who moreover flaunt them with intolerable arrogance. But when asked what he now offered them, Catiline merely names the same things—wealth and power—not moral reform. But they accept his offer, and cement their cruel and insane brotherhood by each partaking of the proffered goblet of wine mixed with blood, thus pledging themselves to secrecy and utter loyalty to their leader.[12] It is a terrible picture, to which modern parallels are only too easy to find, of wholehearted commitment to crime by men who have ceased to believe in ordered society.

One of the conspirators did, nevertheless, break faith, though from no moral scruples: Q. Curius was trying to win back the waning affections of his mistress Fulvia when he boasted of the power and wealth which would soon be his, and so revealed the conspiracy.[13] The news thus divulged destroyed any hopes Catiline might have had of election to the consulship, and Cicero, a 'new man', was elected.[14] Catiline's preparations became more active and more frenzied. His colleague Manlius was raising a secret army in Etruria, while in Rome he watched for an opportunity to murder Cicero.[15] But the consul was vigilant, and not only in guarding his personal safety: his Catilinarian speeches, following upon written evidence of the activities of Manlius, forced Catiline's hand.

At this point[16] Sallust pauses to observe the grim paradox of the situation: that Rome, whose power extended over the whole area of the world, had so many ungrateful citizens. In a wide-ranging survey of the causes of this national sickness, the historian translates the grievances expressed by Catiline into specific social and historical questions: gross disparity in wealth is aggravated by the ever-increasing numbers and political presence of the city mob, whose hopes of relief and recognition have been alternately raised and dashed as popular and aristocratic leaders have precariously held the reins of power. Sallust does not go back to the Gracchi, or even to Marius in this excursus, so that it is in no real sense an exhaustive, Thucydidean analysis of antecedent causes. He refers only to the events which the participants themselves experienced: the tyranny of Sulla; the consulship of Pompey and Crassus, during which some of the people's powers were restored; and Pompey's departure for the Mithridatic War, after which the optimates recovered their lost influence, and now seemed impregnable to any attacks short of revolution.

Further evidence, implicating those conspirators who were still in Rome, was secured through representatives of the Allobroges (a Gallic tribe under Roman rule), who were visiting the city and had been approached with a view to their cooperation in the uprising.[17] But they decided on loyalty to the Republic, and disclosed the names of their contacts, together with documentary evidence in the form of a signed and sealed undertaking that their troubles would be at an end if they supported the conspiracy. Cicero acted promptly. He arrested Lentulus,

Cethegus, Statilius, Gabinius and Caeparius. The city greeted the news with mixed joy and shock:[18] joy at the disclosure of the plot, shock at the names of the arrested men. Lentulus was a praetor, and the others were of senatorial rank. If such men could be involved, why not some of their more influential colleagues? Suspicion fell upon Crassus and Caesar also; but the former's great wealth protected him from open attack, while the latter evaded the brandished swords of some of the more extreme knights, and played a prominent part in the debate on the fate of the captured conspirators. Sallust gives a version of his speech,[19] in which he opposed their execution, and that of the Younger Cato,[20] who carried the day by invoking the pristine Roman principle of severity towards traitors. The five men were taken to an underground dungeon, where their necks were broken. Sallust's description of the scene leaves no doubt that he considered this punishment to be deserved.[21]

The news of these executions had an immediate effect upon the insurgents. The weaker spirits wavered and fell away, leaving a hard core of desperate men. Catiline decided at first to postpone the rebellion until he could recruit more support, and set off for Gaul with this purpose in mind. But his retreat was cut off and he was surrounded by two consular armies. The chosen battlefield was enclosed and rough, unsuitable for cavalry or long-range targeteering. The infantry cast aside their spears and fought it out hand-to-hand. Catiline was prominent and ubiquitous in the fray; but when he saw the tide of battle turned irreversibly against him, he threw himself into the thick of the enemy and was run through by a welter of blades.[22]

Like Thucydides, Sallust was composing contemporary history and on certain occasions appears to be writing as a witness of events or as a confidant of witnesses. Minute details which thus became available to him often appear in his account, such as the fact that Cicero led Lentulus by the hand into the senate,[23] that Caesar was threatened as he left that assembly,[24] and that Catiline died in the middle of the enemy ranks.[25] But the function of these *minutiae* is dramatic rather than historical: their purpose does not differ from that of his descriptions of scenes at Rome following the tidings of the insurrection,[26] and the later news of the arrest of Lentulus,[27] neither of which postulates autopsy on the historian's part, only imagination. The first of these descriptions is worth quoting in full as the precursor of many such scenes portrayed by Roman historians:

> These precautions struck the community with terror, and the aspect of the city was changed. In place of extreme gaiety and frivolity, the fruit of long-lasting peace, there was sudden and general gloom. Men were uneasy and apprehensive; they put little confidence in any place of security or in any human being; they were in a mentality neither of peace nor of war; and each measured the peril by his own fears. The women, too, were in a pitiful state of anxiety, raised suppliant hands to heaven, bewailed the fate of their little children, asked continual questions, trembled at everything, and throwing aside haughtiness and self-indulgence, despaired of themselves and their country.

For concentrated emotional and psychological content this would be difficult to improve upon, and requires no analysis. Sallust has set out here and elsewhere to present events in the most memorable way in order to represent the various aspects and implications of the danger. The *Catiline* is therefore not history, but a historical tableau, condensed, dramatized and spiced with detail.

It is nevertheless interesting to see in what respects it falls short of being a full and accurate account. In the first place, although the names of Caesar and Crassus are mentioned as suspects, none of the latter's earlier machinations, on which these suspicions were founded, is mentioned. Crassus had tried several tricks either to gain political support, as when he proposed the full enfranchisement of the Transpadane Gauls, or to secure command of an army, as when he produced a forged will of Ptolemy X bequeathing his kingdom to Rome, which would require armed supervision in Egypt for its implementation. Although Crassus was far too shrewd to support the conspiracy openly, he undoubtedly shielded Catiline against the worst effects of his earlier blunders, and was therefore in some measure responsible for the conspiracy.

More striking is the relatively small role assigned to Cicero, who in his own opinion was the single voice and mind behind the defeat of Catiline. Personal bias against Cicero may be summarily ruled out. Sallust had read many of Cicero's speeches and political writings, and probably admired them. He introduces him as an 'excellent' (*egregius*) candidate for the consulship of 63 B.C.[28] At the critical moments Cicero is made to show shrewd-

ness and resource.[29] His First Catilinarian speech is called
'brilliant and beneficial to the Republic'[30] (*luculentam et utilem
reipublicae*); later he is gratuitously called *optimus consul*;[31] and
there is no suggestion that his execution of the conspirators was
illegal, as was later alleged: on the contrary, the death of Lentulus
and his partners is described as 'worthy of their character and
their crimes'. Nevertheless, a reader of the *Catiline* of Sallust
who subsequently turns to the relevant speeches of Cicero, the
Catilinarians, the *Pro Murena* and the *Pro Sulla*, might be
excused for thinking that they were referring to two different
conspiracies. Of course, Cicero treasured that consular year in
his memory and wrought about it a self-apotheosis which was
felt to be overdone even in his own time. But Sallust omits certain
of Cicero's actions: in particular, the last three Catilinarians and
his defence of Murena, the consul-elect for 62 B.C., against a
charge of bribery, all of which were important for the maintenance
of order and morale in Rome. Fortunately it is unnecessary to
look beyond Sallust's own pages for an explanation:[32]

> But within my own memory there have appeared two men of
> outstanding merit, though of different character, Marcus Cato and
> Gaius Caesar. Since the occasion has presented itself, their nature
> and way of life I have decided to disclose to the best of my ability
> rather than pass them over in silence.

There follows a comparison of the two men. Cato was renowned
for his probity, austerity and severity, Caesar for his liberality,
respect for friendship, industry and ambition. The reason for
Sallust's choice now becomes plain. These two men are the
representatives of the old and the new in Roman politics and
morality. Cato recalled his illustrious ancestor in his adherence
to the pristine virtues of strict patriotism, incorruptibility and
observance of the law. Caesar was the modern popular leader, who
championed the cause of the under-privileged in return for their
support in the realization of his personal ambition. He was the
disciple of persuasion, expediency and flexibility, who carefully
planned his political career from the outset, and aimed at nothing
less than sole domination.

In view of Caesar's subsequent career, and Sallust's personal
attachment to him, his prominence comes as no surprise. But
surely other statesmen exercised more influence than Cato?

What of Crassus and Pompey, who three years later joined Caesar in the irresistible First Triumvirate? Sallust, however, is not concerned with evaluating the various forces operating in the political struggle, but with indicating the extremes of moral and spiritual change which had transformed Rome from a stable city into a hot-bed of sedition. His neglect of Cicero is thus to be explained by the fact that the orator was essentially a civilian in a city at war, a man who excelled in the arts of peace—letters and administration—and who strove throughout his life to reconcile the forces which were conspiring to foment revolution. Cato, whose attempts to ensure senatorial predominance (which Sallust fails to bring to light) were no more successful than Cicero's efforts to achieve a 'harmony of the orders' (*concordia ordinum*), represented one of the two extremes, contumacious and intransigent, and therefore a cause of the disruption which destroyed the republic. There is no clearer demonstration of the moral rather than narrowly political interest of the *Catiline* than the attention he accords Cato.

Sallust's interest in character is circumscribed by certain moral preconceptions. The notion of *virtus*, 'the quality of a man', (which leaves much to the imagination), is central to his treatment. Catiline had certain manly qualities—strength, vigour and endurance—but *virtus* was unattainable without the right mental disposition (*ingenium*), which in Catiline's case was evil and depraved; so that what would have been eloquence, bravery, pride and generosity in a man with a good *ingenium* became indiscretion, audacity, arrogance and prodigality in Catiline. His career was foredoomed once his moral baseness became ingrained: he plundered, murdered and deceived his way to perdition, pursuing a course from which his *ingenium* would not permit him to deviate. This strait-jacket of moral causation affects all Sallust's formal characterizations and detracts from their individuality. But he finds scope for greater perspective and penetration when he animates his characters with the spoken word. Catiline's speeches admirably illustrate his powers of leadership, his sense of grievance and his determination, positive qualities which provided the real impetus to the rebellion. The speeches of Caesar and Cato, however, provided two forms of characterization—that of the individuals, and that of the age itself; they also form the intellectual climax of the monograph. Sallust's debt to the speeches assigned by Thucydides to Cleon and Diodotus soon becomes plain. Caesar, like Diodotus, seeks to banish all emotion from the deliberations, and quotes good precedents from Roman history (an approved rhetorical device) for a dispassionate approach to political problems. He adds that the present atmosphere is the fault of the orators who have introduced pity and anger into the debate. He then argues that the exaction of the capital penalty from citizens without trial would create a further precedent that might be cruelly abused in the future; and finally proposes that the conspirators be imprisoned for life in various municipalities throughout Italy. Cato, like Cleon, reintroduces righteous anger, and his speech is full of emotional references to home, family and the altars of the gods, which the conspirators have sought to overthrow. This antithesis between justice and expediency, familiar to readers of Thucydides, assumes a new significance when observed in the context of Roman history. The fact that Cato represented the old Roman standards and Caesar the new points to a development in political *savoir-faire*, which has caused the replacement of crude, uncomplicated notions such as those of right and wrong by the more sophisticated ones of long-term interest and diplomacy. (This contrast is brought out best when older nations have diplomatic dealings with younger ones, as when the Greeks first confronted the Romans, and in modern times in the dealings, often frustrating to both sides, between the European and the emergent African nations.) Cato laments the change, and hankers after the days when the dictates of justice were observed to the letter, as they were by the hero Manlius Torquatus, who killed his own son for attacking the enemy in disobedience to orders. What possible alternative can there be to the death penalty, even in these days of equivocation, for men to have plotted against their own country? In his single-minded insistence on justice, Cato ignores a useful argument from expediency: that prompt and drastic action against the captured conspirators might cause some of those still at large to have second thoughts. Sallust, not wishing to complicate the issue, reserves his observations on this for the narrative. His obvious satisfaction at the adoption of Cato's proposal, which had been advocated by other speakers but had appeared to be losing ground as a result of Caesar's brilliant counter-argument, affirms two important aspects of his thought: that the state could survive so long as purely moral arguments continued to command respect, and so long as there remained statesmen who could put these arguments with force and conviction.

The *Jugurthine War* the second of the two monographs is broader both in its literary conception and in its central theme. As in the *Catiline*, Sallust is the best authority for his own choice of subject. He says:[33]

> I am about to write about the war which the Roman people waged against Jugurtha, the Numidian king: first, because it was a great and violent war, and secondly because it brought the first challenge to the arrogance of the nobility.

The ruling house of Numidia had been related to Rome through ties with certain families of the Roman nobility. This peculiarly Roman arrangement was called *clientela*, or 'clientship', and involved obligations of mutual friendship and help. The war in question, which was fought intermittently between 110 and 107 B.C., and was therefore past history to Sallust, arose through dynastic troubles. The death of King Micipsa in 118 left three equal claimants to the throne, his sons Adherbal and Hiempsal, and his nephew Jugurtha, who had earned an equal inheritance with his cousins by showing exceptional qualities of courage and leadership. The two brothers objected to this arrangement, and quarrels arose leading to a war which Jugurtha, who was far abler than his cousins, won with ease. But he offended Rome when he allowed his troops to kill some Italian merchants during the sack of the city of Cirta. News of this insult to Roman dignity precipitated, or rather revived, the political struggle that had been begun some twenty years earlier by Tiberius Gracchus. The popular party seized upon Jugurtha's excesses as a consequence of the indecision and corruptibility of the oligarchs. They could point to the existing clientship, and extrapolate from it the thesis that the nobles concerned, under the influence of bribery, had put Jugurtha's private interests before those of Rome. Henceforth the monograph is concerned with two contests, one external and military, the other domestic and political. The interplay between these two struggles is further diversified and enriched by a wider variety of contrasts to pure narrative than is to be found in the *Catiline*: moralistic passages, private conversations, letters, and a geographical excursus on Africa, in addition to character-sketches and speeches.

The *populares*, taking advantage of the events, succeeded in having Jugurtha brought to Rome in order to answer for his actions. Though nominally a captive, he managed to influence his contacts among the aristocracy, and we can be sure that the argument of a patron's obligations to his client was reinforced by the most persuasive of material enticements. The result of his negotiations was that he left Rome a free man, though with lightened pockets, even after having another troublesome cousin, Massiva, murdered while his case was *sub judice*. 'A city for sale, and doomed to fall to the earliest buyer it can find'[34] was certainly an exaggeration of the extent of corruption in high places at Rome in 110 B.C.; but that even a palpable degree of venality had been discerned by a foreigner like Jugurtha, to whom this description is attributed by Sallust as a parting shot, spelt incalculable danger to Rome's imperial aspirations. The *populares*, meanwhile, continued to exert pressure. A campaign was begun with the ultimate object of stripping Jugurtha of his usurped power; but it ended in humiliating defeat because of the irresolute leadership of its effete patrician general, Aulus Albinus. When the consul for 109, Q. Caecilius Metellus, took over the army, he found it in very bad shape: no watches were being kept, soldiers came and went as they pleased, and camp was moved only when the stench of excrement became too great to bear or when supplies ran short. Sallust has nothing but praise for the manner in which Metellus restored discipline, and subsequently did much to restore Roman self-respect by his successful conduct of operations.[35] But he was unable to capture the elusive prince, who while at large would remain a living affront to Roman dignity. The *populares* were therefore able to intensify their campaign, and now found a candidate for the consulship from their own ranks, Gaius Marius, a soldier of some twenty years' experience, who was serving on Metellus's staff. In the post-election speech which he assigns to him,[36] Sallust stresses his plebeian background and freedom from the aristocratic refinements of culture and diplomacy. His ambition was sharpened through a clash of personalities with Metellus, who advised him not to canvass for the consulship, an office which was above his station.[37] Having obtained leave to return to the city, he canvassed without scruple, unfairly criticizing Metellus's conduct of the war, and boasting that if he were elected consul and given the command, he would deliver Jugurtha to the people in chains within a few days. Meanwhile Metellus suffered further frustration in his attempts to entrap Jugurtha; and Marius, enjoying the advantage of having done nothing, either for good or ill, against the prince, was elected consul and successor to Metellus in the African command (108 B.C.).

Marius had a large measure of material success, capturing several important towns and considerable booty, and impressing the Numidians with the strength and mobility of Roman arms. He extended both the scale of operations by recruiting from the poorer class of citizens (previously military service had been confined to those possessing a stipulated amount of wealth), and its scope. Thus placed under increased pressure, Jugurtha was forced into the alliance with his neighbour, king Bocchus of Mauretania, which eventually brought his downfall. But talents quite different from those possessed by the rough, forthright soldier from Arpinum were needed in order to realize his election boast. Fortunately they were to hand: L. Cornelius Sulla, a quaestor serving on his staff, shared one thing with Marius—a desire for glory—but in other respects he was his complete antithesis.[38] Cultivated, affable and diplomatic, he was the very man to succeed with words where deeds had failed. He negotiated with Bocchus and persuaded him to betray Jugurtha into his hands, and so brought the war to an end.[39]

Sallust's choice of the Jugurthine War as the subject of his second monograph is both understandable on personal grounds (his acquaintance with the country through his sojourn there as governor), and justifiable on historical grounds as a turning point in the political struggle at Rome. He blames the *nobiles* for the initial disruption, saying that the Gracchi 'disclosed the crimes of the few',[40] but finds the plebs guilty of the same '*insolentia*' when they in their turn find themselves in the possession of unbridled freedom.[41] As in the *Catiline*, events centre around personalities, and Sallust shows the same impartiality in his estimation of these. Metellus is incorruptible, and a thoroughly competent general, whom Sallust does not blame for military failure; but he suffers from arrogance ('*superbia*'), the common fault of the nobility,[42] and it is this that alienates Marius, at whose hands he suffers the humiliation of political defeat, which is made the more painful by that same fault of arrogance. Marius and Jugurtha are portrayed more subtly, in that their characters are seen to change under the influence of events and personalities. Sallust's portrait of the young Jugurtha, no doubt idealized in order to draw deeper contrast, may owe something to Xenophon's portrait of Cyrus in the *Anabasis*: comely, vigorous and gifted, his prowess in the manly arts was matched only by his modesty.[43] But exposure to corrupting influences caused him to aspire to power; and the first of these influences was the Roman nobility.[44] Certain of these men made his acquaintance while he was serving in the Roman army in the siege of the Spanish city of Numantia. They became impressed by his ability and cultivated him with promises of their support in the event of his deciding to seize the throne of Numidia on the death of Micipsa. Jugurtha was finally driven to action by the hostility of his cousins, who begrudged him his share of the kingdom. The words attributed to Micipsa on his deathbed, with which he adjured Jugurtha to remain on friendly terms with his cousins, now assume an ironic double significance. He said: 'It is not with armies and treasuries that you furnish your kingdom with protection, but with friends, whom you can neither coerce with arms nor buy with gold: it is by devotion and loyalty that they are won. But what greater tie of friendship is there than that between brother and brother? What outsider will you find loyal if you are at enmity with your own kindred? I deliver to you a kingdom which will be powerful if you are good, but weak if you are evil. For harmony makes small states grow, while discord brings the greatest empires into decline.'[45] It is almost as if Jugurtha listened only to the first sentence of this advice, and formed his own views as to choice of friends and methods of retaining their services. Later, realization of the power of money caused him to overreach himself when, faced with a rival to his throne, he had him murdered even while he himself was preparing to face trial in Rome. And then, abandoning fifty sureties to their fate, he sailed in haste back to Africa.

Marius's character is also seen to evolve. He begins as an honest, industrious and able soldier, interested not in wealth but in glory:[46] a second Cato, in fact. Moreover, sacrificial auspices have assured him that he was destined for greatness (one of the few occasions when Sallust introduces religious matters), so that a desire for the state's highest honours was not unreasonable. This sketchy account of Marius's political aspirations conceals a steady ascent of the *cursus honorum* which had begun with the tribuneship some ten years earlier. Later, in representing his quarrel with Metellus as a moral turning point, at which embitterment replaces good will, Sallust omits to mention the patronage which Marius had enjoyed from the family of the Metelli during much of his early career. Faced with the bigoted opposition of a diehard aristocrat, Marius (not unreasonably, we are made to feel) throws scruples to the winds and seeks popularity by the most unmilitary means, the relaxation of discipline and denigration of his commander.[47] Thus thwarted ambition changes his whole character for a time. During his canvassing campaign he is made the mouthpiece of all the familiar popular slogans; but one theme receives especial prominence, that of his practical services to Rome as a soldier, which he compares with the aristocrats' empty boast of illustrious ancestry, and dynastic alliances cemented long ago.[48] This theme is apposite not only to Marius's career but to the problems of the age. The Italian allies of Rome were making increasingly urgent demands for political recognition for their services in her wars, and finally resorted to arms in order to win their demands.

If moral schematism is the main cause of Sallust's incomplete account of Marius's early career, it is the monograph form itself that prevents us from seeing his total contribution to Roman history. His reform of the army, vaguely hinted at by Sallust in the description of his preparations for his African campaign,[49] altered the whole character of Roman politics. Soldiering now became a profession instead of an unwelcome and impoverishing interlude between civilian occupations. Moreover, through the Senate's failure to assume the responsibility, pay henceforth was found by the generals in command, who consequently came to enjoy the loyalty of their troops as a personal instead of a symbolic sentiment. As the provider of their livelihood, the general received not merely connivance, but the active encouragement of his soldiers to seize power. With such a weapon of political advancement in their hands, successive commanders established the subsequent pattern of republican decline: Marius, Cinna, Sulla, Lepidus, Crassus, Pompey, Caesar, Antony and finally Octavian (Augustus) each led his army against the state and enjoyed varying periods of autocratic control, until at last the constitution itself was adapted to autocracy and stability was restored. But Sallust leaves us with a vision of Marius as the hope for the future, the spearhead in the attack on aristocratic privilege, whose only faults are those of anyone of ability whose just ambitions have been opposed.

The remaining character in which the historian shows an interest is that of L. Cornelius Sulla, to whom he assigns the second of the pen-portraits in the monograph.[50] Sulla resembles Marius in two respects only, but they are important ones: bravery and his desire for glory. This is an interesting representation of Sulla, for other traditions have made pleasure his primary concern, and military success a mere means to that end. The pleasure motive is certainly present in Sallust's portrait, but is subordinated to that of glory. In other respects he is the antithesis of Marius: of noble extraction, cultured, clever, sociable and a master of dissimulation, the ideal man for the situation in which he found himself. Sallust is, for his own reasons, disposed to emphasize Sulla's good fortune (a quality which that general claimed for himself): unlike Marius, who had to make his way against opposition, Sulla found himself in circumstances which appeared to be tailor-made for his particular talents. The words with which Sallust concludes the sketch— 'As to what he did later, I do not know whether I should speak of it with shame or disgust'—might as appropriately have been said of the later career of Marius, which ended in a bloodbath of his enemies and his own timely death in 86 B.C.

The interpretation of the events themselves is subject to the same kind of distortion. Was corruption the sole reason for the Senate's initial handling of the war? There was a compelling reason why Rome should not undertake a major war outside Italy at this time: the threat of a massive invasion from the north by Germanic tribes, who had already inflicted two damaging defeats on Rome's armies. Jugurtha and his troubles, by contrast, offered no serious challenge to Rome if left unmolested, but could inflict incalculable damage upon her prestige if she elected to join issue with him in the Numidian wastes. And what of the motives of the opposition? The knights concealed beneath their popular alliance the stark motive of profit: if there were a war, they would obtain transport and supply contracts; and when Jugurtha was defeated Numidia would be more secure for the pursuit of their trading interests. A disinterested historian would not have taken the upsurge of popular wrath after the fall and sack of Cirta at its face value.

Enough has been said to expose the limitations of Sallust's *Jugurthine War* as an historical account. It remains to resume and complete the examination of its literary qualities. His efforts to achieve greater depth and perspective than in the Catiline are entirely successful. In addition to the infusion of variety and colour by means of a number of different kinds of relief from narrative, the narrative descriptions themselves contain a degree of detail and dramatic force unmatched in the earlier monograph. One passage is worth quoting in full:[51]

Not far from the river Muluccha, which separated the realms of Jugurtha and Bocchus, there was in the midst of a plain a rocky hill which was broad enough for a fortress of moderate size and very high, and accessible only by one narrow path; for the whole place was naturally steep as if it had been made so by art and design. This place Marius aimed to take by supreme effort, because it held the king's treasures, but in this case his success was the result of chance rather than skill; for the fortress was well supplied with arms and men, besides having an abundance of grain and a spring of water. The situation was impracticable for mounds, towers and other siege works, while the path to the fortifications was extremely narrow and had precipices on either side. Mantlets were pushed forward with extreme danger and to no purpose; for when they had gone but a short distance they were ruined by fire or by stones. The soldiers could not keep their footing before the works because of the steepness of the hill nor operate within the mantlets without peril; the bravest of them were killed or wounded, and the rest gradually lost courage.

After Marius had spent many days in great labour, he was anxiously considering whether he should abandon the whole attempt as fruitless or await the favour of fortune, which he had so often enjoyed. For many days and nights he had been a prey to indecision when it chanced that a Ligurian, a common soldier of the auxiliary cohorts, who had left the camp to fetch water, noticed near the side of the fortress which was farthest from the besiegers some snails creeping about among the rocks. Picking up one or two of these and then looking for more, in his eagerness to gather them he gradually made his way almost to the top of the mountain. When he found that he was alone there, the love of overcoming difficulties which is natural to mankind seized him. It happened that a great oak had grown up there among the rocks; it bent down for a little way, then turned and grew upward, as is the nature of all plants. With the help, now of the branches of the tree and now of projecting rocks, the Ligurian mounted to the level of the fortress, while all the Numidians were intent upon the combatants. After examining everything that he thought would be useful later, he returned by the same way, not heedlessly, as he had gone up, but testing and observing everything. Then he hastened to Marius, told him what he had done, and urged him to make an attempt on the fortress at the point where he himself had mounted, offering himself as a guide and leader in the dangerous expedition.

Marius thereupon ordered some of his staff to go with the Ligurian and look into his proposal, and each of them, according to his temperament, pronounced the attempt difficult or easy; on the whole, however, the consul was somewhat encouraged. Accordingly, out of all his horn-blowers and trumpeters he chose the five who were most agile, and with them, four centurions as protection. He put them all under the command of the Ligurian and set the day for the attempt.

Now, when the Ligurian thought the appointed time had come, he made all his preparations and went to the spot. Those who were going to make the ascent, following the previous instructions of their guide had changed their arms and accoutrements, baring their heads and feet so as to be able to see better and climb among the rocks more easily. They carried their swords and shields on their backs, but took Numidian shields of hide, because they were lighter and would make less noise when struck. Then the Ligurian led the way, fastening ropes to the rocks or to old projecting roots, in order that with such help the soldiers might more easily make the ascent. Sometimes he lent a hand to those whom the unusual nature of the route alarmed, and where the ascent was unusually difficult, he would send men ahead one by one unarmed, and then follow himself bringing the arms. He was first to try the places which it seemed dangerous to attempt, and by often climbing up and returning the same way, and then at once stepping aside, he lent courage to the rest. In this way, after a long time and after great exertion, they at last reached the fortress, which was deserted at that point because all the men, as on other days, were face to face with the enemy.

Marius had devoted the whole day to keeping the Numidians intent upon the battle; but as soon as he heard that the Ligurian had accomplished his purpose, he began to urge on his soldiers. He himself went outside the mantlets, formed the tortoise-shed, and advanced to the wall, at the same time trying to terrify the enemy at long range with artillery, archers and slingers. But the Numidians, since they had often before overturned the mantlets of the enemy and set fire to them, no longer protected themselves within the walls of the fortress, but spent day and night outside, reviling the Romans and taunting Marius with madness. Emboldened by their successes, they threatened our soldiers with slavery at the hands of Jugurtha.

In the meantime, while all the Romans and all the enemy were intent upon the conflict, and both sides were exerting themselves to the utmost, the one for glory and dominion and the other for safety, suddenly the trumpets sounded in the rear of the foe. Then the women and children, who had come out to look on, were the first to flee, followed by those who were nearest to the wall, and finally by all, armed and unarmed alike. Upon this the Romans pressed on with greater vigour, routing the enemy, but for the most part only wounding them. Then they rushed on over the bodies of the slain, eager for glory and each striving to be first to reach the wall; not one stayed to plunder. Thus Marius's rashness was made good by fortune and he gained glory through an error of judgment.

This is much more than a narrative of action: it is a minute and graphic portrayal of the triumph of individual ingenuity and audacity over fearsome natural difficulties, in which Fortune plays her customary rôle of helper to the bold. There is a deliberate dramatic division. First, Marius finds the difficulties which originally inspired him to attempt the capture of this fortress to be greater than he had expected. Like his men, he is losing heart, when one of them discovers an undefended point of access. (Xenophon has a parallel to this example of initiative on the part of a private soldier.)[52] Marius then investigates the position and decides to adopt the Ligurian's plan. The crucial ascent, the centre-piece of the episode, is noticeably the richest section in descriptive detail. Finally follows the assault, in which surprise plays an important part. Throughout we are made aware of psychological factors: the desire for glory, which is gratified by the conquest of difficulties, the fears and anxieties engendered by the dangers, and the swift change from confidence to panic on the part of the defendants. There is also a particular interest in the nature of the land itself, the main factor which made the war 'atrox', and which Sallust was able to describe from personal knowledge. These qualities contribute to a narrative of a professional accuracy and dramatic intensity which no historian since Thucydides had been able to recapture.

CHAPTER 6

Livy

THE TRANSFORMATION of the Roman state from Republic to Empire was a gradual, though by no means painless process, foreshadowed by two centuries of continual change in her domestic and foreign politics. Precedents for autocracy abounded. Augustus Caesar was not the first Roman since the ancient kings to assume sole control of the government. With their characteristically practical sense, the Romans had always been prepared, in times of emergency, to waive their republican principles and appoint a single ruler with absolute but temporary powers to decide and act with despatch. The pages of Roman history are studded with the names of famous *dictatores*, as these men were called, like Camillus, who reorganized the army after the Gallic Invasion of 390–386 B.C., and Fabius Maximus, who, in the words of the poet Ennius, 'by attrition single-handed restored our fortunes', after the disasters at Lake Trasimene and Cannae in the Second Punic War. As Rome's dominions increased, her boundaries lengthened and became more distant. Emergencies became more frequent but less pressing, and accordingly the need for the consuls and other senior officials to combine civilian with military duties was diminished; indeed, the growth and increasing complexity of both these branches of the public service called for a division of labour. But whereas the number of military commitments tended to multiply, that of eligible commanders dwindled. Some patricians found soldiering distasteful, and were glad to forego its *al fresco* pleasures, while others, on achieving the consulship, by which they were assured of a lucrative provincial command the following year, were reluctant to face the dangers of campaigning during their consular term. Hence the way lay open for the able but low-born *condottiere*, who appeared in the person of Gaius Marius. He provided not only leadership but also reform of the army, modernizing its equipment, its formations and its training methods, abolishing the property qualifications for prospective recruits, and making military service a profession open to all who wished to face its dangers and reap its rewards. The new army proved itself in combat with the Cimbri, the Teutones and the Tigurini; but the democratic spirit of Marius's reforms and his own personal success at their expense alienated the Senate, so that they declined to assume the responsibility for paying his recruits. The army now became the queen in the political chess-game, and was naturally disposed to confer its allegiance upon the individual who identified himself with its fortunes—its own commander in the field. With armies supporting their generals against the state, a successful military career could lead directly to political pre-eminence, as happened in the cases of Marius and Sulla. Following upon these, the career of Gnaeus Pompeius, whose road to power was paved with ambiguous intentions and extraordinary commands (in other words, commands conferred in defiance of the stipulated limits relating rank to age, the *cursus honorum*), further illustrates the impotence of the civilian government against its more ambitious generals. But his ultimate failure showed that politics still counted for something, and his conqueror, Julius Caesar, set the ultimate example of success with a carefully planned political career in which the *cursus honorum* was not violated, and a consistent stand was taken on the side of popular reform. Pompey became a consul almost before he became a senator, having begun his career at the head of a private army which he had raised in support of the oligarch Sulla. As consul in 70 B.C. he sponsored popular reforms, restoring the powers of the tribunes which Sulla had taken away; but he ended his career in the oligarchic camp once more, the tool of a caucus of senatorial diehards. Caesar rose constitutionally through the offices of quaestor, aedile, pontifex maximus and praetor to the consulship in 59 B.C. Thereafter his enemies, sensing danger in his lawful progress, sought to destroy him. It was only at this point of his career that he concentrated upon acquiring military experience and support as the ultimate *force majeure* against openly professed opposition. Once attained, the summit might have been held through the same diplomatic skills as he had displayed during his ascent. But he abandoned these, and with them all recognition that republican sentiment was alive still in the minds of some, including his closest friends. His self-appointment as permanent dictator was the culmination of a series of insults, and enabled his assassins to defend their act with the argument that tyrants deserve to die.

When, after a further fifteen years of civil war, Augustus emerged in 30 B.C. as the undisputed master of the Roman world, few but the most impractical idealists yearned for the Republic, at least in the form in which it had been discredited in their lifetime. Augustus himself, born a year after the Catilinarian Conspiracy, might reasonably have endorsed the judgment of his adoptive father Julius Caesar, who described the Republic as 'a mere name, without form or substance'. In fact he did the opposite: in his own account of his career, preserved in a famous inscription at Ankara (the *Monumentum Ancyranum*), he claimed to have 'restored the Republic', basing this claim upon the fact that he refused the dictatorship and assumed no office in violation of republican usage. The stark fact of his absolute power refutes the first claim: but the substantial truth of the last two invites further, though necessarily brief investigation of one of the subtlest exercises in the dissimulation of autocratic power ever devised by the human mind.

Augustus refused regular consulships after 23 B.C., and assumed the offices of tribune and proconsul, leaving the most coveted republican offices, the consulship and the praetorship, open to all who could qualify for them. The tribuneship enabled him to identify himself, as had Caesar, with the interests of the people, and for that reason he outwardly attached the more importance to that office. It also enabled him to introduce his own legislation and veto any of which he disapproved. The proconsulship, reinforced with certain special powers, provided him with the ultimate sanction through its conferment of command over most of Rome's armed forces. Thus equipped, Augustus enjoyed unchallengeable supremacy without abolishing the republican offices; and he further fostered the illusion of a republican revival by conducting his own private life with a minimum of pomp and extravagance. It is tempting, and no doubt partly correct, to assume that the cautionary example of Caesar's brief rule profoundly influenced Augustus: dormant republican sentiment might yet be fatally rekindled by arrogance or even by tactlessness; and there is no defence against the determined assassin. But if Augustus had been preoccupied solely with self-preservation, he would have answered to Thucydides's description of the sixth-century tyrants of Greece ('they achieved nothing worthwhile'),[1] instead of being Rome's most constructive emperor. The many reforms which he enacted during his reign of forty-four years (he died in A.D. 14 at the age of seventy-six) all show a deep understanding and respect for the virtues which had made Rome great in the past, and a concern for their revival and adaptation to the present. With the republican constitution apparently preserved, corresponding measures must be taken to re-establish the moral climate of that Saturnian age. Sexual morality had been one of the worst casualties of the revolution, and its decline had struck at the foundations of society—the institution of marriage and the birth of legitimate children. Augustus made adultery a statutory offence carrying a penalty of exile; encouraged marriage by removing old class barriers and imposing penalties on those who remained single after the age of twenty-five; and stimulated procreation by giving precedence to candidates for public office in accordance with the numbers of their children. Youth also came under the emperor's surveillance: he promoted the growth of clubs for young men, both in Rome and in the municipalities of Italy, in which surplus time and energy were canalized into military exercises such as riding and mock fighting. The third institution which he reformed was the state religion. On the material level, he built two new temples in Rome and restored many old shrines. He also invested the priestly colleges with new honours, thus re-establishing them in the public consciousness. The spiritual aspect he approached through the family and the individual, paying particular attention to the household gods (*lares*) and promoting active participation in religious observance by inaugurating and reviving sacred anniversaries and festivals.

Thus fashioned with imaginative insight and moderation, the New Society enjoyed the further advantage of being allowed to burgeon and mature in peace. This boon earned for him the undying gratitude of his subjects, among whom those with the greatest talent for expressing it also had the most reason. Although literature draws its most exciting material from war, an atmosphere of settled calm must prevail before art and reason can conspire to produce a large-scale masterpiece. So stable and permanent did the regime of Augustus appear to the civilized world that the flow of foreign writers and teachers to Rome began once more. One of the most distinguished of these, Dionysius of Halicarnassus, made Rome the centre of a vigorous crusade for the revival of Attic Greek as a literary language. He also wrote a history of Rome from her foundation to the First Punic War, in twenty books. But his crusade met with stiff local competition, for the Augustan Age saw the final achievement by Latin authors of parity with the Greeks, who had for so long been their models and their mentors. Virgil, the greatest Latin poet, was approaching his creative peak with his *Georgics* at the time of Augustus's accession, and went on to celebrate the new era in his *Aeneid*, in which he linked the foundation of Rome with the Homeric legend of the siege and fall of Troy and the wanderings of the Trojan prince Aeneas, the son of Venus, whom Virgil made the ancestor of Augustus through the *gens Julia*. Horace turned from his earlier *Satires* and trenchant *Epodes*, written in the troubled years of revolution, to compose many verses which reveal genuine enthusiasm for the principate, and even personal affection for the *princeps*. But nowhere do we find a more fervent patriotism, a more serious concern for peace and internal political harmony, or a more obvious appreciation of the leisure conferred by it, than in the extant remains of the 142 books in which the historian Titus Livius traced the story of Rome from its foundation (signified by the title of the work, *Ab Urbe Condita*) to his own times.

Biographically, Livy is the most obscure of the great historians: we hardly know anything about his life. The most explicit evidence we have, that of St. Jerome, assigns his birth to the year 59 B.C. and his death to A.D. 17, but both these dates may be too late by as much as five years. Patavium (modern Padua) is at any rate firmly established as his birthplace. Time and circumstances allow a tentative amplification of his early life. He probably remained in his native city until he reached adulthood, neither serving in the army nor travelling abroad in order to complete his education. The character of his environment therefore demands scrutiny. In Livy's day, Patavium was a haven of republican conservatism in the stormy sea of the Roman revolution which raged during the historian's adolescence. His decision to remain aloof from the struggle was partly due to the influence of this environment; but had he been so inclined, there was probably no physical impediment to his participation. It therefore seems likely that he made a deliberate choice which was determined by an innate preference for a quiet life of study and contemplation. The length of his history and the amount of sheer labour expended upon its composition also suggest that he started early and pursued his goal with extraordinary tenacity and single-mindedness. It has been calculated that a modern equivalent of Livy's rate of composition would be an average of a 300-page book each year for forty years. Even with the stimulus of a few best-sellers, not many modern writers can match such fecundity. More significant from our point of view, however, is the fact that Livy breaks with the established Roman tradition that the historian should also be a man of action.

Each as long as a book of Thucydides, but covering on average five years to the Athenian's three, Livy's 142 books narrated some 770 years of Roman history. Of these books only 35 survive in an unabridged form; Books I–X, and XXI–XLV. These reach the year 167 (the missing decade, XI–XX, containing the First Punic War and the Pyrrhic War). The loss of his account of his own time deprives us of a definitive criterion of his ability; but the surviving corpus still represents the longest native Roman history that we possess, and is more than sufficient to enable us to form a coherent picture of his aims and methods, if not of his achievement.

It is pertinent to begin by qualifying Livy's relationship with Augustus. To begin with, one may be certain that he was not insensitive to the mood of renewed hope and national purpose which the emperor had conjured out of the darkness and despair of civil war. To this extent he was as 'Augustan' as Virgil or Horace. But it would be quite wrong to assume that he wrote as the official historian of the principate, colouring the events of the past, and taking every opportunity, either by allusion or by direct reference, to praise the work of the emperor and conceal his errors. In the first place, the loss of the contemporary portion of his narrative has removed all direct evidence, and deduction must depend on surmise or, worse still, on symbolism involving the transference of personalities and situations from earlier to later times. In the second place, such servility was unnecessary, for Augustus was liberal-minded and tolerant of criticism. A story told by Tacitus, that Augustus called Livy a Pompeian,[2] but that this did not damage their friendship, indicates clearly that he put his own interpretation upon events. But the fact that they remained good friends suggests that they shared a common view of the most important problems of the day. In particular, the national qualities which Livy illustrates and vindicates in his long story of Rome's past are the same as those to which Augustus attached such importance in his plans for the New Society.

Viewing seven centuries of steadily growing Roman power and influence, Livy was in an even better position than Sallust to exploit the advantage enjoyed by the historian of Rome over his Greek counterpart—that of studying the long-term evolution and progress of a civilization. But on what aspects of the often monotonous story does he wish his readers to focus especial attention? He answers this question in his Preface, and further explains his choice:[3]

> Here are the questions to which I should like every reader to give his close attention: what life and morals were like; through what men and what policies, in peace and in war, empire was established and enlarged. Then let him note how, with the gradual relaxation of discipline, morals first subsided, as it were, then sank lower and lower, and finally began the downward plunge which has brought us to present time, when we can endure neither our vices nor their cure.
>
> What chiefly makes the study of history beneficial and fruitful is this, that you behold the lessons of every kind of experience as upon a famous monument; from these you may choose for your own state what to imitate, and mark for avoidance what is shameful in conception and shameful in its result. For the rest, either love of the task I have set myself deceives me, or no state was ever greater, none more pious or richer in good examples, none where avarice and prodigality came into the social order so late, or where humble means and thrift were so highly esteemed and so long held in honour. For it is true that the less men's wealth was, the less was their greed. More recently, wealth has imported avarice, and excessive pleasures the longing to carry wantonness and licence to the point of ruin for oneself and of universal destruction.

The concept of history as a storehouse of examples for imitation and avoidance is not new, nor is that of a pattern of decline. What arrests attention is the positive optimism implied by the reference to choice for imitation and avoidance (is Livy here addressing Augustus, the only man able to exercise such a choice at the time of writing?), and the patriotic pride which causes him to mitigate his assertion of general decline with the statement that Roman virtues held their ground longer than those of other eclipsed powers. He elaborates on this theme in many places throughout his history, but one passage summarizes well his theory of the origin of Rome's greatness. It occurs in a hortatory speech by the young Scipio Africanus. After saying that in most of her wars Rome has been victorious only after sustaining terrible defeats, he gives examples of her resilience from past wars with Etruscans, Gauls and Samnites, together with some of more recent memory at the hands of Hannibal and the Carthaginians. He then concludes with these words: 'Amid this wreckage of her fortunes, one thing remained intact and immovable, the courage of the Roman People (*virtus populi Romani*).'[4] Here there are two concepts, not one—courage (literally, 'manly qualities'), and perseverance. All Rome's enemies might readily be conceded courage: what distinguished her from them was the ability to recover from one catastrophe after another, to swallow defeat and fight back. It was in this spirit that she faced the worst of her dangers, the might and the guile of Hannibal. Book XXII, in which are recounted her most crippling reverses, ends on a defiant note with this comment by the historian:

> Yet all these disasters and defections never made the Romans so much as mention peace, either before the consul returned to Rome, or after his return had renewed the remembrance of the terrible loss sustained. On this latter occasion, indeed, such was the high spirit of the country, that when the consul returned after this great disaster of which he himself had been the chief cause, all classes went in crowds to meet him, and he was publicly thanked because 'he had not despaired of the republic'.

Later the citizens display the same magnanimity and public-spiritedness when they applaud the consul for proposing that they should replenish the impoverished treasury from their private funds.

But this ancient counterpart of the 'spirit of Dunkirk', essential as it was for survival in war, represented only one facet of the central Roman virtue, which they themselves called '*constantia*'. Still on the subject of foreign relations, Livy takes every opportunity of furnishing examples of Rome's good faith in the observance of treaties and international law, such as it then was. Sometimes, indeed, they were over-scrupulous, as on one occasion they are criticized by the historian for 'wasting time in sending embassies'.[5] This reliability in the matter of agreements was rewarded by the loyalty of most of her allies, some of whom reciprocated nobly, like the Saguntines, who 'respected their loyalty as allies even to their own destruction'.[6] A different aspect of the same basic quality appears in her domestic politics, especially in the early, unsettled years: it is respect for established law and custom (*mos maiorum*). Dissension and rivalry there certainly were, as patricians and plebs pressed their rival claims for sovereignty; but Livy always succeeds in leaving his readers with the final impression that behind these periodic hostilities there lay in both camps a deep-seated distaste for the intrusion of violence into political argument. It was this sense of respect for parliamentary rights and procedure that enabled a speaker like Appius Claudius Crassus, a man with a reputation for extreme oligarchic views, to receive a fair hearing from the popular assembly when he warned that acceptance of the democratic proposals of the tribunes Licinius and Sextius would confer upon the plebs the same unbridled power that had hitherto been deplored in the patricians.[7] After due allowance has been made for rhetorical display, the tone underlying most political debates is moderate, even when the subject under discussion is of vital importance. No reader of the long dialogue between Scipio Africanus and Fabius Maximus on the question of extending the Second Punic War to Africa[8] would realize how controversial the issue was or to what extent the personal fortunes of the two speakers depended upon its outcome. Unlike Nicias in a debate on a similar question in Thucydides, Fabius has no hard things to say about the ambition of his younger rival, but merely states politely that he prefers to secure the state's safety by first finishing the war in Italy, and then crossing a friendly sea to Carthage.[9] Scipio replies with respect, and after refuting Fabius's argument forcefully but impersonally, proceeds to explain constructively how he proposes to implement his strategy.[10] He concludes with an explicit repudiation of personal abuse.[11] The loss of historicity resulting from Livy's desire to portray Roman self-control is probably considerable.

The same moderation and amenability to order and discipline made the Romans good soldiers: Livy accepts Polybius's estimation of the part played by military efficiency in Rome's success. Nowhere is discipline more important than on the battlefield itself, and there is no more astounding story of its observance than Livy's account of the treatment of his son by the consul Manlius Torquatus, who, after the young man had slain an enemy in defiance of orders, addressed him as follows:[12]

> Titus Manlius, since you have respected neither consular authority nor a father's dignity, and despite our edict have left your place to fight the enemy and, so far as you were able, have broken military discipline, whereby the Roman state has to this day stood unshaken, thus compelling me to forget either myself or the republic, we will sooner endure the punishment of our wrongdoing than suffer the republic to expiate our sins at a cost so heavy to herself. We shall set a stern example, but one which will be salutary for the young men of the future. For myself, I am moved not only by a man's instinctive love for his children, but by this instance you have given of your bravery, misguided though it is by a false notion of honour. But since the authority of the consuls must either be established by your death, or by your impunity forever abrogated, and since I think that you yourself, if you have a drop of my blood in you, would not refuse to restore by your punishment the military discipline which has slipped and fallen—go, lictor, and bind him to the stake.

Whereupon the son was flogged to death in the manner prescribed by the law for his offence, to the horror of all those present. But Livy leaves us in no doubt as to the effectiveness of the punishment:

> Nevertheless the brutality of the punishment made the soldiers more obedient to their general; and not only were guard-duties, watches, and the ordering of outposts, everywhere more carefully observed, but in the final struggle also, when the troops had gone down into battle, that stern act did much good.

A Roman father could legally slay his son for disobedience, but here the issue is not one of the defiance of parental authority, important as this was to the Roman mind, but of the very survival of the state, which depended upon military discipline. Whereas in most other armies the punishment of Titus Manlius might have provoked mutiny, the Romans knew and acknowledged that Torquatus had acted unselfishly and in the common interest.

A more general interest in the nature of Rome's military strength caused Livy to make a long and interesting comparison between the armies of Rome and that of Alexander the Great, which ends with the proud boast that Rome had never been defeated in an infantry battle.[13] Elsewhere, in his descriptions of battles, the limits of his military knowledge are often painfully exposed. Since he had never personally participated in a battle, it is understandable that his descriptions of static scenes are markedly more effective than his commentaries on the ebb and flow of the hand-to-hand conflicts. Taking these mobile pieces first, there is little in his account of the battle of Cannae[14] that suggests the operation by Hannibal of a well-rehearsed manoeuvre (perhaps bias also plays a part here)—that of the retiring centre, the encircling wings and the final ring of steel. According to Livy, this manoeuvre involved only a part of the Roman army, and was not in itself decisive; but he otherwise supplies no centre of gravity on which the whole battle hinges: rather the Romans are defeated piecemeal in a series of unconnected, Homeric engagements. But in the same battle we may contrast his description of the preliminary dispositions, in which he is obviously more at ease. There is something Herodotean about the colour and ethnic variety; but due place is also found for necessary details:[15]

> The total number of the infantry who were that day ranged in line [i.e. on the Carthaginian side,] was forty thousand, that of the cavalry ten thousand. Hasdrubal commanded the left wing; Maharbal the right; Hannibal himself, with his brother Mago, was in the centre. The sun, whether the troops were purposely so placed, or whether it was by chance, fell very conveniently sideways on both armies, the Romans facing the south, the Carthaginians the north. The wind, called Vulturnus by the natives of those parts, blew straight against the Romans and whirled clouds of dust in their faces till they could see nothing.

That Livy himself knew where his strength lay is suggested by his account of the battle of the Metaurus.[16] Here he describes an array which probably had no time to assemble, since battle was joined as soon as the Roman army came up with Hasdrubal. In dealing with sieges, which contain both mobile and static elements, Livy tends to over-simplify, and shows little interest in the many devices and variations of attack and repulse which had been developed over centuries of this type of fighting. Even the novel machinery created by the genius of Archimedes to defend Syracuse is not described in any great detail,[17] and certainly not to an extent which the historian's professed admiration for his originality would lead the reader to expect. Livy's most useful contribution to military history is his account of the organization of the old Roman army, which contains valuable information concerning the numbers, weapons and functions of the different divisions.

A further aspect of the Roman national character which Livy sought to portray was the place of religion in its life and its attitudes. Here, as with other historians, it is necessary to distinguish between personal belief and the obligation to report. And report he does: his catalogues of prodigies are among the fullest and most colourful in the ancient historians. The following is irresistible:[18]

Several portents were announced that year. The more they were believed by simple-minded and pious people, the more numerous were the reports of them. At Lanuvium, within the temple of Juno Sospita, crows, it was said, had built a nest; in Apulia a palm with green leaves had caught fire; at Mantua an overflow of the river Mincius had had the appearance of blood; at Cales it had rained chalk, and at Rome blood in the cattle-market; in the Insteian quarter an underground spring had burst forth with such a gush of water that some jars and casks on the spot were overturned and swept away, as it were by the force of a torrent; lightning had struck a public hall on the Capitol, a temple in Vulcan's field, a walnut tree and a public road in the Sabine country, as well as the city wall and a gate at Gabii. Soon there was talk of other miraculous occurrences. The spear of Mars at Praeneste had moved of its own accord; an ox in Sicily had spoken; a child in its mother's womb in the Marrucine country had shouted 'Ho! Triumph!'; and a woman at Spoletum had been turned into a man; an altar had been seen in the sky at Hadria, with forms of men around it in white apparel. And even at Rome itself, within the city, a swarm of bees had been seen in the Forum, and immediately afterwards, some persons declaring that they had seen armed legions in the Janiculum, roused the citizens to arms. Those who were on the Janiculum at the time declared that no person had been seen there except the ordinary inhabitants of the hill. For these portents expiation was made with victims of the larger kind by the direction of the diviners, and a day of public prayer was appointed to all the gods who had shrines at Rome.

The second sentence gives some indication of his opinion of the credibility of his account. It is also perhaps easier to find natural explanations for the first group of phenomena, most of which are perfectly normal occurrences. But when unlikely visions and sounds are witnessed by few people, and testimonies are contradicted, the historian is clearly implying doubts, and inviting the reader to share his impression that some at least of these manifestations were fictitious. Nevertheless they are legitimate historical material, both because they reflect popular anxiety at the time and because they induced an official reaction: they also play a useful dramatic rôle. Their presence is also partly attributable to the fact that prodigies were recorded in the city's religious calendar, from which much of Livy's material ultimately derives. But perhaps a deeper purpose, suggested by the following statement, underlies their inclusion:[19]

> I am not unaware that, as a result of the same disregard that leads men generally to suppose nowadays that the gods foretell nothing, no portents at all are reported officially, or recorded in our histories. However, not only does my mind, as I write of ancient matters, become in some way or other old-fashioned, but also a certain conscientious scruple prevents me from regarding what those very wise men of former times thought worthy of public concern as something unworthy to be reported in my history.

Interpreted literally, this passage implies no more than that Livy found prodigies useful as a means of keeping his finger on the pulse of ancient life and of imparting an antique hue to the colour of his narrative. But reverence also enters into his explanation, and it is difficult not to see Livy's position in the light of Augustus's measures for the revival of the state religion.

Nevertheless, the part played by religion in Livy's history is not sufficiently active and positive to amount to an official crusade: here, as elsewhere, Livy shows his independence. It is difficult to extract any definite personal opinions. The reasoning ascribed to Numa, the second king of Rome and the architect of her religious system—that the inculcation of religious fear into the populace was necessary when fear of the state's enemies had been temporarily removed—was a conventional view which the historian may have happened to share.[20] Perhaps we come nearer to discovering Livy's own attitude when we note the frequency with which he refers to instances of religious observance, and, even more significantly, of its neglect or abuse. Paradoxically, these lead to a negative conclusion, for in only two cases does he imply any connection between them and subsequent events, and in both these cases he expressly says that individuals and not the state were affected:[21] for the rest, no suggestion, even in cases of great triumph or disaster, that the course of events was directly determined by the observance or neglect of religious rites. Livy's own position must remain obscure, and our present purpose is best served by summarizing the part played by religion in his history. He sets out to show that a state with a strong priesthood and universally practised rituals is assured of a healthy body-politic, and a good reserve of confidence in times of adversity. He sees no reason to question the existence of divine powers further than this. This phenomenological attitude is paralleled in his view of history in general: his interest is less in minute scientific inquiry than in the observation of the broad principles governing the growth and decline, on both the physical and moral plane, of cities and nations.

Having such aims as these, and living in a somewhat inhibiting environment, Livy might be expected to exhibit few startling political views; and this is salutary in a historian who is covering so long a period. Whereas Sallust's indignation against the oligarchic factions of his day may be admissible in a history of that period alone, such bias would do irreparable damage to a complete history of Rome. Livy tries, on the whole successfully, to reflect the various views held at the time about which he is writing. In particular, his account of the early struggles between patricians and plebs maintains a high standard of impartiality. One short personal judgment contained in this account is illuminating. During the year 491 B.C., when the patricians were smarting under the effects of the first secession of the plebs, a large quantity of grain was imported from Sicily. Some patricians saw this as an opportunity to recover their lost power, since at that time the Senate had the authority to decide at what price it should be sold. One of their number, Marcius Coriolanus, proposed to use the corn as a bargaining implement against the plebs, by threatening to set a high price upon it if they should refuse to restore full sovereignty to the patricians. Commenting on this extreme proposal, Livy says: 'It is less easy to say whether it would have been right to do this than it lay, I think, within the Senate's power to have made such conditions.'[22] The absence of detailed information on this early period, of which Livy is acutely conscious, commends this empirical attitude. He tries as far as possible to avoid general issues of right and wrong, and confines praise or blame to individuals. However, he does show a certain prejudice against the popular elements. This is manifested through the words used to describe their behaviour: their outcries are like storms (*procellae*);[23] their spokesmen, the tribunes, act in frenzy (*furor*)[24] and violence (*vis, violentia*).[25] On the other hand, patricians of established dignity and prestige, like the Decemvirs who tried to solve the problems of the constitution in the middle of the fifth century, are treated with great respect even when their performance does not match their reputation.

Much more clearly drawn is Livy's attitude to Rome's various neighbours. Here his patriotism exercises a strong influence. He states it as his view that Rome's allies and subjects tolerated her rule because it was fair and moderate, and because they accepted the Romans as their superiors.[26] Those who take Rome's side are glowingly portrayed, even those of less than immaculate character, like Massinissa, the king of Numidia; while on the other side, he often represents Rome's enemies as cruel and perfidious. It is no accident that the most deeply blackened opponent is also the most dangerous that Rome faced—Carthage. In the short preface to his narrative of the Second Punic War,[27] he stresses the peculiar hatred which existed between the two sides, but follows this statement with the famous story of how Hannibal was steeped in hatred of Rome from boyhood. Unlike Polybius, who says that Hannibal's decision to make war on Rome dated from his assumption of the command of the Punic army in Spain, Livy tells how he was made by his father, as a boy of nine years, to swear eternal hatred of Rome. The pen-portrait of Hannibal which follows directs the reader even more forcefully towards the cause of the war. After praising his personal magnetism, his resourcefulness and his powers of endurance (as events compelled him to), he concludes with this scathing indictment:[28]

These great virtues in the man were equalled by monstrous vices: inhuman cruelty, a worse-than-Punic perfidy. Absolutely false and irreligious, he had no fear of god, no regard for oaths, no scruples.

For a more balanced and analytical estimate of Hannibal we must turn to Polybius.[29] But Livy is here denigrating not so much an individual as a people. The use of the proverbial expression '*Punica fides*' (which is, of course, absent from Polybius's more detached portrait) colours the whole of Livy's picture, and universalizes it: these are the vices of a nation, appearing in their extreme form in its ablest and most zealous citizen. Livy's portraits of the collective character of other nations are less vivid because they are not thus personalized: but we read that the Gauls are factious and headstrong, and lack staying power; while the Greeks are better at talking than fighting, and immoderate in their emotional reactions. Most nations suffer from flaws of character which are found to correspond to one of the cardinal virtues of the Romans.

On the Roman side the collocation of customs and men adumbrated in his preface is faithfully maintained, but it cannot be said that the danger of losing individuality, inherent in the subordination of personal to national characteristics, is altogether avoided. The early heroes suffer especially. The semi-mythological stories of this period turn mainly upon violent action in which glory or ignominy is achieved: bravery, cowardice, arrogance and popular sympathies are the qualities variously exhibited by these figures; and the permutations of these are limited. Later we find some more interesting characterization. Flaminius before Trasimene is portrayed as a man over-nourished by good fortune, which has stimulated his natural rashness and made him prey to the wiles of a percipient enemy. As the disaster unfolds, the character of Flaminius is kept constantly to the fore, and imparts to the whole episode the flavour of a cautionary tale.[30] The presence of Fabius Maximus is felt over a much longer period. The correctness of his policy is demonstrated by the plight of his Master of Horse, Minucius, who eventually confesses his error and honours Fabius with the name of 'Father'[31] (an image which grows). His avowed aim is not to do nothing but, in whatever is done, to let reason and not fortune be the guide. Later he appears in the debate with Scipio already alluded to,[32] in which he advocates the completion of the war in Italy before the invasion of Africa. This debate lies at the crossroads of Roman history not only because of the immediate strategic question raised in it, but because of the conflict of personalities which foreshadows and symbolizes a major change in the character of Roman politics. On the foreign front, the antithesis between the circumspection and caution of Fabius and the extrovert enterprise of Scipio corresponds with the contemporary question of Rome's future, whether she should extend her sphere of interest beyond the shores and natural boundaries of Italy, Sicily, and Sardinia. In domestic politics, Scipio invites comparison, by his attention to his personal prestige and powers of popular appeal, with Julius Caesar, and even Augustus, who attached such importance to his tribunician power. Livy lays particular emphasis on this aspect of Scipio's character in his pen-portrait:[33]

> Scipio was an object of admiration not only because of his actual qualities, but because of a certain technique he had perfected since his youth of displaying them. To the people he represented many of his actions as beheld in visions at night, or implanted in his mind by the gods, either because he was as susceptible to superstition as they were, or in order that men might carry out his orders without hesitation as though they had emanated from an oracle.

Fabius, on the other hand, appeals to constitutional procedure, which at this time meant initial senatorial approval, in the matter of the decision as to whether to invade Africa. He also alludes to his seniority and past services and the lessons of Roman misfortunes in similar previous enterprises, and reproves Scipio for placing desire for personal glory before the good of the state. But it is upon Scipio that our attention is made to dwell: he undoubtedly has the better of the argument. Winning his audience's good will at the outset with an open admission of his honest ambition, he proceeds to argue the advantages of an aggressive policy, adducing the unhappily recent example of Hannibal's success, and outlining a new mental approach to foreign policy based upon opportunism and adaptability—the very approach which brought Rome her later conquests. After his speech we have a further allusion to Scipio's ambition and reliance upon popular support when Livy mentions that he was reported as having intended to bring the matter of the African expedition before the popular assembly if the Senate should refuse to ratify it.[34]

Livy's pen-portrait of Scipio contains another recurrent

quality of the popular leader—the assertion of semi-divinity, or at least of communication with the gods. This had been found useful by Alexander the Great in the more susceptible East, and was later exploited by the emperors of Rome in the same regions. Scipio employs it with studied moderation, using it only to win the confidence and obedience of the common people, whether they were soldiers or civilians. Another quality which later dynasts found it useful to lay claim to, good fortune, also finds its first claimant in Scipio Africanus. But a thorough reading of the books which he dominates (XXIV–XXX) reveals a more balanced and complete portrait of the ideal general. Livy refers to one character-istic occasion on which Scipio, after making an important discovery through careful research, ascribed it to a divine, though unnamed informant,[35] but he ensures through many examples that we should be in no doubt as to his professional thoroughness in the mundane matters of logistics and adminis-tration, in addition to his more romantic qualities of courage, personal example and understanding of his men. Idealism is not allowed to go too far, and limitations are admitted: Livy recog-nizes that Scipio was less successful as a politician than as a general,[36] a judgment with which modern opinion is in sub-stantial agreement.

Livy's accounts of clashes of personality such as that of Scipio and Fabius may be said to fall short of realism in that they fail to bring to light the violence and bitterness of the factional struggles in which these men were engaged; nor do we receive so much as a glimpse of the more shady private intrigues which were undoubtedly transacted between men of outward probity, and which a Herodotus or a Xenophon would have enjoyed reporting. But here again essential characteristics are not lost. Livy's Roman politicians keep pace with the changing times, and reflect the new forces operating on the political scene. The ancient figures, like Coriolanus and Appius Claudius, display the pristine severity and intractability of an all-powerful oligarchy; Scipio, the new consciousness of the growing importance of 'the breezes of popular favour'; and the Elder Cato, to whom Livy assigns a pen-portrait comparable to those accorded Hannibal and Scipio,[37] is the first thoroughly successful 'new man', who combined plebeian ancestry with the old Roman standards (which an effete aristocracy was beginning to lay upon the altar of philhellenism), and reached the highest offices, the consulship and the censorship, by dint of sheer ability. Personalities like these play a dynamic as well as a colorific part in the development of Livy's story.

Most of what has so far been observed of Livy's life, qualifications and preconceptions will have conditioned us not to apply the highest standards of historical accuracy to his work. The sources available to him and his selection and arrangement of them aggravate rather than mitigate this weakness. As to his sources, Livy is himself under no illusions: of early history he says that not only its antiquity but the paucity of contemporary written records renders it obscure,[38] an opinion which he underlines by condensing the first 365 years of Roman history into five books. This statement is, however, misleading inasmuch as it implies that Livy consulted original sources: astonishingly to the modern student, he drew his material exclusively from literary sources. Distortion is thus liable to occur at two stages, and two different combinations of bias, competence and intention are embodied in Livy's final product, his own and that of his source. Livy's dependence on literary sources gives rise to a further difficulty: some of them are Greek, and although his knowledge of that language was adequate for the translation of straightforward passages, he occasionally mistranslates when the unfamiliarity of a word coincides with his own ignorance of the subject. For example, in a translation of Polybius's narrative of an underground battle between Romans and Aetolians,[39] unable to imagine the conditions of such an engagement, Livy has both sides defending themselves with *doors*[40] ($\theta\acute{\nu}\rho\alpha\varsigma$) instead of *shields* ($\theta\nu\rho\epsilon o\acute{\nu}\varsigma$, the word used by Polybius). The provenance of these novel means of protection, and the manner in which they were manipulated so that their bearers could also fight, are understandably left to the reader's imagination. Opportunities for errors such as this are mercifully few, but the possibility of misinterpretation of arguments and discussions, which can lead to serious distortion of events and situations, is always present when Livy is translating from a Greek source. But how often such distortions occur must, in the absence of all the original Greek sources except Polybius, remain unknown.

The main sources employed by Livy may be briefly mentioned. For the first ten books he used his contemporary Aelius Tubero, the *popularis* Licinius Macer, and Valerius Antias. This combination probably enabled him to strike a happy balance between the traditional, popular and rhetorical elements present in the earlier accounts. In Books XXI–XXX Polybius and Coelius Antipater were used in conjunction with Valerius Antias; and in Books XXXI–L these three were joined by Claudius Quadrigarius. Here again there was scope for judicious eclecticism: Polybius being strong on Eastern affairs and military operations, Coelius with his wide reading and accuracy providing some essential annalistic detail, and Valerius contributing valuable political knowledge. With such varied and talented sources at his disposal Livy might be expected to have produced a version of events which avoided extreme views and came as near to factual truth as was humanly possible. But his practice was not to amalgamate but to select, not to seek a *communis opinio*, but to reproduce one version substantially as it stood, sometimes appending, in the manner of Herodotus, a brief reference to a contradictory account, but unlike him rarely commenting on its credibility. Inevitably many errors arise from this practice, and even more inconsistencies; duplications even, as when he appears to describe Hannibal's movements in the winter of 218/217 twice. Again, Livy's concern to celebrate the glory of Rome's past and the triumph of her national virtues does not encourage confidence in his invariable choice of the true version.

When due attention has been drawn to the limitations of Livy's history, two of its qualities render it certain of a permanent place in the canon of the world's great histories. In the first place, thanks to his great industry, professional historians are furnished with many mundane but essential facts—the names of consuls, the terms of treaties, the foundation of colonies, the organization of provinces and the details of reforms. Livy is the most important surviving source for Roman history. Secondly, when we try to envisage the amount of labour involved in the composition of 142 books of history, our calculations should include the effort which he expended on the form as distinct from the content. Livy did not merely copy his sources: he recast them in a style which, from a purely literary standpoint, was as new and original as Homer's version of the siege of Troy or Virgil's version of the story of Aeneas. Steeped in Ciceronian rhetorical theory, and profoundly influenced by that orator's style, Livy probably spent more time upon the literary composition of his history, which included many full-length speeches, than upon the study and comparison of his source-material.

Thus we come to consider the aspect on which Livy himself would have wished his work to be judged—its literary style. The rhetorical method of composition employed by Livy, the origin of which is to be traced back through Cicero to Isocrates and his school, shared some of the aims of oratory itself. It sought to win and retain the attention of a listening audience, and did so by two main means. It replaced the missing element of spectacle (with which theatrical and other forms of mass entertainment were liberally endowed) by the infusion of emotive colouring into the narrative and the live speech, consisting of descriptive or rational material capable of arousing fear, pity, wonder or elation. Secondly, the material was so arranged as to achieve the maximum variety, both in subject matter and in dramatic content. This quest for variety is skilfully adapted to the annalistic framework to which Livy, true to his vocation as a historian, adheres throughout. The occasional sacrifice of chronology to artistic arrangement is mainly restricted to the confusion of the order of events within a year, and rarely results in the attribution of an event to the wrong year. Livy's reliance upon historical fact as the basis of his composition is firmly established by the marked superiority, from the literary as well as the historical point of view, of his accounts of episodes on which he had reliable and detailed information. Conversely, incidents like the stand of Horatius Cocles and episodes like the Gallic Invasion of 390–386 B.C. are recounted with rather less vividness and dramatic force than their importance merited. The honest historian does not try to clothe the mouldering bones of a lost tradition in false flesh: the participants in these obscure events act out their accredited parts with little individuality, and Livy signifies his lack of interest in them by the identifiably commonplace character of the rhetorical embellishments which he uses upon them. But when he has a wealth of historical detail at his disposal he is immeasurably more individual and effective. It is with the aid of such detail that genuine colour and life, and also organic structure, can be conferred upon a narrative. Livy's account of Hannibal's crossing of the Alps, based on Polybius's narrative but diverging in presentation, admirably exemplifies this:[41]

Then they reached a canton, which, for a mountain district, was densely populated. Here Hannibal was all but cut off, not by open fighting, but by his own peculiar arts, treachery and ambuscade. Some old men, governors of the fortresses, came to him as envoys, with assurances that, warned by the salutary examples of the misfortunes of others, they preferred to make trial of the friendship rather than of the might of the Carthaginians; that thereupon they would obediently do his bidding; and they begged him to accept supplies, guides for his march, and hostages as a guarantee of their promises. Hannibal, feeling that he must not either rashly trust or slight them, lest refusal might make them open enemies, gave them a gracious answer. He accepted the offered hostages, and used the supplies which they had themselves brought to the road, but he followed the guides with his army in fighting order, not as if he was among a friendly people. His van was formed of the elephants and cavalry, while he marched himself in the rear with the main strength of the infantry, anxiously reconnoitring at every step. The moment they entered the narrow pass, dominated on one side by an overhanging height, the barbarians sprang out of their ambuscades in every direction, attacking in front and rear, discharging missiles and coming to close quarters, and rolling down huge stones upon the army. It was on the rear that the enemy pressed with the greatest force. The infantry-column wheeled and faced him; but it was proved beyond a doubt that, had not the rear been well strengthened, a terrible disaster would have been sustained in that pass. Even as it was, they were brought to the extremest jeopardy, and were within a hairsbreadth of destruction. For while Hannibal was hesitating about sending his men into the defile because, though he could himself support the cavalry, he had no reserve in his rear for the infantry, the mountaineers rushed on his flanks, and having cut his line in half barred his advance. One night he had to pass without his cavalry and his baggage.

Next day, as the barbarians were less active in their attacks, the army was again united, and fought its way through the pass, but not without loss, which, however, fell more heavily on the beasts of burden than the men. From this point the mountaineers became less numerous; hovering round more like brigands than soldiers, they threatened now the van, now the rear, whenever the ground gave them the chance, or stragglers in advance or behind offered the opportunity. The elephants, though it was a tedious business to drive them along the narrow precipitous passes, at least protected the troops from the enemy wherever they went, inspiring as they did a peculiar fear in all who were unused to approach them.

On the ninth day they reached the top of the Alps, passing for the most part over trackless slopes, and by devious ways, into which they were led by the treachery of their guides. Two days they encamped on the height, and the men, worn out with hardships and fighting, were allowed to rest. Some beasts of burden too, which had fallen down among the crags, found their way to the camp by following the army's track. The men were already worn out and wearied with their many miseries, when a fall of snow coming with the setting of the Pleiades added to their sufferings a terrible fear. At daybreak the march commenced, and as the army moved wearily over ground all buried in snow, languor and despair were visibly written on every face, when Hannibal stepped to the front, and having ordered a halt on a peak which commanded a wide and distant prospect, pointed to Italy and to the plains around the Po, as they lay beneath the heights of the Alps, telling his men, 'It is the walls not of Italy but of Rome itself that you are now scaling. What remains,' he added, 'will be a smooth descent; in one, or at the most two battles we shall have the citadel and capital of Italy in our grasp and power.'

The army then began to advance, and now even the enemy attempted nothing but some stealthy ambuscades, as opportunity offered. The remainder of the march, however, proved far more difficult than the ascent, as the Alps for the most part on the Italian side have a shorter and therefore steeper slope. In fact the whole way was precipitous, narrow and slippery, so much so that they could not keep themselves from falling, nor could those who had once stumbled retain their foothold. Thus they tumbled over one another, and the beasts of burden over the men.

Next they came to a much narrower pass with walls of rock so steep that a light-armed soldier could hardly let himself down by feeling his way, and grasping with his hands the bushes and roots sticking out around him. The place had always been naturally precipitous, and now by a recent landslide it had been broken away sheer to a height of a thousand feet. Here the cavalry halted as if it must be the end of their route, and when Hannibal wondered what delayed the march, he was told that the rock was impassable. Then he went himself to examine the spot. There seemed to be no doubt that he must lead his army round by pathless and hitherto untrodden slopes, however tedious might be the circuit. This route, however, was impracticable; while on last season's unmelted snow lay a fresh layer of moderate depth. The foot of the first comer found a good hold on the soft and not very deep drift, but when it had once been trampled down under the march of such a host of men and beasts, they had to walk on the bare ice beneath, and the liquid mud from the melting snow. Here there was a horrible struggle. The slippery ice allowed no firm foothold, and indeed betrayed the foot all the more quickly on the slope, so that whether a man helped himself to rise by his hands or knees, his supports gave way, and he fell again. And here there were no stalks or roots to which hand or foot could cling. Thus there was incessant rolling on nothing but smooth ice or slush. The beasts broke through, occasionally treading down even to the lowest layer of snow, and when they fell, as they wildly struck out with their hoofs in their efforts to rise, they cut clean to the bottom, till many of them stuck fast in the hard and deep-frozen ice, as if caught in a trap.

At last, when both men and beasts were worn out with fruitless exertion, they encamped on a height, in a spot which with the utmost difficulty they had cleared; so much snow had to be dug out and removed. The soldiers were then marched off to the work of making a road through the rock, as only by that way was a passage possible. Having cut into the stone, they heaped up a huge pile of wood from great trees in the neighbourhood, which they had felled and lopped. As soon as there was strength enough in the wind to create a blaze they lighted the pile, and melted the rocks, as they heated, by pouring vinegar on them. The burning stone was cleft open with iron implements, and then they relieved the steepness of the slopes by gradual winding tracks, so that even the elephants as well as the other beasts could be led down. Four days were spent in this rocky pass, and the beasts almost perished with hunger, as the heights generally are quite bare, and such herbage as grows is buried in snow. Amid the lower slopes were valleys, sunny hills too, and streams, and woods beside them, and spots now at last more worthy to be the habitations of men. Here they set the beasts to feed, and the men, worn out with the toil of road-making, were allowed to rest. In the next three days they reached level ground, and now the country was less wild, as was also the character of the inhabitants.

The narrative is informed by dramatic contrasts, which promote emotional variety. It begins with a paradox—Hannibal almost suffering disaster, not through fighting but as a result of his own over-subtlety. The ordeal of the ascent, as the army runs the gauntlet of enemy ambushes through the pass, is made the more vivid by the historian's ability to identify the different units and the part they played. As they climb higher, the nature of the fighting changes and natural problems supervene. The narrative reaches a climax, both physical and emotional, when the army, utterly exhausted, takes a brief rest on the summit. An optimistic item, the return of some of the lost beasts, is followed by a pessimistic one, a heavy fall of snow, and this prompts Hannibal to take cognizance of the low state of the army's morale. But subsequent events invest his confident assertion with a terrible irony. In them there is both paradox and anticlimax: it ought to be easier to go down than up, and the enemy was no longer giving trouble. The narrative now concentrates on the physical problems, and here again detail plays a dynamic part, as for example in the description of the increasing treachery of the snow as it became impacted under the tread of successive marchers, and again when the beasts of burden become immobilized. The negotiation of the final hurdle is the most spectacular part of the narrative, combining hard labour and ingenuity in an extraordinary degree; and this is followed immediately by an idyllic scene of peace and sylvan repose. Rhetoric plays no part independently of the narrative, but is merely used to underline the elements of dramatic contrast already present in a well-known story.

Pitched battles might be thought to offer even better opportunities for the exhibition of rhetorical skill than the above episode; but here again Livy's best battle-narratives are those which are based on the most precise information, in which the rhetoric is allowed to arise naturally out of the situation. His description of the Battle of Zama, which decided the Second Punic War, may be quoted in full as an illustration of this:[42]

> For this contest two of the most clearly distinguished generals, and two of the bravest armies of the two wealthiest nations went forth on that day following, when they would either crown the many distinctions they had won hitherto, or bring them to nothing. Consequently a wavering between hope and fear confused their spirits; and as they surveyed now their own battle-line, now that of the enemy, while weighing their strength more by the eye than by calculation, the bright side and at the same time the dark was before their minds. What did not occur to the men of their own accord the generals would suggest in admonition and exhortation. Hannibal kept recalling to their minds the achievements of sixteen years in the land of Italy, so many Roman generals, so many armies wiped out completely, and brave deeds of individuals, whenever he came to a

soldier distinguished in the record of some battle. Scipio would recall the Spanish provinces and recent battles in Africa and the enemy's admission, in that on account of fear they could only sue for peace, and yet had been unable to abide by the peace on account of their ingrained perfidy. Furthermore, as his conference with Hannibal had been in private and could be freely altered, he gave it the direction he desired. He divined that as the Carthaginians went out into battle-line, the gods had given them the same omens as when their fathers fought at the Aegates Islands. The end of the war and of hardship was at hand, he said, the spoils of Carthage within reach, and return home to their native city, to parents, children, wives and household gods. So erect did he stand as he spoke, and with so happy a look on his face that one would have believed him already the victor.

Thereupon he drew up in the first line the *hastati*, behind them the *principes*, and in the rear the *triarii* closing the formation. However, he did not form cohorts in close contact, each in advance of its standards, but rather maniples at a considerable distance from each other, so that there should be an interval where the enemy's elephants might be driven through without breaking up the ranks. Laelius, whom he had previously had in his service as lieutenant, but in the present year as quaestor, assigned not by lot but by decree of the senate, was posted with the Italic cavalry on the left wing, Massinissa and the Numidians on the right. The open passages between the maniples of the front line of troops Scipio filled with *velites*, the light-armed of that day, under orders that, upon the charge of the elephants, they should either flee behind the ranks in the line, or else dashing to right and left and closing up to the maniples in the van, should give the beasts an opening through which they might rush among missiles hurled from both sides.

Hannibal, in order to create a panic, drew up his elephants in front— and there were eighty of them, a number he had never before had in any battle. Next in order he placed the Ligurian and Gallic auxiliaries in combination with Balearic and Mauretanian troops; in the second line Carthaginians and Africans and the legion of Macedonians. Then, leaving a moderate interval, he drew up a reserve line of Italic soldiers, most of them Bruttians, more of whom had followed him under compulsion and of necessity than of their own consent, as he retired from Italy. As for the cavalry, he also placed them on the wings: the Carthaginians held the right wing, the Numidians the left.

In an army made up of so many men who had no language, no custom, no law, no arms, no clothing and general appearance in common, nor the same reason for serving, exhortation took various forms. To the auxiliaries was offered pay in cash, to be greatly increased by a share in the booty. The Gauls had their own inbred hatred of the Romans fanned into flame. Ligurians were offered as an incentive to victory the rich plains of Italy, once they were brought down from their rugged mountains. Mauretanians and Numidians were frightened by Hannibal with the prospect of Massinissa's tyrannical rule. To different nations different hopes and fears were displayed. The Carthaginians' attention was called to the walls of their city, to household gods, tombs of ancestors, children and parents and terror-stricken wives, to destruction and servitude on the one hand, and on the other to rule over the world, to the absence of any ground between the extremes of fear and hope.

Just as the general was thus speaking among the Carthaginians, and the national leaders among their countrymen, mainly through interpreters, since foreigners were intermingled, trumpets and horns sounded on the Roman side, and such shouts were raised that the elephants turned against their own men, especially against the left wing, the Mauretanians and Numidians, Massinissa easily increased their panic and stripped that end of the line of its cavalry support. A few of the beasts, however, being fearlessly driven into the enemy, caused great losses among the ranks of the lightly-armed, though suffering many wounds themselves. For springing back to the maniples the light-armed made way for the elephants, to avoid being trampled down, and then would hurl their lances from both sides against the beasts doubly exposed to missiles. Nor was there any slackening in the javelin-fire of the men in the front lines until these elephants also, driven out of the Roman line and into their own men by missiles showered upon them from all sides, put the right wing, the Carthaginian cavalry itself, to flight. Laelius, on seeing the enemy in confusion increased their panic.

On both sides the Punic battle-line had been stripped of its cavalry when the infantry clashed, now no longer matched either in their hopes or in their strength. And there were what seem small things to mention, but at the same time were highly important in the battle: a harmony in the shouting of the Romans, which consequently was greater in volume and more terrifying; on the other side discordant voices, as was natural from many nations with a confusion of tongues; for the Romans a battle of little movement, as they pressed on into the enemy by their own weight and that of their arms; on the other side repeated charges at high speed but with less power. Consequently at the first attack the Romans at once dislodged the enemy's line. Then beating them back with their shoulders and the bosses of their shields, being now in close contact with men forced from their position, they made considerable progress, as no one offered any resistance, while as soon as they saw that the enemy's line had given way, even the rear line pressed upon the first, a circumstance which of itself gave them great force in repulsing the enemy. On the enemy side, so far was their second line, the Africans and Carthaginians, from supporting the auxiliaries as they gave way, that on the contrary they even drew back from fear lest the enemy, by slaying the men of the first line if these stoutly resisted, should reach themselves. Accordingly the auxiliaries suddenly retreated and, facing their own men, some found refuge in the second line while others, having been refused aid shortly before, and also admission now to the ranks, slashed at those who would not make way for them. And by this time there were almost two battles in one, since the Carthaginians were forced to engage with the enemy and at the same time with their own men. Nevertheless even so they did not admit the panic-stricken, angry men into the line, but closing up their ranks, they forced them out upon the wings and into the empty plain on this side and that outside of the battle, in order not to contaminate their own line, still intact and fresh, with soldiers alarmed by the flight and their wounds.

But such heaps of bodies and arms had covered the place where the auxiliaries had stood shortly before that to make their way across was almost more difficult than it had been through the dense mass of the enemy. Accordingly the men of the front line, the *hastati*, pursuing the enemy wherever they could over heaps of bodies and arms and through pools of blood, broke up both their maniples and their ranks. The maniples of the *principes* also began to waver, as they saw the unsteady line in front of them. When Scipio saw this he ordered the recall to be sounded at once for the *hastati*, and after withdrawing the wounded to the rear line, he led the *principes* and the *triarii* to the wings, in order that the centre, composed of the *hastati*, might be safer and steadier. Thus began an entirely new battle. For they had reached the real enemy, their equals in the character of their weapons and their experience in war and the celebrity of their deeds and the greatness whether of their hopes or of their dangers. But the Romans were superior both in numbers and in spirit, because they had already routed the cavalry, had already routed the elephants, and were already fighting against the second line, having repulsed the first.

At the right moment Laelius and Massinissa, who had pursued the routed cavalry for a considerable distance, returned and dashed into the rear of the enemy line. That charge finally worsted the enemy. Many were overpowered and slain in the battle-line, many were scattered in flight over the open plain around, and as the cavalry were in complete possession, they perished everywhere. Over twenty thousand of the Carthaginians and their allies were slain on that day. About the same number were captured, together with one hundred and thirty-two military standards and eleven elephants. Of the victors about fifteen hundred fell.

The all-important scene-setting for this, one of the most decisive battles in world history contains contrasting elements: the psychological and subjective, through which are portrayed the feelings of the combatants and their leaders' interpretation and exploitation of these feelings; and the physical and objective, through which the historian gives a detailed account of the numbers and disposition of the various units on each side. Like Herodotus, Livy is fully aware of the colourfulness of mixed nationalities; but he improves on Herodotus's catalogue of the Persian host by describing their different fears and hopes. The battle itself begins with a surprise attack and a paradox, Hannibal being once again hoist with his own petard, this time his elephants. The corporate discipline of the Roman side, symbolized by the concord of their battle-cry, contrasts with the multilingual tumult of Hannibal's cosmopolitan host; so too does the manner of their advance, which is slow, even and strong, compared with the swift but unpenetrative thrusts of the enemy. The climax of the battle is reached in the second phase when Romans confront Carthaginians, the 'real enemy'. Most battles are decided by a single *coup* executed at a moment when matters are upon a razor's edge, and Zama was no exception. 'Opportunity' and 'the psychological moment' are also rhetorical concepts long recognized in oratorical theory. After the timely blow has been struck matters are brought to a swift conclusion. The outcome of the battle has been foreshadowed almost from the beginning, and has ceased to be in doubt after the paradoxical spectacle of Punic units engaging in battle with one another. The horrific scene which follows that episode also contains a paradox, as piles of corpses and pools of blood, not live men, impede the Roman advance. But this whole section is a complex of many rhetorical devices in which emotions, tactics, ethnic colour and surprise contribute varying effects, sometimes supplying contrast, at others combining to produce a cumulative result. Generally speaking, Livy's technique of contrast is most clearly seen at work in his arrangement of whole episodes. This passage is followed by a relief from carnage and fighting as the historian stands back to assess the generalship of the two leaders. Then follow further contrasting episodes, Scipio's plundering of Hannibal's camp and Carthaginian peace moves. Occasionally, however, variation, surprise and antithesis are employed in a concentrated form, especially in passages portraying strong emotion, like the following, in which Livy describes the reception given at Rome to the news of her first major defeat at Hannibal's hands in the Battle of Lake Trasimene:[43]

> The misfortunes of the beaten army were not more numerous than the anxieties which distracted the minds of those whose relatives had served under Flaminius. All were utterly ignorant of how this or that kinsman had fared; no one even quite knew what to hope or to fear. On the next day, and for some days after, there stood at the gates a crowd in which the women even outnumbered the men, waiting to see their relatives or hear some tidings about them. They thronged round all whom they met, with incessant questions, and could not tear themselves away, least of all leave any acquaintance, till they had heard the whole story to the end. Different indeed were their looks as they turned away from the tale which filled them with either joy or grief, and friends crowded round to congratulate or console them as they returned to their houses. The women were most conspicuous in their joy and their grief. At one of the very gates, a woman un-expectedly meeting a son who had escaped died, it is said, in his embrace; another who had had false tidings of her son's death and sat sorrowing at home, expired from excessive joy when she saw him entering the home.

This tableau of mixed and changing emotions represents Livy's *chiaroscuro* technique in its most concentrated form, and is the more remarkable in that the action described is not in itself violent or climactic. Comparable insight into psychology and emotional intensity is to be found rarely elsewhere.

From narrative we turn to speeches. Livy employs two distinct kinds, corresponding respectively with the Herodotean and the Thucydidean tradition. Of the former—brief addresses at important turning points of the narrative—the greatest number is to be found in the earlier books. These are ancillary to the narrative rather than independent of it. Their purpose appears to be to highlight the climax of a narrative by dramatizing and summarizing its rational elements. They usually have a distinctly artificial ring. For example, Publius Valerius, during the plebeian agitation in 460 B.C., is made to speak as follows:[44]

'What means this, tribunes? Are you going to overturn the state under the auspices of Appius Herdonius? Has he who could not arouse the slaves been so successful in corrupting you? With the enemy over your heads do you choose to quit your arms and legislate?' Then, turning to the crowd, he continued: 'If you feel no concern, citizens, for your city, or for yourselves, at least fear your gods, whom the enemy hold captive. Jupiter Optimus Maximus, Queen Juno, and Minerva, and the other gods and goddesses, are beleaguered; a camp of slaves is in possession of the tutelary gods of your country; does this seem to you the appearance of a healthy state? All these foes are not merely within our walls, but in the citadel, above the Forum and in the Curia; the people meanwhile are assembled in the Forum, and in the Curia sits the Senate; as when peace reigns supreme, the senator gives voice to his opinion, the other citizens vote. Should every patrician and plebeian, the consuls, the tribunes, gods and men, all have drawn the sword and helped; have rushed upon the Capitol; have brought liberty and peace to the most august house of Jupiter Optimus Maximus? Father Romulus, grant thou to thy descendants that spirit in which thou didst in former times regain the citadel from those same Sabines, when they had captured it with gold; bid them advance by that road where thou didst lead, and thy army followed. Lo, I the consul will be the first, so far as a mortal can emulate a god, to follow in thy footsteps!'

The string of rhetorical questions (a figure of speech which Livy also introduces into his narrative) serves to dramatize and summarize; but why does he strive at such condensation? Why, further, is the progress of the argument allowed to suffer through brevity? The probable reason does Livy some credit: he had no clear idea of what was said on this and on other critical occasions in the early period, or any reliable information concerning the character and oratorical style of the leading figures. He is therefore content to provide a brief synopsis of the main arguments demanded by the situation and appropriate to the idealized view of early Roman politics which he wished to propound.

Full-length speeches, with conventional rhetorical topics and divisions in the Thucydidean tradition, are correspondingly found with the greatest frequency in those parts of the history where firm knowledge of events and personalities has replaced mythology and conjecture. In these the rhetorical structure is built upon a reliable foundation of known character and motivation, just as his best narratives are those in which he is able to provide the most detail. In fact, detailed information, used to serve the rhetorical argument, is a prominent feature of some of Livy's longer speeches. A good example of this is a long hortatory speech (the least likely genre for such material) which Publius Scipio somehow finds time to deliver to his troops before the Battle of Ticinus:[45]

Soldiers, if I were leading into battle the army I had with me in Gaul, I should have thought it needless to address you. What use, indeed, could there be in words of encouragement to the horsemen who gloriously defeated the enemy's cavalry at the Rhône, or to the legions with which I pursued that same enemy in his flight, finding in his retreat and in his refusal to give battle the equivalent of victory? Now, since that army, having been levied for Spain, is fighting there, as the Senate and people of Rome willed that it should, with my brother Gnaeus Scipio in command, and under my auspices, and since I have volunteered to command in this battle, that you may have a consul to lead you against Hannibal and the Carthaginians, I, a new commander over new soldiers, am bound to say a few words.

I would have you know both the enemy and the conditions of the war. You have to fight, soldiers, with the men whom you vanquished by sea and land in the former war, from whom for twenty years you have exacted tribute, from whom you have wrested as prizes of the contest provinces which you now hold, Sicily and Sardinia. In this battle, therefore, there will be in you and in them the spirit which belongs respectively to the victors and the vanquished. Even now they are going to fight, not because they are confident, but because they are compelled. For surely you cannot think that the very men who declined battle with their army at its full strength, have found more confidence now that they have lost two-thirds of their infantry and cavalry in crossing the Alps. But you will say that though they are but few, they have such stout hearts and bodies, that scarcely any strength can bear the brunt of their resolute attack. No; they are nothing but ghosts and shadows of men, half-dead with hunger, cold, filth and misery, bruised and maimed amid crags and rocks; add to this their limbs frost-bitten, their fingers stiffened by the snow, their arms shattered and broken, their horses maimed and feeble. Such is the cavalry, such the infantry with which you are going to fight. It is not an enemy, but the last remnant of an enemy that you will have before you: and what I fear most is that when you have fought, it will be the Alps that will seem to have conquered Hannibal. Yet perhaps it was right it should be so, and that the gods, without human aid, should begin and all but terminate a war waged against a treaty-breaking leader and people, while we, who next to the gods have been grievously wronged, merely finish off what they have begun and almost ended.

I have no fear that any of you will think that I am talking grandly in order to encourage you, while in my heart I feel otherwise. I might have gone with my army to Spain, my allotted province, for which I had started, where I should have a brother to share my counsels and be the companion of my dangers, Hasdrubal instead of Hannibal as my foe and an unquestionably less formidable war. But as I was sailing along the shores of Gaul, on hearing the rumours about this enemy I landed, sent my cavalry on and advanced my camp to the Rhône. In an action fought with my cavalry, the only portion of my army with which I had the opportunity of fighting, I vanquished the enemy. His infantry, which hurried on with the rapidity of a flight, I could not overtake, and so I returned with all possible speed to my ships, made this long circuit by sea and land, and now almost at the foot of the Alps have met this dread foe. Can you think that I have stumbled on him unexpectedly, when seeking to shun a conflict, rather than that I am confronting him on his very track, challenging him and forcing him to fight? It is a joy to me to discover whether in the last twenty years the earth has suddenly produced another race of Carthaginians, or whether they are the same as they were when they fought at the Aegates Islands, whom you then let go from Eryx at a valuation of eighteen denarii for each man. And this Hannibal, is he, as he boasts, a rival of Hercules in his expeditions, or the man whom his father left to pay tax and tribute and be the slave of the Roman people? Were it not that his crime at Saguntum is driving him on, he would surely look back, if not on his conquered country at least on his home and his father, and on those treaties in the very handwriting of that Hamilcar who, at our consul's bidding, withdrew his garrison from Eryx, accepted with murmurs and lamentation the hard terms imposed upon Carthage, and consented to give up Sicily and pay tribute to Rome.

So I would have you fight, soldiers, not merely with the feelings you have towards any other foe, but with a peculiar wrath and fury, as if you saw your slaves suddenly bearing arms against you. You might have destroyed them by that worst of all human punishments, starvation, when they were shut up in Eryx; you might have crossed with your victorious fleet into Africa, and within a few days effaced Carthage without a struggle. But we gave quarter when they begged

it; we released them from blockade; we made peace with the conquered; we took them under our protection in their sore distress
during the African War. By way of return for these boons, they come
following the lead of a young madman, to attack our country. And
would that this battle were only for your honour, and not for your
safety. It is not for the possession of Sicily and Sardinia, which were
formerly in dispute, but for Italy that you now have to fight. There
is no other army behind you to bar the enemy's way if we do not
conquer; there are no more Alps, during the passage of which new
forces can be raised. Here, soldiers, you must make a stand as if we
were fighting before the walls of Rome. Let every man of you assure
himself that he is defending with his arms not himself, but his wife
and his little children; and let him not confine himself to thoughts of
his family; let him reflect again and again that the Senate and people of
Rome are now anxiously watching our prowess, and that such as shall
be our strength and resolution, so too in the future shall be the fortune
of that great city and of the empire of Rome.

The chief qualities of this speech, and those which save it at
certain points from becoming mere rodomontade, are the amount
of historical detail, the characterization of the speaker, and the
rhetorical arrangement; each of which is worthy of closer
examination. The first two of these may be taken together,
because the portrayal of Scipio's heady confidence, which
transcends his immediate need to encourage his men, is greatly
enhanced both by the pervasiveness of the first person, through
which the speaker gives details of his career and his achievements,
and by his temerity in bombarding his audience with volley upon
volley of half-truths and untruths. It is true that at this point
Rome had suffered no serious defeats at the hands of the
Carthaginians; but readers of Polybius (and therefore perhaps of
the fourth pentad of Livy) would know full well that the
Carthaginian acceptance of defeat at the end of the First Punic
War was in no sense the act of a nation reduced to abject impotence. Certain of her forces were still intact, including the
garrison at Eryx, which Hamilcar only surrendered on the
instruction of his home government. Finally, the arrogance of
Scipio's injunction to treat one of the most sophisticated peoples
of the Mediterranean like rebellious slaves is too blatant to be
anything other than a piece of characterization introduced in
order to adumbrate the sequel according to the time-honoured
formula of the nexus of *hybris* and *nemesis*.

To the student of classical rhetoric, this and most of the other major speeches in Livy exhibit many standard devices and techniques. It begins with a form of antithesis approved by rhetoricians, and found in the prologues of many speeches of the Attic Orators and Cicero—a conditional clause expressing an unreal situation, followed by a statement of the real situation ('. . . but now, as it is . . .'). The central theme, which is the prospect of victory, is introduced with a summary statement of the superiority established during and since the First Punic War. This is followed by a somewhat specious *a fortiori* argument in which the enemy's confidence before crossing the Alps is compared to their likely mental state after their terrible experience. This is also an example of argument from probability, which became established very early in the Greek rhetorical tradition because it was considered superior to argument from direct evidence, which could be fabricated and corrupted. This the speaker exploits with colour and force, using the rhetorical objection and refutation ('But you may say that those who survived the crossing will be superhuman: to which I reply . . .'); the rhetorical correction ('It is not an enemy, but the remnant of an enemy') and the vivid amplification of the mountaineers' sufferings. The latter part of this centre-piece sees the speaker inviting the audience to relate these general considerations of their advantages to his own personality. He explains how he has chosen to fight with them rather than in a less dangerous theatre of war because he is personally confident of victory. The Carthaginian leaders are by contrast portrayed as men branded with the double stigma of perfidy and defeat. The concluding paragraph, in accordance with convention, is charged with the most emotive material, designed to arouse wrath against the enemy, awareness of the seriousness of the task ahead, and a sense of the glory that is to be won by victory.

Every ancient speech should be examined with one eye upon the rhetorical handbooks: but the main purpose of this procedure is to see in what ways a skilful writer has adapted the rules to suit his own purposes. In this speech Livy has given especial prominence to the personality of Scipio and his own assertion of it, both by giving a *principium a sua persona* in the prologue in the approved manner, and by allowing the speaker's person to reappear and hold the stage during the last half of the main argument. This is an original device. Perhaps the speech represents what Scipio actually said, faithfully reproduced by a diligent source: more likely Livy, or his source, is indulging in a shrewd piece of characterization.

Speeches in which strong personality is lacking tend to adhere more closely to standard rules and conventional divisions. The Campanian ambassadors to Rome in 343 B.C., who are seeking an alliance against the Samnites,[46] use similar arguments to those attributed by Thucydides to the Corcyreans, who were on a similar mission: the theme of *justice* followed by that of *expediency*, and the corresponding topics of the promise of future gratitude and the prospect of greater strength through the combination of forces. Again, at other times it is the importance of the situation that has prompted the historian to put the issues in a rhetorical form, perhaps as an *aide-mémoire* to his readers, most of whom would have had a rhetorical training. The speech assigned to Appius Claudius in Book V seems to belong to this category.[47] The occasion is a dispute between the classes which threatened to denude the Roman army besieging Veii. It was vital to Rome's future reputation among the cities of central Italy that this Etruscan stronghold, situated only a few miles away, should be taken. Appius is here cast not in the rôle of Rome's saviour through his eloquence, but merely as the mouthpiece through which 'the rhetoric of the situation' is expounded. Personal colouring is sacrificed to convention: the introduction contains the prescribed *captatio benevolentiae* (the speaker's effort to ingratiate himself to his audience), in spite of the reputation for arrogance and *hauteur* shared by all members of the Claudian family. The central theme is the reassertion of the national virtues of bravery and perseverance, and this is broadened to embrace not merely the present situation but its implications for the future. Rome's position as leader of a confederacy had to be guarded by action and example. Coming at this point in Livy's story, immediately before the Gallic invasion and the subsequent temporary dissolution of the confederacy, this theme has prophetic as well as contemporary significance, and contributes materially to the rational content of this period of Livy's Roman history. It is in this kind of speech that Livy applies to greatest effect the Ciceronian principle of *amplificatio*, the widening of the rhetorical horizon by the inclusion of examples to support precepts and the deduction of far-reaching conclusions from premises based on present experience.

The study of 'life and morals, men and policies', which Livy promises his readers in his introduction, afforded endless scope for rhetorical elaboration. To a writer with Livy's training in rhetoric, living in an age when declamation was growing into a public spectacle, to which were attracted those citizens of a more civilized bent who found blood-sports distasteful, the temptation to saturate his history with rhetoric was strong—too strong, indeed for some of his contemporaries. Regarding his performance it is worth making two points, one admitting his surrender, the other asserting his resistance to this temptation. Rhetoric overflows from the speeches into the narrative: it is seen in the frequent rhetorical questions, the periodic sentence structure, and his use of metaphorical and poetic colouring in his language. On the other hand, the proportion of Livy's history devoted to speeches is smaller than that in Sallust's monographs, and only half that in Thucydides. His love of rhetoric rarely leads him to invent the occasion as well as the content of a speech, but is seen rather in the length at which he allows some of his speakers to dilate on inappropriate occasions. One instance of this is the speech delivered to his troops by Publius Decius before a night attack,[48] for the successful execution of which surprise and secrecy were essential. His long and impressive oration, if it had been historical, would have acted like a protracted clarion call to the slumbering enemy. But such extreme examples as this are rare, and serve mainly to remind us of the importance of creative artistry in Livy's conception of historiography.

We are now in a position to form some general conclusions concerning Livy's achievement. As to his reliability as a purveyor of historical information, nothing useful can be said that does not take account of the literary sources upon which he exclusively relied. His account of the early period must, in the absence of contemporary documents, remain an imponderable mixture of legend and fact. His later narrative is vertebrated by reliable magistrate lists, which provide a generally sound chronological framework. But whenever great upheavals occur, which throw strong light on individuals, classes, policies and the national character, distortion creeps in, reflecting the view of the source with which Livy finds himself in the greatest sympathy. To this must be added his own shortcomings—his ignorance of military matters and practical politics—which prevent him from correcting the mistakes of his sources. But after everything possible has been said in adverse criticism, his triumph in his main aim— the portrayal through her history of the character of a great nation, her martial spirit, her religion, her perseverance and her moderation, all changing and developing under the influence of many vicissitudes—is undeniable; and when history is thus elevated to the status of a witness to a lasting phenomenon, the truth is more important than the facts.

CHAPTER 7

Tacitus

'POWER TENDS to corrupt; absolute power corrupts absolutely.' The ambiguity of Lord Acton's oft-quoted dictum is sometimes overlooked. Usually the two statements are taken to apply to the unspecified object of the verb 'corrupt', in other words the holder of the power; but a possible interpretation would be to regard that verb as intransitive, referring back to its subject, 'power', and implying that the nature of power itself causes its own degeneration, especially when it is unquestioned. According to both interpretations the dictum is conspicuously and progressively exemplified in the history of the early Roman Empire. Freedom died with the First Triumvirate, was interred with the Second, and was revived, fleetingly and in conception only, in the minds of a few theorists after the accession of Augustus. That emperor enjoyed advantages peculiar to his times and his position as a pioneer: any workable alternative to civil strife was deemed worth the experiment, and the recent example of Caesar's fate provided a warning against excess. The worst civil disturbances of Augustus's reign, the riots of 23 and 19 B.C., expressed not popular resentment against despotism, but a demand that the *princeps* should assume greater powers. To the aristocracy, however, the principate presented a different face. The republican offices, unattainable by the masses, still survived to tantalize the men on whose ancestors they had conferred real power. Now the emperor not only superseded their offices with his *imperium maius*, but controlled entry to the senatorial order and ascent of the constitutional ladder. Turning in disappointment from honest ambition to material gain, the young aristocrat was faced with scarcely less forbidding barriers: the emperor kept vigilant watch over the wealth of the provinces through his procurators, and commanded the armed forces. He also chose a policy of containment rather than expansion beyond the existing frontiers of the empire, and thus limited the opportunities for acquiring military glory. With the possibility of pre-eminence effectively removed, the young aristocrat might yet sublimate his personal ambitions by service to the state in an age of reform; but, deprived of their accustomed powers of initiative, many potential senators lost interest in the business of government. Augustus experienced increasing difficulty in filling the state offices, recruiting senators and stimulating debate. In the face of such apathy, a less shrewd emperor might have abandoned all attempts at the artificial maintenance of republican institutions and openly assumed autocratic control. Augustus, with a sure feeling for the national mood at all levels, adopted the only course likely to reconcile the aristocracy to its subordinate rôle. He privately enlisted the aid and counsel of a few men of experience and good will, and contrived, through various timely dispensations, to widen, if not actually to strengthen, the powers of the Senate. By these and other means the principate of Augustus ran its natural course without serious opposition, in spite of the universal loss of freedom.

In the matter of the succession, however, bad luck and mismanagement conspired to bring the dynasty to the verge of collapse on the first, as upon subsequent crises. Tiberius was Augustus's fifth choice, having survived the emperor's grandchildren Gaius and Lucius and his son-in-law Agrippa, and his own brother Drusus. Nothing was in his favour, not even the appetite for empire, at least in the form established by his predecessor. By profession a soldier, and by birth and temperament an aristocrat, he found it difficult for the first reason to exercise power without appearing to do so, and for the second to inspire popular acclaim. He was used to giving orders and seeing them obeyed, while his Claudian blood rendered him unsympathetic towards the people, their vulgar tastes and their base desires. Self-knowledge, a valuable attribute in most circumstances, served Tiberius ill, causing him to approach his thankless task with a diffidence which the enemies of the principate decried as hypocrisy. Finally, there was his constitutional position. Under Augustus, Rome had still been, in theory, a republic, in which no single citizen could appoint another to a position of power. Tiberius was therefore doing no more than keeping faith with the Augustan ideal of a constitutional principate when he insisted upon receiving the formal nomination of the Senate to his position. But this gesture was, like others, misunderstood; and, having inherited serious problems from Augustus without the prestige with which to surmount them, Tiberius must have been sorely tempted to impose his rule by conventional tyrannical methods; but it was the circumstances outlined above rather than any deliberate policy on his part that gave rise to the first symptoms of oppression and absolutism, the treason trials. As a result of his decision to spend the last years of his reign in retirement, these and other weapons of tyranny, wielded in the hands of others, brought the principate into evil repute; but the army remained loyal and the provinces were well administered. Moreover he had a successor whose lineage and appearance boded well, so that when he died in A.D. 37, the transition from one *princeps* to another was effected without difficulty.

If any reign was calculated to shatter Augustan illusions, it was that of his great-grandson Gaius ('Caligula'). Clinical diagnosis from the behaviour of persons in the remote past, reported, often out of context, by hostile witnesses, is a patently hazardous procedure: but many of the acts of Gaius bore the stamp of an unhinged mind. The throne vacated by his murder in A.D. 41 was quickly filled by the Palace ('Praetorian') Guard. Their choice, the halting, havering, senescent Claudius, uncle of Gaius, seemed unpropitious, but his turned out to be the only Julio-Claudian reign in which performance exceeded promise. His scholarly interest in history and law made him alive to the possibilities of revival and adaptation of ancient usage; but nearly all the changes he made were aimed at a greater centralization of power upon the emperor. Unlike Augustus and Tiberius, who made sincere efforts to win the partnership of the Senate, Claudius appointed members of his own household to newly-created administrative posts which carried extraordinary powers. The result was an imperial bureaucracy on the lines of the old Hellenistic monarchies, the main concept of which was that the kingdom was the monarch's private estate. This centralization of power was somewhat invalidated by the emperor's personal weaknesses, his tendency to be dominated and deceived by his staff and by his womenfolk; so that at his death by poisoning at the hands of his wife Agrippina the Younger the principate, after initial signs of recovery, was almost as unpopular as it had become under Gaius.

Nero's reign went well so long as he delegated the business of government to his able advisers Seneca and Burrus. Left to his own devices after their retirement and the murder of his mother, he showed that his real interests lay elsewhere than in government, but found his position useful for securing multiple victories in the cultural festivals of Greece. However, the fleeting excursions which he made into government in his later years removed the last vestiges of republican sovereignty. But even his failure to designate a successor did not produce, at his death, a strong movement in favour of constitutional government. On the contrary, the throne was now a permanent institution, and for a year (A.D. 68–9) it was an open prize, to be contended for with military power and won by the general with the strongest army. Of the four emperors who mounted it, three were summarily unseated: successively Galba, Otho and Vitellius. Finally Vespasian, the governor of Judaea, assured of his army's support and joined by contingents from other provinces, resolved to try his chances, and a new dynasty, the Flavian, came into being. Flavius Vespasianus was a firm, responsible emperor, who combined frugal domestic administration with a determination to balance the claims of the different provinces to the benefits of Romanization. But his decision to base his power upon the office of censor set a tone of uncompromising autocracy which persisted throughout the Flavian dynasty. The reign of his elder son Titus was too brief to affect the image of the principate, but his younger son Domitian, in the fifteen years of his reign until his murder in A.D. 96, demanded the abject servility of his subjects, expressed in the appellation '*dominus et deus*'. The good aspects of his reign, his administration of the provinces and his able selection of personnel, have been largely obscured beneath the catalogue of crimes bequeathed by a uniformly hostile tradition.

The foregoing brief account of the first two dynasties of imperial Rome serves to introduce the historian Cornelius Tacitus, for their fortunes are his main concern. His birth is to be assigned to the early years of Nero's reign, probably to A.D. 56 or 57. The early years of his public career therefore fell within the reign of Vespasian, a most fortunate contingency in view of his special talents: for it was Vespasian who restored to respectability the art of oratory after the jealousy of Nero had driven almost all forms of artistic performance underground. The appointment of the famous Quintilian as the first state-salaried professor of rhetoric set the imperial seal of approval upon the art, and the young Tacitus was one of many who participated in its revival. He practised it in all three current media—the schools of rhetoric, the law-courts and the Senate. His marriage, however, in A.D. 77 to the daughter of Julius Agricola, who governed Britain and was one of the most distinguished military men of his day, permits the safe deduction that he won his spurs on the field of battle or through strenuous service under the eyes of that exacting general. Armed with this family link, Tacitus proceeded to an unimpeded succession of offices: the quaestorship in 81 or 82, a tribuneship or aedileship not long afterwards, followed by a priesthood; and the praetorship in 88. After that, a posting abroad, probably entailing the command of a provincial legion, and perhaps culminating in a proconsulship. Then four unaccounted years (93–6), but years when it was healthier to be obscure, for they saw the worst excesses of Domitian's tyranny. The second half of the year 97 marks the summit of his public career, for it was then that he attained the consulship. Competition for the post in that year was keen, for the opinion was current that with the enthronement of Cocceius Nerva, a senator with no family connections with previous emperors, a republican principate had at last come into being, and republican offices might once more carry real power. At this time Tacitus was exercising his oratorical talents rather than his talents for history. One trial is recorded in which he played a successful part in company with his friend Pliny the Younger: between them they secured the exile of a provincial governor named Marius Priscus on the grounds of extortion. Tacitus probably continued to prosper under the enlightened principate of Trajan, though the only firm date we have is A.D. 112–13, the year of his proconsulship in Asia. Of his subsequent life nothing is known, except that it was probably spent in the writing of his greatest work, the *Annals*.

Sixteen books of the *Annals* are known to us, but of these most of Book V and part of Book XVI, and Books VII to X in their entirety are lost; while there is every reason for believing that the work originally comprised eighteen books. The *Annals* narrate the history of Rome under the Julio-Claudian emperors after the death of Augustus (A.D. 14). They mark the culmination of an active literary life, being preceded by the *Histories*, a work of

twelve books, of which the first four and a part of the fifth
survive. The *Histories* probably followed the Flavian dynasty to
its demise with the death of Domitian in A.D. 96; but the first
four books are taken up with the revolutionary Year of the Four
Emperors (A.D. 69), thus constituting the most detailed extant
historical account of any single episode of Roman history, and
suggesting in what direction Tacitus's interests lay at the time of
writing. The *Histories* were preceded by two monographs, one on
the life of his father-in-law Agricola, a work which has always
been popular in Britain because it is concerned chiefly with
Agricola's experiences as governor of that province; and a study of
Germany, a work with an ethnological and geographical rather
than a biographical bias. Before these he wrote a *Dialogue on
Orators*, an imaginary discussion among contemporary men of
letters on the subject of great orators of the past, the interest of
which from the present point of view is twofold: it confirms
Tacitus's interest in practical oratory, and, by its central thesis
that the art has suffered a progressive decline, prepares us for
the mood of present disillusionment and pessimism for the future
which characterizes his historical writing.

It is with this paradox that the examination of Tacitus's two
main historical works begins, concentrating for the time being
mainly upon the *Annals*. It is in the introduction to the *Histories*,
however, that the answer is to be found to the question of why
a man who enjoyed such a successful career should be so critical
of the age in which he lived. There he writes:[1]

I shall begin my work with the year in which Servius Galba and
Titus Vinius were consuls, the former for the second time. My choice
of starting-point is determined by the fact that the preceding period
of 820 years dating from the foundation of Rome has found many
historians. So long as republican history was their theme, they wrote
with equal eloquence of style and independence of outlook. But when
the Battle of Actium had been fought and the interests of peace
demanded the concentration of powers in the hands of one man, this
great line of classical historians came to an end. Truth, too, suffered
in more ways than one. To an understandable ignorance of policy,
which now lay outside public control, was in due course added a
passion for flattery, or else a hatred of autocrats. Thus neither school
bothered about posterity, for the one was bitterly alienated and the
other deeply committed. But whereas the reader can easily discount
the bias of the time-serving historian, detraction and spite find a

ready audience. Adulation bears the ugly taint of subservience, but malice gives the false impression of being independent. As for myself, Galba, Otho and Vitellius were known to me neither as benefactors nor as enemies. My official career owed its beginning to Vespasian, its progress to Titus and its further advancement to Domitian. I have no wish to deny this. But partiality and hatred towards any man are equally inappropriate in a writer who claims to be honest and reliable. If I live, I propose to deal with the reign of the deified Nerva and imperial career of Trajan. This is a more fruitful and a less thorny field, and I have reserved it for my declining years. Modern times are indeed happy as few others have been, for we can think as we please, and speak as we think.

The story upon which I embark is one rich in disaster, marked by bitter fighting, rent by treason, and even in peace sinister. Four emperors perished violently. There were three civil wars, still more campaigns fought against the foreigner, and often conflicts with combined elements of both . . .

The passage proceeds with a catalogue of the disturbances which beset the empire during the Flavian principates, and a following, shorter account of the brighter aspects of the period is no more than a tribute to those hardier spirits who bore the universal burden of tragedy with fortitude. What aspects of the principate affected Tacitus personally? In this passage he shows where his main ambition lay, and how it had been thwarted by the very emperors who had conferred upon him most of the honours which would have satisfied other men. He accepts the need for autocracy, but cannot forgive the principate for its suppression of the freedom of tongue and pen. The *Dialogue on Orators* bears witness to his early literary interests and ambitions, while the above passage touches upon his contempt for sycophancy. Silence was therefore enjoined, at least on controversial subjects. The traumatic effect of inactivity upon a creative writer is to be seen throughout this introduction. He is obsessively preoccupied with the forces of dissolution, and states that he has chosen the years of his prime for the narration of the most turbulent years of recent history. But there are salutary signs also: pessimism is not a bad quality in a historian, especially when he is a man of ripe experience in public life. Reassuring too is his undertaking to remain free from partiality and hatred, which he repeats in his introduction to the *Annals*. To what extent he honours this pledge we shall see in due course.

The concept of freedom, especially freedom of utterance, is never allowed to remain in the background for long, and on occasion even prompts the historian to make a brief digression. In one of these a pointed contrast is made with the republic:[2]

> In spite of repeated popular pressure, Tiberius refused the title 'Father of his Country'. He also declined the Senate's proposal that obedience should be sworn to his enactments. All human affairs were uncertain, he protested, and the higher his position the more slippery it was. Nevertheless, he did not convince people of his republicanism. For he revived the treason law. The ancients had employed the same name, but had applied it to other offences—to official misconduct damaging the Roman State, such as betrayal of an army or incitement to sedition. *Action had been taken against deeds, words went unpunished.* The first employer of this law to investigate written libel was Augustus, provoked by an immoderate slander of eminent men and women. Then Tiberius, asked by a praetor whether cases under the treason law were to receive attention, replied: 'The laws must take their course.' Like Augustus he had been annoyed by anonymous verses. These had criticised his cruelty, arrogance and bad relations with his mother.

But another episode, concerning the case of Cremutius Cordus, who had argued that his encomium of the republican Brutus, which had incurred the emperor's displeasure, would have gone unnoticed if Tiberius had not perceived, quite correctly, that some of its strictures against tyranny were applicable to himself, is followed by these words:[3]

> Cremutius walked out of the Senate, and starved himself to death. The Senate ordered his books to be burnt by the aediles. But they survived, first hidden and later republished. This makes one deride the stupidity of people who believe that today's authority can destroy tomorrow's memories. On the contrary, repressions of genius increase its prestige. All that tyrannical conquerors, and imitators of their brutalities, achieve is their own disrepute and their victims' renown.

This passage reflects Tacitus's sympathy with an earlier generation of shackled men of letters. What of his own life and times? His introduction to the *Agricola* furnishes the parallel:[4]

> Great indeed are the proofs we have given of our powers of endurance. Ancient times viewed the utmost limits of freedom, we of servitude; robbed by an inquisition of the common use of speech and

hearing, we should have lost our very memory with our voice, were we as able to forget as to be dumb. Now at last our breath has come back; yet in the nature of human frailty remedies are slower than their diseases, and genius and learning are more easily extinguished than recalled. Fifteen years have been taken out of our lives, while youth passed silently into age; and we are the wretched survivors, not only of those who have been taken away from us, but of ourselves.

In the past four generations freedom has been lost and regained, but the scars left on sensitive minds are permanent. Ready at first to see in isolated acts of the emperors indications of its partial restoration, under the tyranny of Domitian even the most sanguine republican bade a bitter farewell to freedom, an act which poisoned the mind beyond the power of any subsequent placebo. The most gifted writers of this age were those who wrote in protest, the satirists Juvenal and Martial; and Tacitus, whose pessimism is the natural expression of an ingrained and irreversible disillusionment.

Pessimism also had good precedents. Sallust, whom Tacitus so much admired, Asinius Pollio, and even Livy, saw Roman history as a story of material growth but moral decline. More specifically, Tacitus, while grudgingly accepting the necessity of the devolution of power upon one man, deplores the consequent eclipse of the aristocracy, of which he is a part. For him and his class, ordered society and peace had had to be bought at the price of humiliation:[5]

> This was a tainted, meanly obsequious age. The greatest figures had to protect themselves by subserviency; and in addition to them, all ex-consuls, most ex-praetors, even many junior senators competed with each other's offensively sycophantic proposals. There is a tradition that whenever Tiberius left the Senate-house he exclaimed in Greek, 'Men fit to be slaves!' Even he, freedom's enemy, became impatient of such abject servility.

The psychological consequences of self-abasement, which is contrary to human nature, are dire: men turn upon their equals and their inferiors and gratify their frustrated power-lust through deeds of horror. Hence the willing part played by senators in the treason-trials and other acts of injustice and cruelty. Another consequence of the same curtailment of power is their recourse to self-indulgent extravagance, the opiate of the politically deprived, examples of which are scattered throughout Tacitus's pages. In a state in which the nobility still held the political offices but lacked political power, such ostentation was natural. Indeed, since the new order had been forced upon them by historical circumstances outside their control, they are not to be blamed for their reaction, which is in accordance with the laws of human nature. Tacitus is their spokesman, and his history is to some extent the expression of the anger and resentment of four generations of frustated aristocrats, focussed on the person of the emperor:[6]

What interests and stimulates readers is a geographical description, the changing fortune of a battle, the glorious death of a commander. My themes on the other hand concern cruel orders, unremitting accusations, treacherous friendships, innocent men ruined—a conspicuously monotonous glut of downfalls and their monotonous causes. Besides, whereas the ancient historian has few critics—nobody minds if he over-praises the Carthaginian (or Roman) army—the men punished or disgraced under Tiberius have numerous descendants living today. And even when the families are extinct, some will think, if their own habits are similar, that the mention of others' crimes is directed against them. Even glory and merit makes enemies —by showing their opposites in too sharp and critical relief.

Tacitus aims to keep the aristocracy to the forefront of his story, and to highlight the successes and misfortunes of its worthiest representatives, usually to the discredit of the *princeps*. In the Annals a succession of senators is paraded across the stage, sometimes being introduced gratuitously at their death. Crispus is a typical decadent *eques*, who, by not aspiring to the highest offices, enjoyed luxury beyond his station and exercised power through discreet influence on the *princeps* and his immediate advisers. Quirinus, a man of similar background and character, was recommended for posthumous honours by Tiberius. By contrast, in his purely laudatory necrologies of Lentulus and Domitius, Tacitus shows bias in favour of the established patrician families as against the foregoing *parvenus*. The object of these minor portraits is to show, by their success or failure, the kind of characters that fitted into their times. This is most clearly to be seen in the sketch of the famous author and *bon viveur* Petronius Arbiter:[7]

Gaius Petronius deserves a brief obituary. He spent his days sleeping, his nights working and enjoying himself. Others achieve fame by energy, Petronius by laziness. Yet he was not, like others who waste their resources, regarded as dissipated or extravagant, but as a refined voluptuary. People liked the apparent freshness of his unconventional and unselfconscious sayings and doings. Nevertheless, as governor of Bithynia and later as consul, he displayed a capacity for business. Then, reverting to a vicious or ostensibly vicious way of life, he had been admitted into the small circle of Nero's intimates, as Arbiter of Taste: to the blasé emperor, smartness and elegance were restricted to what Petronius approved. So Tigellinus, loathing him as a rival and expert hedonist, denounced him.

Petronius fits perfectly into the setting of Nero's court—too perfectly, as it turned out, for his own good.

Important as these minor portraits are as indications of the character of contemporary society, their function is to provide background only. For most of the narrative, our attention is ineluctably drawn towards the chief characters of the grim drama, the emperors and their families.

First, Tiberius, whose reign occupies the first six books of the *Annals*. Recent experience combined with a settled tradition to influence the picture which Tacitus presents. Domitian began well and degenerated into a paranoic tyrant: he was said also to have admired Tiberius and studied his state papers. Tacitus found the tradition to be too superficial, but paid lip-service to it by making frequent references to a 'report' concerning the emperor's less creditable activities. For the historian's own view we must discount these rumours. Tacitus represents Tiberius initially as secretive, devious, vindictive and cruel; but we are enabled, by consulting his résumé of relevant details of the reign of Augustus in the opening ten chapters of the *Annals*, to perceive that these qualities were induced as much by circumstances as by nature. Tiberius was insecure: the first murder of his reign was that of Agrippa Postumus, a possible rival; and another more serious rival was Germanicus, emperor designate by the orders of Augustus. Nevertheless, Tiberius did not resort to stark auto-cracy, as a weaker man might have done, but turned to the republican institutions, the consuls and the Senate. But he also had to face a mixed reception from the state as a whole. Vividly, the mixed feelings about Augustus after his death, given at length and with thorough historical insight, serve to evoke the mood with which many Romans faced the new principate, which was unhallowed by conquest or constitution; and we are forced to sympathize with Tiberius, whose entire life had been governed by reasons of state. The contrast between the initial positions of Augustus and Tiberius runs deep through these early chapters, and on the whole Tiberius emerges with the greater credit. Unlike his predecessor, who started as a military adventurer and reached the summit through revolution, Tiberius had risen through merit in an ordered society, assuming responsibilities and earning preferment. He was, moreover, a member of one of the most illustrious republican families, which had always achieved all the honours it had desired under the old system.

But there is much more. Like Augustus, Tiberius found the Senate unwilling to participate in government, but anxious not to be ignored. He therefore took the only course open to him, to assume more and more personal power while appearing to consult the senior body. This sometimes involved him in dissimulation when his intentions conflicted with the views expressed in the house. But on the whole we are made to feel the wisdom of his rule: apart from the fact that a reign which survived a bad beginning to last twenty-three years could not have been devoid of statesmanship, Tacitus makes a real effort to reveal his positive achievement. At least for the first half of his reign, administration at home and abroad was efficient and reasonably humane. Officials were well-chosen and prosperity safeguarded. Tacitus states his explicit approval of Tiberius's disdain for popularity and paternalism (the bane of the later empire), and saw in his dislike of personal homage and admiration for those who spoke freely a regard for the old republican virtues. From the various crises of his reign, especially those involving the provinces, the empire generally escapes unscathed, thanks to his sagacity. The only substantial charge made by Tacitus against Tiberius is that his habit of dissimulation included a general concealment of his own worst faults, which finally emerged (though without direct witnesses and specific accusations) during his retirement on Capri. If this is true, it remains to his lasting credit that he wore the mask for so long in the interests of Rome.

Further, and deeper light is cast upon the character of Tiberius in the utterances ascribed to him. Careful reading of a long letter addressed to the Senate in Book III[8] reveals not only the qualities already mentioned, but also a serious view of his own rôle as servant extraordinary of the empire: conscious of the difficulties facing a monarch, who alone receives the blame for the vices and misfortunes of his time, but remains steadfast in his determination to do his duty. In a speech at a later meeting[9] he repudiates divine honours and wishes only that his temporal faculties should remain unimpaired while he holds the reins of government. In another speech,[10] in which he replies to Sejanus's request for the hand of the Younger Livia, the emperor's technique of equivocation and dissimulation is brilliantly characterized; but Tiberius is also made to say that, whereas self-interest may be deemed to be the only criterion of action in a private citizen, an emperor must consider public opinion.

Tacitus's picture of the complex character of Tiberius must therefore be judged to contain elements both of detestation and of admiration. He knew that a good statesman, and a monarch to an eminent degree, must possess a certain ruthlessness, and faces the danger of the erosion of his nobler qualities through continual exposure to freely exercised power. It is this rather than any preconceived intention to denigrate the name of Tiberius (a task which was no longer necessary), that caused Tacitus to draw attention to the dark side of his character.

In the absence of a Tacitean portrait of Caligula, the emperors who show the strongest contrast to Tiberius are the first three of those who appear in the *Histories*, Galba, Otho and Vitellius; but their characters will be considered in greater detail when the *Histories* are looked at separately. Of the remaining emperors in the *Annals*, Claudius is incompletely portrayed because some of Tacitus's narrative is lost; but what we have seems to owe much to the ridicule poured upon him by immediate posterity. Faced with the incredible fact of his wife's celebration (in public) of a marriage ceremony with one C. Silius, he could only stand in stupid amazement and ask his entourage: 'Am I emperor? Is Silius still a private citizen?'[11] A little later, his freedmen managed to arouse him to anger sufficiently to pronounce judgment on the adulterer; but he still wavered over the fate of Messalina, until she was finally dispatched out of hand. Later, when the news of her death was brought to him, he showed no sign of emotion, but called for more food and drink and indulged himself in apathetic gluttony. He was to Tacitus 'a man without sentiment, devoid of passion and without motive, save for that inspired by others'.[12] It is an unconvincing portrait simply because the historian, while depriving him of the credit for the many reforms and innovations introduced during his reign, has made no effort to discover the true inventors, but has been content merely with vague referenccs to the power wielded by his freedmen and his wives.

After due allowance has been made for the greater volume of Tacitus's surviving account, Nero, a far less meritorious emperor, is much more convincingly portrayed. His irresponsibility, stimulated by lust for Poppaea Sabina, and his preoccupation with frivolous artistic accomplishments, are made more dangerous as his reign proceeds by his sensitivity to unpopularity, which receives its most wounding shock at the revelation of the Pisonian Conspiracy. Here is a genuine example of a typically Italian extrovert personality, who courts attention and yet reacts violently to the reception accorded to him, because his exhibitionism conceals acute self-doubt. Tacitus is well aware of the danger to the principate posed by such a character, and it is for this reason that he defends the sometimes questionable devices of Seneca and Burrus for preserving its prestige (devices which included condoning the murder of Agrippina). Shades of Tiberius and Caligula cloud Nero's last years, and the Julio-Claudian dynasty draws to a close in an atmosphere of almost universal detestation for the person of the emperor.

The part played by the Julio-Claudian women receives a deserved prominence, since their activities contributed substantially to the fortunes and misfortunes of the dynasty. Tacitus took a conventional view of women, considering that they are full of art and malice, but frail and fickle in their resolve. But almost all the royal ladies acquit themselves of the last half of this indictment, as do not a few commoners, notably the slave-woman Epicharis, whose silence under extreme torture is horrifically described:[13]

> Nero now remembered the information of Volusius Proculus and consequent arrest of Epicharis. Thinking no female body could stand the pain, he ordered her to be tortured. But lashes did not weaken her denials, nor did branding, nor the fury of the torturers at being defied by a woman. So the first day's examination was frustrated. Next day her racked limbs could not support her, so she was taken for further torments in a chair. But on the way she tore off her breastband,

fastened it in a noose to the chair's canopy, and placed her neck inside it. Then, straining with all her weight, she throttled the little life which was still in her. So, shielding in the direst agony men unconnected with her and almost strangers, this ex-slavewoman set an example which particularly shone when free men, Roman gentlemen and senators, were betraying, untouched, their nearest and dearest. For Lucan and Senecio and Quintianus gave away their fellow-conspirators wholesale.

An age of tyrannized and emasculated men produced women with masculine characteristics. The royal house is full of them. The redoubtable dowager empress Livia, and Agrippina mother and daughter, re remarkable for their masculine obsession with the perpetuation of the dynasty through their own line, and for their fearless tenacity and ruthless lack of scruple. But the historian's greatest art is lavished upon the two queens who used their sexual endowments to the most advantage, Valeria Messalina and Poppaea Sabina. Yet these two, outwardly the most feminine of women, shared a masculine trait: a complete detachment in their attitude to personal relationships, which enabled them to receive and discard lovers without any deep sense of gratification or loss. This is how Tacitus describes the treatment of Montanus, one of Messalina's paramours:[14]

> Rejection, too, awaited the defence of an unpretentious but good-looking young gentleman, not a senator, Sextus Traulus Montanus, whom within a single night Messalina, as capricious in her dislikes as in her desires, had sent for and sent away.

To be executed as an associate of the condemned empress after so short an association seems a little hard; but empresses make dangerous bedfellows. Tacitus's character-sketch of Poppaea underlines in full measure the contradiction between appearance and reality, conventional femininity and contemporary morality:[15]

> Poppaea had every asset except goodness. From her mother, the loveliest woman of her day, she inherited distinction and beauty. Her wealth, too, was equal to her birth. She was clever and pleasant to talk to. She seemed respectable. But her life was depraved. Her public appearances were few; she would half-veil her face at them, to stimulate curiosity (or because it suited her). To her, married or bachelor bedfellows were alike. She was indifferent to her reputation —yet insensible to men's love, and herself unloving. Advantage dictated the bestowal of her favours.

Livia is less than fairly treated by Tacitus, who, because she is the most important of the royal ladies, feels it the more necessary to conform her to his pattern. His obituary of her is on the whole favourable, but prior to that he has attempted to blacken her character by insinuations that she may have had a hand in the removal of each of the rivals to her son Tiberius. Tacitus's willingness to incorporate into his narrative rumour and scandal (which reflects the nature of much of his source-material) is here seen at its worst. The Younger Agrippina receives even harsher treatment, but with more justice, for there can be little doubt that she murdered Claudius and attempted to govern the empire in the name of her son Nero. Her violent death, which she had herself anticipated, was the result of an excessively open and direct pursuit of power, in the course of which she encountered a will no less stubborn and proud than her own, a will which she tried to break by incestuous advances. It is from Tacitus above all that we learn the extent, and the limits, of female influence in the imperial house. The model of success is undoubtedly Livia, who survived to the age of eighty-six, when she died a natural death. Her secret is discretion. She is rarely found in the centre of the stage, but is portrayed as a paragon of republican womanhood (with a few concessions to contemporary manners), who plans and schemes through her menfolk and induces them, unperceiving, to identify their interests with hers.

Dynastic matters continue to occupy our attention when we come to consider the most distinctive aspect of Tacitus's work, his selection and arrangement of material. Here again we shall chiefly be concerned with the *Annals*. Tacitus had access to sources of greater variety and detail than most of his predecessors —formal histories, memoirs (a growing genre under the empire) state papers, archives and personal reminiscences; so that necessity no less than artistic requirements enjoined stringent selection. As to arrangement, the *Annals* are divided into groups of six books or hexads. The first of these narrates the principate of Tiberius, the second those of Caligula and Claudius, and the third that of Nero. It will be clear that, in spite of the chrono-logical evenness implied by the title, equal treatment is not given to the four reigns. The twenty-three years under Tiberius and the sixteen years under Nero (assuming that Books XVII and

XVIII follow the latter's reign to its conclusion), each occupy six books, while in the six allocated to the four years under Caligula and the thirteen under Claudius, it is evident that the former receives disproportionate coverage. In the narrative of the reigns of Tiberius and Nero, the structure is governed by a conception, altogether apposite in their cases, of a scheme of good administration followed by a decline. At the point of change comes the main crisis of the reign, after which its character alters. In the case of Tiberius, the death of Germanicus, apparently a serious setback to Tiberius because of his popularity and the suspicious circumstances which surrounded his death, in reality made him more secure, at least for a few years, because Augustus had intended that Germanicus should ultimately become emperor, and had made Tiberius adopt him as his heir. The major crisis comes with the death of Drusus, Tiberius's own son, who was more than a mere heir: he was the safeguard of the Claudian dynasty against the continued arrogations of the Julians. Book III has begun with an account of the Elder Agrippina's journey to Rome with the ashes of Germanicus, and her rapturous popular reception there. She and her children were a living challenge to the regime, being armed with the blessing of the revered Augustus; but the succession was secure for the Claudians so long as Tiberius had an heir of his own house. With the point of change at the beginning of the fourth book, the irony of events is enhanced: in order to escape the importunities of the surviving Julians, Tiberius enlists the services of an outsider with ambitions of his own, the villainous Sejanus, who not only alters the character of the reign of Tiberius, but arranges for the murder of Drusus. Throughout the *Annals* Tacitus follows the principle established by Livy of alternating events at home with those abroad; but a comparison between the events of Books I–III and those of Books IV–VI in both spheres shows the forces of discord, tyranny and decay gaining a stranglehold upon the empire. As Tiberius's reign proceeds, we read less and less about events in the provinces, which from other sources we know to have been well-governed under him: in Book VI we hear nothing about provincial affairs until well past half-way. Finally Tiberius has to come to a decision about the succession, and here Tacitus's penetration into one of the problems which most interested him is seen at its most impressive:[16]

After the death of Junia Claudilla—whose wedding with Gaius [Caligula] I recorded elsewhere—Macro induced his own wife Ennia to pretend she loved the prince and entice him into a promise of marriage. Gaius had no objection if it helped him towards the throne. Temperamental though he was, intimacy with his grandfather [Tiberius] had taught him dissimulation. The emperor knew this, and hesitated about the succession. First, there were his grandsons. Drusus's son Tiberius Gemellus was nearer to him in blood, and dearer. But he was still a boy. Gaius was in the prime of early manhood. He was also popular, being Germanicus's son. So his grandfather hated him. Claudius too was considered. He was middle-aged and well-meaning, but his weakmindedness was an objection. Tiberius feared that to nominate a successor outside the imperial house might bring contempt and humiliation upon Augustus's memory and the name of the Caesars. He cared more for posthumous appreciation than for immediate popularity.

Dynastic problems had pursued Tiberius from before his accession to his deathbed, and Tacitus's account of his reign reflects this fact by its structure. Nero's reign is more complicated. The operative forces are seen at the outset of Book XIII: his mother, the Younger Agrippina, by whose agency he had attained the throne, and who threatened to begin his reign with a bloodbath; Seneca and Burrus, who were to succeed in curbing her ambitions to rule; and Nero himself, who soon revealed a will of his own. Nero's determination to free himself from his mother is tactfully harnessed by Seneca, who encourages him to murder Britannicus, Claudius's son whom Agrippina rashly sponsors, and to gratify his passion for Poppaea and so further estrange himself from his mother. The point of change to decline is less well-defined, and hangs suspended somewhere between the psychological breaking-point, Nero's murder of his mother in A.D. 59, and the death of Burrus and retirement of Seneca in A.D. 62. Both these events occur in Book XIV, which becomes the pivotal book of this hexad. Chronology is less carefully harmonized with space than in the first hexad: two books dispose of eight years (54–62), leaving four for the remaining six, and as in the first hexad, more tumultuous years. The Pisonian Conspiracy, belonging to the year 65, with over three books to go but only three years of Nero's reign, has repercussions, recounted at length, in the form of a steady stream of judicial murders and enforced suicides. Tacitus's arrangement of the events of Nero's reign serves above all to underline the effect of an irresponsible *princeps* upon his dynasty and upon the empire in general. The crisis is reached when he becomes liberated from his mother and his inherited statesmen; when allowed to choose his own adviser he picks Tigellinus,[17] a less able counterpart of Sejanus, although unlike Tiberius, he was in real need of an able *socius laborum*. It is likely that a large part of the lost Books XVII and XVIII are given over to an account of Nero's cultural pleasures, a fitting conclusion to a reign that had been a theatrical act from the beginning.

Three-quarters of the intervening hexad are lost, but the attribution of the first surviving fragment, some way through Book XI, to the year A.D. 47 leaves seven years to be narrated in one and a half books, while the preceding four and a half have been allowed to cover six years. The reign of Caligula (37–41), an example of the most abrupt decline imaginable, must have provided much material to Tacitus's taste; whereas Claudius, because of his uniform if unspectacular success, which could not be made to fit any scheme of decline, failed to arouse his interest and probably suffered accordingly.

From the overall structure of the *Annals* we turn to a more detailed examination of Tacitus's selection and arrangement of his materials. Under his pen history is not merely reconstructed, but recreated in such a way as to convey his impression of the nature of the *Zeitgeist*. This is a legitimate application to historiography of a principle, which the Greeks called *poeēsis*, whereby original material is adapted, by means of omission, emphasis and location, to serve the writer's conception of what is most important. Historians of contemporary or near-contemporary events, like Thucydides and Tacitus, had the advantage over others of a wider choice of materials to manipulate and adapt to their purpose; but they were correspondingly restricted in their use of 'poetic licence' by the knowledge that their first readers would know many of the facts. Nevertheless, the choice of what to include and what to omit rested with the historian, as did the prerogative of ascribing motives, assigning praise or blame, and estimating character. In addition to all this, he could decide the order in which to present his story.

The annalistic framework, which many historians found to be an impediment to the momentum of their narrative, is skilfully exploited by Tacitus. Episodes have their uses. He sometimes begins them with a startling deed of evil in order to restate one of his main themes. The bane of political murder is introduced at the beginning of the reign of Tiberius with the murder of Agrippa Postumus,[18] and at the beginning of Nero's reign with the murder of Junius Silanus.[19] No less important is the end of an episode, which is often rounded off with a gnomic expression, summarizing its main implication in accordance with the rhetorical tastes of the day. The earlier of the above episodes ends with the maxim: 'Responsibility to one man alone, that is the law of monarchy.'[20] Conclusions of episodes are also often marked by pregnant anticipatory phrases foreshadowing the future, often in gloomy terms. The execution of Messalina is followed by this statement, which, after the best manner of the serial in modern mass-media, engages the reader's attention for the next episode: 'The punishment inflicted was undoubtedly just, but it proved the source of innumerable crimes and a long sequence of public calamities.'[21] We can hardly wait to read of the machinations of her successor to the imperial bed, the Younger Agrippina, which resulted in the death of Claudius, later of his son Britannicus, and subsequently of Agrippina herself. Portents are used for a similar purpose, being regarded by Tacitus as purely hostile manifestations, since he believed that the gods (if such beings existed) confined their intervention in human affairs to the punishment of wrongdoers. The year 64 ends with a list of such omens. The appearance of a comet (which, when it happened not long after the death of Julius Caesar was regarded as his soul taking its place among the gods) was 'a certain prelude to some bloody act to be committed by Nero,[22] and the Pisonian Conspiracy follows immediately in the next chapter. Unlike Livy's gods, those of Tacitus cannot be placated.

It is within such frameworks as these that the annalistic structure operates. The maximum required effect is usually obtained by adhering to the chronological sequence of events. Thus, whereas a historian who valued orderliness above artistry might make a simple dichotomy within a book between domestic and foreign affairs, Tacitus is constantly switching from one sphere to the other. The result of this is that the domestic treason-trials, dynastic intrigues and murders are distributed throughout the whole history: our attention is never averted from them for

long. Key figures, whose part in these events is obscure, are
sometimes gratuitously introduced as suspected agents in the
drama in order that they should similarly be kept before our
eyes. A gradual increase in domestic at the expense of provincial
events is discernible in the first three books of the *Annals*, a
phenomenon which has been noticed elsewhere. But it is of equal
importance to observe the difference in tone of Tacitus's account
of the two spheres. His narrative of the army mutinies which
took place in Pannonia and on the Rhine begin with the following
statement concerning the former:[23]

> While these events were taking place at Rome, mutiny broke out
> in the regular army in Pannonia. There were no fresh motives for
> this, except that the change of emperors offered hopes of rioting with
> impunity and collecting the profits afforded by civil wars. Three
> brigades were stationed in a summer camp with Junius Blaesus in
> command. When he heard of the death of Augustus and the accession
> of Tiberius, he suspended normal duty for public mourning (or
> rejoicing). This was when insubordination and altercation began.

The alleged causes of the mutiny are a vague revolutionary
feeling occasioned by the change of emperor, and too much
leisure. As the account proceeds, our sympathies are drawn more
and more to the government and the generals, who handle the
situation, which has been inflamed by the rantings of numerous
soap-box orators and barrack-room lawyers, with commendable
coolness. The very real grievances of the troops are submerged,
the disturbances quelled. Even the histrionic capitulation of
Germanicus to his men's demands is allowed to pass as expedient.
By contrast, domestic events assume a darker and darker character as they occupy more space, and we are left in little doubt
where the fault for the deterioration lies. In Book I there are
forebodings, but little else to excite dismay. Book II, like its
predecessor, is largely concerned with external events, but
domestic discord is manifested in the impeachment and trial
of Libo Drusus and Appuleia Varilla, the popularity of Germanicus and his death. In Book III, the focus on domestic events
becomes stronger, centring on the trial of Piso and his suicide.
Fewer than twenty of the seventy-six chapters are devoted to the
provinces, and these contain the first civil disturbances of
Tiberius's reign. In Book IV provincial matters receive fewer

than ten chapters: this is the book of Sejanus and the informers, whose unremitting crimes cause the historian to apologize for the monotony of his narrative. Most of Book V is lost. Book VI is more evenly balanced, and Tiberius, in retirement at Capri after ridding the empire of Sejanus, recovers some of our sympathies with some timely clemency and statesmanship before his death, which is marked by the following obituary:[24]

> The son of Tiberius Claudius Nero, he was a Claudian on both sides. From birth he experienced contrasts of fortune. After following his proscribed father into exile, he entered Augustus's family as his stepson—only to suffer from many competitors, while they lived: first Marcellus and Agrippa, then Gaius and Lucius Caesar. His own brother Nero Drusus was more of a popular favourite. But Tiberius's position became more delicate after marrying Augustus's daughter Julia. For he had to choose between enduring her unfaithfulness or escaping it. He went to Rhodes. When he returned, he was undisputed heir in the emperor's home for twelve years. Then he ruled the Roman world for nearly twenty-three.
>
> His character, too, had its different stages. While he was a private citizen or holding commands under Augustus, his life was blameless; and so was his reputation. While Germanicus and Drusus still lived, he concealed his real self, cunningly affecting virtuous qualities. However, until his mother died there was good in Tiberius as well as evil. Again, as long as he favoured (or feared) Sejanus, the cruelty of Tiberius was detested, but his perversions unrevealed. Then fear vanished, and with it shame. Thereafter he expressed his own personality, by unrestrained crime and infamy.

Baffling though this portrait is in some ways—we are left uncertain as to what Tiberius's real nature was—it gives a pattern of the corruption of power, and follows the scheme of the Tacitean account fairly closely. It is also by no means devoid of sympathy.

At an early stage of his career, Tacitus wrote plays. Dramatic purpose and technique is to be discerned in his historical writings. Original crime, foreboding and retribution; surprise, contrast, digression and moral judgment, are devices familiar in history since early Hellenistic times. But Tacitus is able to use them to greater effect than any of his predecessors because he has, in each imperial reign, a single main character and a central theme. The drama of Tacitus's overall plan is, as has been suggested, the tragic *peripeteia*, or change of fortune, here applied to the fortune of the principate. Nero's reign exemplifies this even more clearly than that of Tiberius. It begins more propitiously, in spite of the murder of Silanus, contrived by Agrippina without Nero's knowledge. Seneca and Burrus curtail her nefarious activities and set Nero on the right path. The principate is consolidated by the deification of Claudius;[25] certain powers are returned to the Senate;[26] and we are whisked off to Armenia to hear about frontier problems that are developing there.[27] At Rome the development of the drama centres around the figures of Nero and his mother Agrippina, for which there is no parallel in the first hexad. Court plots and counter-plots, the murder of Britannicus, Nero's affair with the ex-slave girl Acte are paralleled by similar acts of immorality in society at large; but the Senate continues to enjoy renewed prestige. In Book XIV the central drama receives added impetus with the introduction of a third person, Poppaea, to turn the balance against the dowager queen. With taunts she fires Nero, already enamoured of her, with the resolve to rid himself of his mother, who counter-attacks by making incestuous advances to her son. Seeing with surprise the extremes to which she will go, but himself spurred on by the two strongest motives known to man—carnal desire and the lust for power, Nero decides on the most heinous of all crimes, matricide. His preparations are given in detail by Tacitus: Agrippina's suspicions before the voyage on which her ship was supposed to sink, their dispulsion by Nero's polite address to her, the calmness and serenity of the night as the boat put out, her escape from the wreck and her decision to keep her knowledge of the plot secret. Meanwhile, the emperor's first reaction to the news of the miscarriage of the plan is fear lest, should his attempt become known while Agrippina still lived, there might be a revolution, for she was a Julian and a daughter of the ever-popular Germanicus. She must be despatched without delay by a common assassin. Here is Tacitus's account of the death-scene of Agrippina:[28]

> Anicetus surrounded her house and broke in. Arresting every slave in his path, he came to her bedroom door. Here stood a few servants—the rest had been frightened away by the invasion. In her dimly lit room a single maid waited with her. Agrippina's alarm had increased as nobody, not even Agerinus, came from her son. If things had been well there would not be this terrible ominous isolation, then

this sudden uproar. Her maid vanished. 'Are you leaving me, too?' called Agrippina. Then she saw Anicetus. Behind him were a naval captain and lieutenant. 'If you have come to visit me,' she said, 'you can report that I am better. But if you are assassins, I know my son is not responsible. He did not order his mother's death.' The murderers closed around her bed. First the captain hit her on the head with a truncheon. Then as the lieutenant was drawing his sword to finish her off, she cried out: 'Strike here!'—pointing to her womb. Blow after blow fell, and she died.

There follows a complicated picture of the psychological effect of his crime upon Nero. Initially he is tortured by remorse, and he is haunted by visions, associations and portents. Then, with his characteristic shallow cynicism—for a moment he had appeared human, but only for a moment—he allows himself to be reassured by his advisers, concocts a version of what had happened in which Agrippina is accused of a number of crimes against the state. No less shocking than Nero's part in this narrative is that of the leading men of the state and the citizenry at large, who applaud him on his return to Rome. But after a while their attitude changes, when they see Nero indulging in an unbroken orgy of improprieties and trivial pleasures. They had seen the murder of Agrippina as an act of political necessity, and a token of his intention to abolish petticoat government and rule independently. Now, as they see licentious pleasures and exotic foreign cults proliferating under the emperor's patronage, some resent the change which appears to be coming over the national character; and the appearance of a comet thereby turns men's thoughts to the prospect of a new emperor, without perhaps knowing whether it is in order to affirm or to arrest the change that they want a successor to Nero. The spirit of revolution may be fomented by means other than the force of arms.

Tacitus's mastery of the art of suspense is seen by his introduction at this point of provincial matters. There is contrast also: the Armenian campaign under that model general Domitius Corbulo is conducted with all the military efficiency and diplomacy which has won for Rome universal renown, and has made her seem superior to all her subjects; while at Rome the emperor himself has become the slave of outlandish, effete pleasures. This contrast is heightened when the emperor sends one of his freedmen to investigate the state of affairs in Britain.[29] Though the

troops were suitably respectful, mindful of their military oath
to the emperor and seeing that Polycleitus was invested with
the emperor's *auctoritas*, the Britons, not understanding this
subtlety, saw him as a non-Roman upstart and treated him with
derision, marvelling that an army which had completed such a
mighty war should obey a slave. (In the same passage there is one
of Tacitus's several references to barbarians' love of freedom,
made with his usual tone of nostalgia.)

The next contrast is one of place only. The subject is the same:
the increasing arrogance of men of subject or servile status, which
has been incited initially by the emperor's personal licence and
irresponsibility. It concerns the murder of a master by his slave.
The law regarding this crime was that the whole of the servile
household of the murdered man should be executed. In the
present case these numbered over two hundred, so that there
was some cause to question, and some need to defend the law.
The situation affords Tacitus, who was a practised forensic
speaker, the opportunity to display his art in a historical context.
The tone, if not the form, of legal argument is to be found in
many of Tacitus's passages of live speech, but none more than
in the present case, in which the conflict between the spirit and
the letter of the law, one of the major topics of ancient forensic
rhetoric, lies at the heart of the case. One of the speeches is worth
recording in full:[30]

I have often been here, senators, when decrees deviating from our
ancestral laws and customs have been mooted. I have not opposed
them. Not that I had any doubts about the superiority—in every
matter whatsoever—of ancient arrangements, and the undesirability
of every change. But I did not wish, by exaggerating my regard for
antique usage, to show too high an opinion of my own profession, the
law. Nor did I want, by continual opposition, to weaken any influence
I may possess. I wanted to keep it intact in case the country needed
my advice.

It needs it today! An ex-consul has been deliberately murdered by
a slave in his own home. None of his fellow-slaves prevented or
betrayed the murderer, though the senatorial decree threatening the
whole household with execution still stands. Exempt them from the
penalty if you like. But then, if the City Prefect was not important
enough to be immune, who will be? Who will have enough slaves to
protect him if Pedanius's were too few? Who can rely on his household's help if even fear for their own lives does not make them shield us?

Or was the assassin avenging a wrong? For that is one shameless fabrication. Tell us next that the slave had been negotiating about his patrimony, or he had lost some ancestral property! We had better call it justifiable homicide straight away.

Though wiser men have apparently considered and settled the whole matter, may I attempt to refute them? Pretend, if you like, that we are deciding a policy for the first time. Do you believe that a slave can have planned to kill his master without letting fall a single rash or menacing word? Or even if we assume he kept his secret—and obtained a weapon unnoticed—could he have passed the watch, opened the bedroom door, carried in a light, and committed the murder without anyone knowing? There are many advance notifications of crimes. If slaves give them away, we can live securely, though one among many, because of their insecurity; or, if we must die, we can at least be sure that the guilty will be punished.

Our ancestors distrusted their slaves. Yet slaves were then born on the same estates, in the same homes, as their masters, who had treated them kindly from birth. But nowadays our huge households are international. They include every alien religion—or none at all. The only way to keep down this scum is by intimidation. Innocent people will die, you say. Yes, and when in a defeated army every tenth man is flogged to death, the brave have to draw lots with the others. Exemplary punishment always contains an element of injustice. But individual wrongs are outweighed by the advantage of the community.

The issues raised in this speech are of historical interest, not only because they reflect traditional Roman attitudes and beliefs concerning society, but because they indicate the danger in changes which are taking place at the time: the precarious foundation on which an outward stability has been built is exemplified by the necessity of severe, and even unfair punishment of delinquents in the two classes on which the active working of the state depends, the servile population and the army. Add to this the permanent attitudes to change of the laws and to the security of the family hierarchy, and we have a subject worthy of elaboration in a historical work. Tacitus's rhetorical handling of the case (assuming the speech to be his own composition) shows expertise in adapting conventional practice to the situation. The speech begins by establishing the good sense and moderation of the speaker, necessary when so extreme a penalty was being proposed, and in the best rhetorical tradition, by which the introduction of a speech contained a *captatio benevolentiae*. Most of the remainder of the speech consists of forms of argument from probability, the main weapon of proof from earliest times. The final section draws attention to the changing state of society, and closes with the two *sententiae* on exemplary punishment and the advantage of the community, thus satisfying the contemporary taste for such forms of expression, and ending with something memorable for his hearers to take away with them. Nero, ever susceptible to artistry, is persuaded: he lets the law take its terrible course, and the structure of society is for the time preserved.

Soon afterwards we read of the death of Burrus and the retirement of Seneca; and other men of worth, Faenius Rufus and Rubellius Plautus, are disposed of by the rising menace of the new Sejanus, Ofonius Tigellinus.[31] The Senate, cowed by the fate of some of its noblest members, condones Nero's divorce of Octavia and his marriage to Poppaea. The people now become the conscience of the state: statues of Poppaea are pulled down, while those of Octavia are wreathed with flowers. Nero is forced to resort to subterfuge, and has Octavia accused of adultery. The episode closes with one of Tacitus's most pathetic descriptions, the murder of Octavia:[32]

> So this girl, in her twentieth year, was picketed by company-commanders of the Guard and their men. She was hardly a living person any more—so certain was she of imminent destruction: yet she still lacked the peace of death. The order to die arrived a few days later. She protested that she was a wife no longer—Nero's sister only. She invoked the Germanici, the relations she shared with Nero. Finally she invoked Agrippina, in whose days her marriage had been unhappy, certainly, but at least not fatal. But Octavia was bound, and all her veins were opened. However, her terror retarded the flow of blood. So she was put into an exceedingly hot vapour-bath and suffocated. An even crueller atrocity followed. Her head was cut off and taken to Rome for Poppaea to see.

The stage is set for the horrors and the political disintegration that follows. There has been a progressive decline in the character of the emperor, and the ethos of the empire itself, or those parts of it in which he has had direct influence, has declined accordingly. The historian has skilfully linked and orchestrated events by means of association, contrast and suspense, and has generated dramatic power at moments of extreme horror.

If the *Annals* represent the mature achievement of Tacitus, the *Histories*, which are by no means *iuvenilia*, should not be underrated. The four extant books are concerned largely with military matters: it is therefore appropriate to begin by considering his performance in this respect. If has been correctly observed that military affairs as an independent study did not interest Tacitus. But since most major political changes are attended by violence and bloodshed, no historian of revolutionary times can dissociate himself from warfare. The fact that Tacitus devotes the first three books of the *Histories* to the tumultuous year 69, an unprecedented coverage, suggests at first sight that he had a taste for war. But examination of the emphasis and omissions in his story show both his limitations and his intentions. Details of distances marched, and of numbers of detachments and armies are not always given accurately. More or less clear examples of ignorance or neglect of topography are not difficult to find. Strategy, also, is not always clear; though, by contrast, tactical movements, especially those immediately preceding major battles, are for the most part narrated with exemplary clarity, since it is upon these that the impetus of the narrative depends. There are many fine battle-narratives in which accuracy of description contributes to vividness. But what contributes equally to the graphic quality of many of these passages of violent action is Tacitus's technique of 'viewing from the inside', of describing the engagement from the point of view of the participants, constantly drawing attention to their thoughts and feelings as the situation develops. The following narrative illustrates this technique, which owes something to Thucydides:[33]

> The Othonians, meanwhile, had erected a tower on the bank and were discharging stones and firebrands. There was also an island in midstream to which both sides found their way, the gladiators by hard rowing, the Germans swimming down with the current. It happened on one occasion that the latter got across in some strength. Macer then manned some galleys and attacked them, using the keenest of his gladiators. But the latter did not exhibit the same steady courage as the regulars, and found it harder to shoot effectively from the heaving decks than did their enemies, who had a firm footing on the bank. As the frightened men shifted their position, so the boats swayed with their movements, and the rowers and fighters fell over

each other in confusion. The Germans seized their chance. They plunged into the shallow water, held the ships back by the sterns, climbed on board the gangways or drowned their opponents in hand-to-hand struggles. The whole scene was played out under the eyes of the two armies. The Vitellians were delighted, and with corresponding bitterness the Othonians cursed the cause and architect of their defeat.

The outcome of this battle, unlike that of Thucydides's version of the battle in the Great Harbour of Syracuse, with which it has certain points of resemblance, depends not on some undefined chance, but upon the individual courage and moral fibre of the combatants, and their ability to master the conditions. The victors not only enjoy initial advantages, but show enterprise and daring.

Leaving aside detail and techniques, we turn to the main question concerning the *Histories*: what is the central theme of the four extant books? It is no more than the subject of the episode itself: civil war, its nature and its consequences, bloody, internecine; even on occasion parricidal.[34]

A recruit to the Hurricane Legion, one Julius Mansuetus from Spain, had left a young lad at home. Soon after, the boy came of age, and having been called up by Galba for service in the Seventh, chanced to encounter his father in this battle and wounded him seriously. As he was searching the prostrate and semi-conscious figure, father and son recognised each other. Embracing the dying man, the son prayed in words choked by sobs that his father's spirit would be appeased and not bear him ill-will as a parricide: the act was not a personal one, and one single soldier was merely an infinitesimal fraction of the forces engaged in the civil war. With these words, he took up the body, dug a grave, and discharged the last duty to his father. Some nearby troops noticed this, then more and more; and so throughout the lines ran a current of wonder and complaint, and men cursed this cruellest of wars. However, this did not stop them killing and robbing relatives, kinsmen and brothers: they said to each other that crime had been done—and in the same breath did it themselves.

The action arises from the hostile confrontation of armies whose generals no longer have any higher authority to which they owe allegiance; and the seat of that authority is, through the negligence of Nero, now an open prize:[35]

The death of Nero had been welcomed initially by a surge of relief. But it had also evoked a variety of emotions in the Senate, the populace, and the garrison of the capital, as well as in all the many legions and legionary commanders: it was possible, it seemed, for an emperor to be chosen outside Rome.

The 'emperor' here referred to is Galba, and Tacitus goes on to describe his reputed qualities, the most conspicuous being his old age and his unpopularity, his lack of drive and his tendency to be dominated by his subordinates. Tacitus thus kills any expectation of a long reign. Our attention is quickly directed to the mood of the armies in Germany, the first provincial force to manifest that corporate military pride which was to become the motive behind the subsequent wars. Galba had not been their nominee; but it is of great importance to note that, in Tacitus's account, they did not initially have an alternative. He is at pains to show that the revolutionary mood originated in the army: the individual general (in this case Vitellius) arrived to find it already there, and became the agent of his army's ambition.[36] Confirmation of this is to be found in the frequent references to the boastful and emulous pronouncements of the several armies, and their horrible glee at the discomfiture of their rivals in battle. In one passage, men and officers return to the site of the Battle of Bedriacum and delight in retracing its course amid the mutilated corpses of men and horses.[37] The generals, on the other hand, enjoy winning battles and earning momentary renown, but appear to have no long-term ambitions, and still less any sense of destiny. This is clear in the case of Vitellius from Tacitus's account of the origin of his bid for the throne. The troops were spoiling for a fight, the object of which was to show the superiority of their professional skill over that of the other provincial armies, not by fighting Rome's enemies, but by the more telling course of direct confrontation with their rivals. Vitellius is hardly mentioned until, predictably enough, he appears, bent upon currying favour. His personal position is somewhat ambiguous, and eventually he yields to the persuasions of his more positive-thinking subordinates, Caecina and Valens. The chapter concludes with these words:[38]

> Vitellius was a man of lazy temperament, but he wavered under the strong impact of these arguments. The result was an idle longing rather than a real hope.

A little later he draws a sharp contrast between the mood of the general and that of his army:[39]

> The army and its emperor presented a remarkable contrast. The impatient troops demanded action while the Gallic provinces were still unnerved and the Spanish ones undecided. They were not going to be held up by winter or the slow pace of unheroic peace. It was vital, they held, to invade Italy and get hold of the capital. In civil war, speed was the only safe policy, and deeds were wanted, not deliberation.
>
> Vitellius dozed away his time. Quick to take advantage of the privileges of an emperor, he gave himself up to idle pleasures and sumptuous banquets. Even at midday he was the worse for drinking and over-eating. Yet, despite this, their keenness and vigour made his men carry out the duties of their commander as well as their own, just as though he were there to give them their orders and afford the active or lazy the stimulus of hope or fear. Ready and at the alert, they clamoured for the signal to start, and gave Vitellius the title of 'Germanicus' on the spot, though he refused to allow them to address him as 'Caesar' even after his final victory.

Readers of Latin will note how Tacitus has underlined the contrast with short syllables, historic infinitives and clipped clauses in his description of the mood of the army, while that of Vitellius is rendered in verbs in the imperfect tense, longer clauses and a greater frequency of long syllables, in order to portray his inertia.

Vitellius is depicted as indolent and bestial, devoid of ambition beyond the satisfaction of his own private appetites. His successor Otho is also fundamentally idle and luxury-loving; but his good family and breeding have given him a certain elegance, and also a capacity for self-dramatization which the historian exploits for his own artistic purposes. It is this contingency between character and literary opportunism that underlies Tacitus's elaborate portrayal of the final acts of Otho, rather than any admiration. Otho emerges as a man of moderate gifts, but of good connections and experience, who happened to be in the right place at the right time.

Vespasian, the ultimately successful claimant, is the only one who at one point refused to be put forward, and attempted to induce his troops to swear allegiance to Otho.[40] He is a military man in the best republican tradition, the true descendant of

Marius and Corbulo. He makes up his own mind coolly and practically, weighing up his chances and his own qualifications; after which, encouraged by the favourable prophecy of an astrologer (the best military men are superstitious), he embarks on his bid for the throne. The character of Vespasian is one of the few glimmers of hope on a very sombre scene.

But perhaps none of the participants had calculated the full extent to which a civil war would damage the minds of men and the fabric of civilization. Unrestrained by the scruples imposed by custom and law, which the removal of the central authority had thrown into confusion, men yielded to the persuasions of the most vociferous firebrands, and it was these latter that often became the 'king-makers'. But any transactions initiated by them rested upon the most infirm foundations, for the mob which they had moulded to their will was no less susceptible to the blandishments and pyrotechnics of others of their kind. On the death of Vitellius, the historian acidly observes: 'And still the mob reviled him in death as viciously as they had flattered him in life'.[41]

The political disruption is no less great. Old sores are opened, and in the provinces old rivalries among neighbours are revived as opposing factions claim their allegiance. In Rome, the weakness and lack of purpose of the predecessors of Vespasian reach their nadir in the brief reign of Vitellius. His sloth, ignorance and uncertainty make him a mere pawn in the strategy of his lieutenants Caecina and Valens, who thus exercise the privileges of power without its responsibilities. Naturally enough, this licence extends down the chain of command to the lower ranks, and in the formation of the new urban militia rank is given to those who clamour most, not to those who have earned it. But amid all this chaos, a few sane men continued to have sane thoughts:[42]

> For myself, I am quite prepared to grant that in their hearts a few men may have prayed for peace in preference to strife and for a good and honest ruler instead of two worthless and infamous scoundrels. Yet in an age and society so degenerate, I do not believe that the prudent Paulinus expected the ordinary soldier to exercise such self-control as to lay down his arms from an attachment to peace after disturbing the peace from a love of war.

Tacitus goes on to explain his reasons for this pessimistic view. Man's nature leads him to have a vested interest in fomenting revolution, because it is by this means that he may satisfy his lust for power. Aristocrats and *populares* have always shared this common aim. It is a gloomy picture and a gloomy prospect for the future. Two restraints exist: the incompetence of the malefactors themselves, and divine wrath. Tacitus does not believe in the intimate and continuous involvement of the gods in human affairs: rather, they intervene purely for the purpose of punishment. Thus the most outrageous misfortunes to the state, like the rise of Sejanus in the *Annals*, are ascribed, perhaps a little too glibly, to the wrath of the gods, who are incensed with the Roman state. Like Livy, though not quite so assiduously, Tacitus records omens and portents, weaving them into the fabric of his dramatic presentation. But in one passage he states plainly to which agency, human or divine, the course of events is to be ascribed when the two are in competition: [43]

During a speech of Vitellius to his assembled troops, an incident occurred which was spoken of as a prodigy: a flock of birds of ill omen flew overhead in such numbers that they seemed like a dark cloud blotting out the daylight. Then, too, there was the sinister escape from the altar of an ox that scattered the implements of sacrifice and was felled some distance from the altar in a manner contrary to the ritual prescribed for the killing of victims. But the chief portent was Vitellius himself. He knew nothing about active service, and had formed no plans for the future. He was perpetually asking others about the proper march-order, the arrangement for reconnaissance, and the extent to which a military decision should be forced or postponed. Whenever a dispatch arrived, his very looks and movements displayed panic; and, to crown it all, he drank. Finally, bored with camp life, and learning of the defection of the fleet at Misenum, he returned to Rome, frightened by each new blow he suffered but blind to the supreme danger.

Tacitus's view of the world, like that of Thucydides, is sardonic and anthropocentric. Portents may influence the minds of men, but have no significance independently of the human imagination.

Finally, some discussion is necessary of the original aspects of Tacitus's use of live speech. An indication has already been given of his particular interest in oratory, which is revealed in his earliest work, the *Dialogue on Orators*, and his career in the law-courts. In a work of history like the *Annals* there was an opportunity to pursue this interest in a historical way, and to survey the long-term development of oratory in a society in which its rôle was limited, yet at the same time diverse. There is some evidence that Tacitus had this purpose in mind when he composed his speeches, for, unlike those of Thucydides, they show a remarkable range of styles, reflecting the various rhetorical trends. But Tacitus was also aware of personal styles, as his *Dialogue* shows, and his speeches are his most potent medium of indirect characterization. Those assigned to Tiberius provide a valuable counterpart to the generally unfavourable picture that emerges from the body of the narrative. In his utterances the emperor is allowed to express his thoughts on the problems of monarchy. His original style, with its brevity, dignity and ambiguity, was much to the historian's taste, and formed a bond between them and made the composition of his speeches a congenial task. Claudius, by contrast, spoke with excessive bombast and superfluity, further vulgarized by a spurious antiquarianism. Tacitus ignores his oratory except to draw attention to its peculiarities. When Nero speaks at the funeral of Claudius, the historian is quick to report that the text was the work of Annaeus Seneca. The final disgrace had come: an emperor who could not compose speeches. The criticism is less than fair, for Nero was only sixteen years of age, and later showed considerable interest in rhetorical composition. But it illustrates the importance attached to oratory as an instrument of government by Tacitus. It is better, we are assured, even for an absolute ruler to have the power of persuading his people of the correctness of his policies.

Words have power for evil as well as for good, and might even be used as a deterrent to free speech or as a weapon of private vendetta. The hated informers (*delatores*) were orators. The prototype of this breed, and the trade itself, are thus described by Tacitus:[44]

Shortly afterwards Marcus Granius Marcellus, governor of Bithynia, was accused of treason by his own assistant. But it was the latter's partner Romanius Hispo who created a career which was to be made notorious by the villainous products of subsequent gloomy years. Needy, obscure, and restless, he wormed his way by secret reports into the grim emperor's confidence. Then everyone of any eminence was in danger from him. Over one man he enjoyed an ascendancy; all others loathed him. His was the precedent which enabled imitators to exchange beggary for wealth, to inspire dread instead of contempt, to destroy their fellow-citizens—and finally themselves.

It is characteristic of Tacitus's feeling for the dignity of history that he records none of the speeches of this class, but leaves to posterity only the words of some of their more worthy victims. Those of Cremutius Cordus, which echo some of the sentiments which are closest to the historian's heart, and suggest that Tacitus might have seen himself in the speaker's place if he had lived in that age, provide a fitting end not only to this section but to the main body of the chapter:[45]

Senators, my words are blamed. My actions are not blameworthy. Nor were these words of mine aimed against the emperor and his parent, to whom the law of treason applies. I am charged with praising Brutus and Cassius. Yet many have written of their deeds—always with respect. Livy, outstanding for objectivity as well as eloquence, praised Pompey so warmly that Augustus called him a Pompeian. But their friendship did not suffer. And Livy never called Brutus and Cassius bandits and parricides—their fashionable designations today. He described them in language appropriate to distinguished men.

Gaius Asinius Pollio gave a highly complimentary account of them. Marcus Valerius Messalla Corvinus called Cassius 'my commander'. When Cicero praised Cato to the skies, the dictator Julius Caesar reacted by writing a speech against him—as in a lawsuit. Antony's letters, Brutus's speeches, contain scathing slanders against Augustus. The poems of Marcus Furius Bibaculus and Catullus, still read, are crammed with insults against the Caesars. Yet the divine Julius, the divine Augustus endured them and let them be. This could well be interpreted as wise policy, and not merely forbearance. For things unnoticed are forgotten; resentment confers status upon them.

I am not speaking of the Greeks. For they left licence unpunished as well as freedom—or, at most, words were countered by words. But among us, too, there has always been complete, uncensored liberty to speak about those whom death has placed beyond hatred or partiality. Cassius and Brutus are not in arms at Philippi now. I am not on the platform inciting the people to civil war. They died seventy years ago! They are known by their statues—even the conqueror did not remove them. And they have their place in the historian's pages. Posterity gives everyone his due honour. If I am condemned, people will remember me as well as Brutus and Cassius.

If we now ask whether Tacitus has been seen to present his story, according to his own initial undertaking, without anger, hatred or partiality, we must surely accept a negative answer. Both the *Annals* and the *Histories* are full of rancour and personal judgments, coloured by a disturbing willingness to adduce popular rumour in their support. As a member of a class whose right to rule had been eroded for over a century, culminating in a reign of terror which coincided with the time when he himself was on the point of reaching the summit of his career, Tacitus had every reason to lament the demise of freedom. But there is detachment also, and a healthy scepticism. On many occasions he refuses to add his authority to irresponsible stories, like those which incriminated Tiberius in the death of Germanicus and that of his own son Drusus. It is this scepticism, combined with an impressive intellectual penetration, that enables him to define more clearly than any other historian the central problem of the empire—the exercise of power by one man without his self-destruction and without incurring the ill-will of the subject. The reign of Tiberius, and to a lesser extent that of Claudius, emerge as tolerable, and we see that they were so because both were fundamentally responsible emperors who worked actively for concord and prosperity. Nero's natural impulse was to leave the work of government to others, while enjoying the limelight which his position afforded. His decline is traced by Tacitus with great analytical skill in the *Annals*, while in the *Histories* the forces of revolution which he unleashed are exposed amid the horrors of civil war. Above all, Tacitus is a superb stylist, tracing his lineage back to Sallust, the predecessor he most admired, and superseding him by virtue of his grasp of the historical forces in operation in his time, which assisted his artistic talents in the selection and arrangement of the rich material at his disposal.

CHAPTER 8

Some Minor Historians

IF THE volume of their surviving work were taken as the main criterion of merit, several hitherto unmentioned historians would qualify for fuller treatment than those whose work has been examined in the previous chapters. Some, moreover, of these neglected histories would, in certain respects, stand comparison on literary grounds with those of the chosen historians; while nearly all of them frequently shed light on periods and episodes which would otherwise have been lost to posterity, or provide an alternative version when a major historian is guilty of palpable bias. The glib antithesis between quantity and quality will therefore not adequately explain their belated appearance. This is due mainly, and in varying degrees, to their lack of originality, and hence their comparative failure to contribute to the development of the genre.

Beginning with Diodorus of Sicily, we encounter history in its broadest conception. He inherited the idea of universal history from Ephorus, divested it of its Greek orientation, and included the whole of the inhabited world in a compendious *Library of of History*. No less a Greek than Ephorus, he was convinced by two things of the obsoleteness of his 'Hellenocentric' view of the civilized world: he lived, like Polybius, under Roman rule; and, more significantly, he was influenced by a Stoic doctrine which radically affected his attitude to history, that of the brotherhood of man. The placing of his date of birth in the region of the year 90 B.C., probably at Agyrium in Sicily, makes it possible that he acquainted himself with the current teaching of the Stoic philosopher and historian Posidonius on that subject. Like several other Hellenistic historians, he made Rome his centre of study, but he travelled abroad at least as far as Egypt. He probably survived into the Augustan era. There is no evidence that he did anything of note except to write; and the length of his *Library* (forty books, of which fifteen survive in unabridged form)

235

disposes us to doubt whether much time was left for any other creative writing.

The title itself arouses a curiosity which is to some extent satisfied in the eloquent introduction. Here Diodorus engagingly disclaims deep intelligence or insight,[1] and admits the second-hand nature of his material.[2] From other personal utterances it becomes plain that his main interest lies not in creative historiography but in the presentation, in a convenient and readable form, of a comprehensive history of the human race. To increase further understanding of his intentions we may most usefully turn to his application of Stoic doctrine. Two main concepts are involved. The first affirmed that mankind, though separate in space, are brothers in blood, and that this conceptually united world is harmonized and ruled by divine providence. The universal historian becomes the servant of this providence, and will attempt to relate the apparently confused and disconnected events of world history to a central divine plan. Diodorus falls far short of realizing this ideal, and does not seem to have fully grasped the difficulties inherent in it. On the concept of human brotherhood, however, he is frequently articulate, often expressing pity at the sufferings of men at one another's hands. More specifically, the evil of slavery, of which he may have become conscious through his childhood experiences in Sicily, the scene of two servile revolts in living memory (135–132 and 104–102 B.C.), moved Diodorus to write two notable passages describing conditions in gold mines in Spain and Egypt.[3]

Another aspect of Stoic doctrine which affected the form of Diodorus's history is the concept of the utility of history as a medium of education and general benefit. Linked with the universal concept, this finds its logical form in Diodorus's concentration upon imparting information in a simple, straightforward (and, it should be said, often dull) style, but with particular emphasis upon the deeds and memorable utterances of important men, which illustrate good or evil in human endeavour. Most of Diodorus's own personal comments are upon such actions. This interest in individuals and in moral instruction affects his choice of material, a fact which is best illustrated by comparison with the parallel narrative of another author—Xenophon—whose interests lie in a somewhat similar direction. True to his universal conception, Diodorus gives the broader coverage of events outside the immediate theatre of the Ionian War. On the other hand, Xenophon's accounts of battles, though by no means entirely satisfactory, are clearer than those of Diodorus, who too readily resorts to rhetoric. Xenophon also usually scores when it comes to the disclosure of motives and strategy, and is correspondingly less lavish with censure and praise. When we come to the period of Theban dominance, however, Diodorus's pro-Athenian bias, which he derives from his source Ephorus, proves less mischievous than Xenophon's adulation for Agesilaus, and it is mainly from his account that we are able to estimate the genius of Epaminondas. Before the period of the Peloponnesian War Diodorus is scarcely less useful, devoting a whole book to the *Pentekontaetia*,[4] which is scant coverage by other standards, but since Thucydides summarizes these years in thirty chapters[5] it is the fullest continuous account we have. And again, after the more detailed Xenophontine account breaks off in 362 B.C., Diodorus, using Ephorus as his main source, once more furnishes the only consecutive account of these years, while for the period 323 to 302 B.C. he is the main literary authority. Sicilian episodes, which understandably occur frequently, and for which he is indebted chiefly to Timaeus, provide modern historians with much of their knowledge of the early history of that island.

The foregoing facts concerning the scope and value of Diodorus's narrative being undeniable, criticism of his work has been directed mainly against two faults: his superficiality, which from his own terms of reference and the brevity of the human span is inevitable; and his lack of originality. The latter needs definition. Distinction must be made between content and form. He has been called, among other things, a 'scissors and paste historian',[6] and the fact that he depended upon others for his material has led to the wide assumption that he had no style of his own, but copied his sources verbatim. Such assertions are, in the absence of more than a few fragments of some of the original sources, very difficult to prove. On the other hand, recent work on the style of Diodorus, including statistical examination of his sentence structure and vocabulary,[7] has tended to show uniformity, and to lead to the conclusion that he tried, not without success, to forge a style of his own and to create a work of independent merit.

.   .   .

Another émigré Greek historian who took up residence in Rome during the latter part of the first century B.C. was Dionysius of Halicarnassus. He tells us[8] that he arrived in Rome in the middle of the 187th Olympiad (30 B.C.). From other indirect sources it can be deduced that he was in his late twenties at this time, and that he probably had considerable resources or influence to have been able to make the journey from Halicarnassus to Rome at that troubled time. Once ensconced in the great city, Dionysius was allowed to enter into its cultural life and became the leading member of an active circle of *literati*. Both Greeks and Romans comprised this coterie, but they shared a common interest in the purification and promotion of Greek as a literary language, and turned for their models to the orators of fourth-century Athens. Of these the most admired was Demosthenes, who was considered to embody all the major oratorical virtues. But due attention was also paid to the peculiar qualities of his lesser brethren—the smooth periodic virtuosity of Isocrates; the plain, pellucid simplicity of Lysias, which concealed his artistry; and the vehement and exhaustive argumentation of Isaeus, from which Demosthenes learned so much. Dionysius wrote essays on these and other authors, including Thucydides, part of whose introduction (in Book I) he has the temerity to rewrite, omitting chapters 2 to 20 as irrelevant. However, this essay also contains more mature criticism, and is of some interest on the grounds that it explores the possibilities of adapting the best Attic oratorical usages and techniques to the medium of historiography.

Dionysius's choice of history as the medium for his single excursion into creative, as distinct from critical, literature was to a large extent conditioned by time and circumstances. Roman oratory had attained to a brilliant virtuosity in the hands of Cicero (whom Dionysius never mentions in his writings), Caesar and their contemporaries under the free republic, whereas Greek oratory had languished since the fall of democracy in the motherland. Under Augustus, any form of free speech was subject to certain restrictions, and there was no longer any scope for impassioned political harangues. But oratory now became a form of mass entertainment, an alternative, for the more gentle or the more squeamish, to the blood-sports of the Colosseum. The language used in this stage-oratory was Latin, the language of the Roman populace. But in history Greek maintained its continuity, largely because it retained a reading public of intellectuals like the circle of Dionysius. Therefore, in electing to devote his creative talents to the writing of history, Dionysius was choosing the most acceptable medium through which to promote his crusade for the revival of Attic Greek. By further choosing the early history of Rome down to the First Punic War as his subject, he discharged an obligation to his hosts. In his preface he expresses his gratitude to them for their cordial hospitality and offers his work as a token of this gratitude.[9] But he intended it to be much more than this. In his rhetorical writings he had expressed the view that the first duty of the historian was to select a worthy subject. What worthier than the rise to supremacy of the mightiest power of his day? But in the same passage he unwittingly reveals the danger inherent in such a choice. How is a 'great subject' to be defined? Dionysius criticizes Thucydides for choosing a subject inferior to that chosen by Herodotus, since the latter embraces a cosmic war, while the former is concerned with a parochial affair among Greeks.[10] Such a shallow criterion of great historiography raises serious doubts concerning Dionysius's own competence as a historian, whatever his pretensions. And in spite of a considerable measure of solid achievement, these doubts are never wholly dispelled.

His *Early History of Rome (Antiquitates Romanae)* consisted of twenty books, of which the first ten are preserved complete, together with most of the eleventh. In order to study native sources Dionysius acquainted himself with the Latin language (the influence of which is curiously perceptible in the word-order of his Greek). He also shows a commendable appetite for precise information, and is responsible for the preservation of the Servian Census. He had also read Thucydides and Polybius (whom he disliked on stylistic grounds) on the subject of historical causes, understood the distinctions they made and tried to apply them. He paid careful attention to chronology, and is not entirely to blame for the errors which arise from the confusion between the Greek and Roman calendars. In the matter of bias, his obvious admiration for Rome did not prevent him from censuring her politicians when this seemed appropriate. He scrupulously compares his sources in the best Hellenistic manner, and in much the same critical spirit as that which he applies to his learned literary discussions of the authenticity of the speeches of Dinarchus and others. And finally, his pre-conceived 'programme'—to represent Rome's achievement as a continuation of a glorious Greek past by showing that the founders of Rome were Greek in origin—was not in itself an impediment to the truthful presentation of subsequent Roman history.

But these virtues are to some extent cancelled out by the author's preoccupation with form at the expense of content. As a leading rhetorician, he conceived his *magnum opus* in a rhetorical spirit, which in the context of his own day meant that it was designed, like the public declamations, to make the maximum emotional impact on a listening public. An obvious means of achieving this effect in a work of history is to include a high proportion of live speech; and this Dionysius does. After the first two books, orations become frequent, forming about a third of the whole text. In the shadowy context of early Roman history, where little was known for certain of personalities and motives, or in some cases even the existence of some of the leaders named by tradition, the assignment of arguments and characterization could not be made with any serious claim to authenticity. On this view the speeches in the early books of Livy are open to the same criticism as those of Dionysius. But at least Livy's speeches were written in Latin, whereas those of Dionysius take unreality a stage further by having all the signs of their author's reverence for the canon of Attic orators, for Herodotus, Thucydides and Xenophon, from whose pages he has culled many sentiments and verbal expressions. Sometimes whole speeches appear to be modelled on classical originals, like that of Coriolanus advising the Volscians, the model for which is Thucydides's speech of Alcibiades to the Spartans.[11] Often it seems probable that the existence of a classical model to fit the situation, rather than the knowledge that a speech was actually made, has led to the insertion of a speech.

Another aspect of rhetorical technique, amplification, is very much in evidence, and often destroys the historical perspective. Dionysius's narrative of the story of Coriolanus once more provides an excellent example, especially when compared with that of Livy. Dionysius needs forty-eight chapters to deal with it and assigns fifteen speeches to the protagonists: Livy dismisses the episode in half a chapter.[12] It is a story full of tragedy, pathos and torn loyalties, and as such contains rich material for rhetorical display. Livy and Dionysius had access to the same sources, and yet treated the same episode very differently. It might be objected that Livy's reticence may be due in part to embarrassment at the treason of a prominent countryman; but he is elsewhere as ready as Dionysius to censure bad generalship or statesmanship with impartiality. The difference between the two historians is further illustrated by later divergences. The Samnite Wars, a protracted and dreary series of campaigns which lacked the definition of time and space (an essential quality for successful rhetorical treatment) that characterized the Coriolanian episode, were nevertheless probably more fully documented, and were certainly more important for the survival of Rome and the growth of her power. They cover six books in Livy, whereas Dionysius accords them less than four.[13] Altogether it is not unfair to say that it is only when historical importance and rhetorical or dramatic qualities coincide in an event that one can be sure it receives from him the attention it deserves.

Perhaps Dionysius's most original contribution to ancient historical thought is his attempt, in the first two books, to combine within a single narrative the work of many different authorities for the legend of the Greek origins of Rome. Even this, however, is not without its weaknesses, for the more successful his synthesis is, the more completely is early Rome deprived of its native primitive elements—elements whose existence has been firmly established by modern archaeological discoveries. Thus deprived of the credit for experiment and innovation, the early Romans lose much of their vigour and individuality. Nevertheless Dionysius is one of those minor historians we should least want to be without, since his scholarly diligence has enabled us to fill many of the gaps in Livy's account.

The first of the minor Latin historians under the empire to claim attention is Velleius Paterculus. His minor status is self-confessed: he wrote not from purely academic motives, devoting his whole life to research and literary composition, but hastily and for a specific personal occasion, to celebrate the consulship of his friend Marcus Vinicius in the year A.D. 30. The work itself is not a full-length history after the manner of Livy, but an epitome comprehending a thousand years of history. It survives in two books, the first beginning with Homeric times and the legend of Aeneas, and ending with the catastrophic year 146 B.C., when both Carthage and Corinth were destroyed by the Romans. The second book is some six times as long, and becomes progressively more detailed as events draw nearer to the lifetime of the historian.

All the internal evidence provided by his history (and there is little evidence of any other kind) suggests that Velleius was an amateur and an opsimath in the art of historiography. From a study of his style it is apparent that a knowledge of rhetoric, recently and perfunctorily acquired, had not had the time to become refined and disciplined by good taste. On the other hand, as sometimes happens in such cases, where fools rush in, some felicities may emerge of which angels had not dreamed: as when he reaches the consulship of Julius Caesar and prepares the reader for an extended treatment of this episode with a colourful *prosopopoeia*, saying that Caesar 'lays hold of his pen and compels him to linger a while on him'.[14] Generally speaking, his fondness for metaphor and verbal conceits, which might become tedious in a longer work, seem appropriate and ancillary to the lapidary concision necessary in an epitome, and conforms to the rhetorical conventions of the Silver Age, which demanded the expression of ideas in a memorable, and preferably gnomic way. But occasional excesses betray Velleius's inexperience, as when he devotes almost the whole of one chapter (which consequently reads like a rhetorical *suasoria*)[15] to an *apostrophe*, or direct address, to Mark Antony for the murder of Cicero. Elsewhere also, he forgets the scale of his work and digresses, sometimes giving prominence to unimportant people. One of these is of especial interest: he is Marcus Caelius Rufus,[16] a friend of Cicero for whom the orator wrote one of his most famous speeches. The share of the narrative accorded Caelius and certain other men who were in some way or other involved with Cicero suggests not only that Velleius had read some of Cicero's speeches (an assumption which is in no need of proof), but also that he may have employed them as source-material.

The substance of Velleius's history is informed by two related characteristics, its senatorial orientation and its biographical tendency. The connection is most clearly indicated in the more summary sections, in which the chief actors are the scions of the great senatorial houses, whose offices, triumphs and funerals are faithfully recorded, as upon the tablets adorning their ancestral halls. Balanced biographical sketches of such men are not to be expected: Velleius is too involved to admit faults in patricians, and probably lacked the shrewdness to perceive them. *Populares* and *novi homines*, on the other hand, like Mummius and Marius, receive the most cavalier treatment. The Gracchi also are represented as destroyers of the constitution. The result is that we are never permitted to evaluate, or even to view, the underlying forces of revolution.

Nevertheless, with the advantage of access to the crystallized thought of a generation on the subject of the fall of the Republic, Velleius is able to furnish some useful analyses of the more important phases:[17]

> It was in Caesar's consulship that there was formed between himself, Gnaeus Pompeius and Marcus Crassus the partnership in political power which proved so baleful to the city, to the world, and subsequently at different periods to each of the triumvirs himself. Pompey's motive in the adoption of this policy had been to secure through Caesar as consul the long-delayed ratification of his acts in the provinces across the seas, to which, as I have already said, many still raised objections; Caesar agreed to it because he realised that in making this concession to the prestige of Pompey he would increase his own, and that by throwing odium on Pompey for their joint control he would add to his own power; while Crassus hoped that by the influence of Pompey and the power of Caesar he might achieve a place of pre-eminence in the state which he had not been able to reach single-handed. Furthermore, a tie of marriage was cemented between Caesar and Pompey, in that Pompey now wedded Julia, Caesar's daughter.

Though not very profound, this is the sort of analysis which would assure an Advanced Level student of a good mark in an answer on the First Triumvirate. Velleius is also responsible for some useful chronology, while his broad cultural interests are reflected in the chapters devoted to literary history, which once again perhaps signify his debt to Cicero, whose style in the *Brutus*, a dialogue on the history of oratory, may have influenced these chapters. A final impression of a writer with a considerable natural flair, attempting a marriage of forms—biography, rhetoric and epitome—which a more experienced writer would have eschewed; coming near to success for brief moments, but suffering ultimate betrayal at the hands of his own lack of historical insight, would not be an uncharitable one with which to leave Velleius Paterculus.

The life of Appian of Alexandria coincided with what many subsequent historians have judged to be the Golden Age of the Roman Empire, the principates of Trajan, Hadrian and the Antonine emperors. He was born about A.D. 95, and probably attained the biblical span. A provincial by birth and by choice, he pursued his career in his own country and sought beyond local honours only an office which permitted him to remain in his native land, that of procurator, or the emperor's fiscal representative. Prior to his appointment to this high office he had been a frequent visitor to Rome on his country's business, and had earned a reputation as a forensic pleader. At the height of his career he was sufficiently well-known to write an autobiography with the expectation that it would be read.

But Appian's only surviving work is a history of Rome from its beginnings, of which eleven books have survived from an original putative twenty-four. Although most of the sources he employs are Roman, he has divested their account of any patriotic bias it may have had, and writes with the detachment of a foreigner furnishing his countrymen, in their own language, with facts concerning the past of the head city of the empire of which they are a part. The empire itself, and the process of its growth, is deprived of the quality of organic inevitability of which Polybius and other admirers of Rome had made so much, by Appian's decision to divide his story into a series of episodes corresponding to the list of her imperial possessions which he gives in his preface. Yet it may well be the case that the resulting picture of isolated and accidental accretion is more accurate than the idealized one.

In this regional and ethnological scheme, however, all sense of continuity is lost, and chronology is neglected. Thus the surviving fragments of Book V follow Sicilian history through two centuries, while Book VI contains a full account of Spain's part in Roman history from the early days of Punic occupation to 25 B.C.; but in neither are precise dates given, and we have to be content with such expressions as 'some time later' and 'not many years after these events'. For one important period of Roman history, however, he abandons this scheme and concentrates on the problems of Rome herself during the period of political disruption, 133–30 B.C., to which he devotes five books.[18] It is in these books that his greatest virtue, his impartiality, is of most service to students of Roman history. His account of the Gracchan episode is unique in giving a balanced presentation of the main issues, and provides a welcome, not to say better-argued, counterblast to the anti-popular protestations of Velleius. Such inaccuracies as he commits arise chiefly from his lack of interest in chronology and his incomplete knowledge of Roman institutions.

It is in his style that Appian disappoints most. Only rarely does he exhibit the ability at argument and debate which his performances in the imperial courts must have contained. Perhaps, after reading Dionysius, we should be grateful for being spared displays of protracted and derivative rhetoric. But Appian's continuous bare narrative, which is rarely relieved by ratiocination, causes us to welcome the few passages of live speech which he includes. These are mostly brief and to the point, and cover no new ground in the development of historical oratory. Appian's main interest, and his chief claim to our attention, is in his narration of fact. In this respect he shows a certain fondness for describing clever stratagems, suggesting that there may be an interesting episode in his career of which we know nothing. He is also capable of elevating his tone under the stimulus of dramatic events. His account of the reception given by the Carthaginian ambassadors to the Roman terms of peace in 149 B.C. is a vivid portrayal of emotion:[19]

> While he [Censorinus, the Roman spokesman] was yet speaking, the Carthaginians lifted their hands towards heaven with loud cries, and called on the gods as avengers of violated faith. Repeatedly and virulently they cursed the Romans, either because they wished to die, or because they were out of their minds, or because they were determined to provoke the Romans to sacrilegious violence to ambassadors. They flung themselves on the ground and beat it with their hands and heads. Some of them even tore their clothes and lacerated their flesh as though they were absolutely bereft of their senses. When at last the frenzy was past they lay there, crushed and silent, like dead men. The Romans were struck with amazement, and

the consuls thought it best to bear with men who were overwhelmed at an appalling command until their indignation should subside, for they well knew that great dangers often bring desperate courage on the instant, which time and necessity gradually subdue. This was the case with the Carthaginians; for when during the interval of silence their calamity came over them, they ceased their reproaches and began to bewail, with fresh lamentations, their own fate and that of their wives and children, calling them by name, and also that of their country, as though she could hear their pitiful and incessant cries like a human being. The priests also invoked their temples, and the gods within them, as though they too were present, accusing them of being the cause of their destruction. So pitiable was this mingling together of public and private grief, that it drew tears from the Romans themselves.

The change of mood gives an element of restraint and realism to the picture. Sometimes, however, Appian's enthusiasm runs away with him, as when, in his narrative of the Battle of Zama, he has Scipio Africanus and Hannibal engaging in a Homeric duel.[20] But such excesses as this are uncharacteristic, except in so far as they typify the prominence given to action over rational processes by Appian.

Certain characteristics are shared by Appian and the next historian to be considered, Flavius Arrianus. Their dates of birth must have been close, A.D. 96 being the year favoured for Arrian. Both were Greeks who attained high rank in the imperial administration, and both wrote history of periods remote from their own time. Both are relatively free from the excesses of rhetoric, and wrote in a plain, unadorned style well adapted to their main purpose, which was to write lucid narrative. But Arrian had pretensions which his contemporary lacked. As governor of Cappadocia under Hadrian from A.D. 131 to 137 (a post of extraordinary distinction for a non-Roman at that time), he acquired considerable military experience and repelled an invasion by the barbaric Alan tribesmen. In one of his minor writings he explains the tactics he used in achieving this feat; while in another he reveals himself as a pupil of the philosopher Epictetus, faithfully recording the main tenets of his master's teaching. A familiar image, that of the soldier-philosopher emerges. Add to this Arrian's early retirement, to the enjoyment of leisure and literary composition for the last forty years of his life (until around 180) and who is to be recognized as his ancient precursor? Arrian was in fact an admirer of Xenophon, had read his *Anabasis*, studied his style and perhaps even modelled his life on that of the Athenian to an extent, for we read that he styled himself 'The New Xenophon.'[21] But with what expedition or campaign could he rival his hero's masterpiece? There was no need to look far. Alexander's expedition marched over the same ground and fought against the same enemy. It was also staged on a far grander scale, and enjoyed the further merit of success. One of the few examples of the influence of rhetoric on Arrian's thought occurs in the passage in which he explains his reason for writing his seven books of Alexander's *Anabasis*. By a peculiar and specious turn of logic, he argues that Alexander's achievements, unlike those of Achilles and many other lesser princes, had never enjoyed the advantage of a historian capable of doing them justice; that Xenophon had bestowed this benefit upon the lesser expedition of Cyrus, magnifying it by his narrative powers; and that he, Arrian, now proposed to pay Alexander the same overdue service, and, in doing so, claimed a place among the great historians of the past by virtue of the greatness of his subject.[22]

In spite of this unpromising beginning, Arrian proves to possess two qualities which make his account the most reliable we have of Alexander's exploits. Firstly, he shows an impressively professional knowledge of warfare, the basic techniques of which had changed little in the 450 years separating his own time from that of his subject. Strategy, tactics and set pieces are, so far as one can judge, generally described with precision and understanding. The second quality is his critical spirit. He inherited the Hellenistic habit of naming and discussing sources. His main authorities, in order of importance, were Ptolemy (Soter—the founder of the Ptolemaic dynasty of Hellenistic Egypt), and Aristobulus, both of whom accompanied Alexander. The trust which he places in Ptolemy, ('because he was a king he was not likely to lie'),[23] seems a little naïve, but is usually justified at points of disagreement by sound military arguments.[24]

But the success of any account of Alexander's conquests must depend ultimately upon the author's estimation of the character and motives of the king himself. Most of the live speech in

Arrian's *Anabasis* serves this end. A sentence in one of these explains the driving force which impelled him to pursue a career of endless conquest.[25]

> I set no limit of labours to men of spirit, save only the labours themselves, such as lead them on to noble undertakings.

And later in the same speech, made to raise the flagging spirits of the Macedonians:

> It is those who endure toil and who dare danger that achieve glorious deeds; and it is sweet to live with courage, and to die leaving behind an immortal renown.[26]

To this idealistic, and therefore unlimited view of war and conquest is to be added a sense of destiny. Alexander traced his descent from those great mythological conquerors Perseus and Heracles[27] (who were also respectively ancestors of the Persian and Greek races), and set himself the task of emulating the victorious careers of both. But Arrian, like Alexander himself, recognized all these claims for their true value, as instruments of propaganda, and accords them and the other semi-divine and romantic aspects of his character, his clemency and his chivalry, less attention than his practical qualities as a general. He represents Alexander as supremely confident,[28] even to the point of taking risks which lesser men would have considered excessive.[29] But in facing all dangers, Arrian's Alexander exposed himself equally with his men, and led them from the front with energy and courage. A pronounced streak of realism and shrewdness is to be observed in many of his actions, including those involving religion: a quality which contrasts him with his chief enemy Darius, who is a constant victim of wishful thinking. All his victories are carefully planned, with just that element of calculated risk which, from the outsider's point of view, imparts flare and genius to the operation.

As a pupil of Epictetus, Arrian was as interested in human foibles as in virtues; and such a training discouraged hero-worship. For his criticisms of Alexander Arrian is probably independent of his sources. He disapproved of Alexander's decision to destroy Thebes, though for diplomatic, not humanitarian reasons.[30] At another point he notes with disapproval the king's over-sensitivity to adverse criticism.[31] But the gravamen of his case against Alexander is that he was, on occasions, 'not master of himself', as when he slew his friend and boon companion Cleitus.[32] According to the Stoic ideal, the essential virtue of the philosopher-king was self-control, and this was a belief to which both Epictetus and his pupil subscribed. Arrian also shows unease at the habit of obeisance which Alexander demanded of his men after observing its practice in the Persian court.

But there is no scheme of decline. Alexander's virtues manifest themselves in word and deed to the last, for he repented his worst actions. When he dies Arrian has this to say of his faults:[33]

> If, however, Alexander committed any error through haste or in anger, or if he went some distance in the direction of Eastern arrogance, this I do not regard as important; if readers will consider in a spirit of charity Alexander's youth, his unbroken success, and those courtiers who associate with kings to flatter but not to improve them, and who will always do so to their detriment. But I do know that to Alexander alone of the kings of old did repentance for his faults come, by reason of his noble nature. . . . But that he referred his birth to a god, even this I do not altogether think to be a grave fault, unless perhaps it was a mere device to impress upon his subjects, and to appear more dignified. . . . Moreover, I feel that the adoption of Persian equipage was a device, both towards the Persians, so that their king might not appear wholly removed from them, and towards the Macedonians, to mark some reversions from Macedonian abruptness and arrogance. . . . And his carousings, as Aristobulus says, were prolonged not for wine, but from a spirit of comradeship.

Arrian's lack of originality or sense of drama deprives him of a place in the first rank of historians; but if diligence, sobriety and technical knowledge count for anything, his *Anabasis* has few rivals among the Greek histories of the Christian era, and bears comparison with its Xenophontine model.

The last full history of Rome was written, like the first, in Greek and by a senator. But Dio Cassius, unlike Fabius Pictor, was not a Roman of patrician stock, but a native of the Bithynian city of Nicaea. Almost two centuries had passed since the exclusive nationalism of Augustus had debarred all but natives of Italy from the highest positions. Some of his later successors were themselves non-Roman: Trajan was a Spaniard, and so was

Hadrian who, as emperor, spent more time away from Rome than in it; while Dio's contemporary Septimius Severus came from North Africa. Dio and his family were typical upper-class provincials of the late second century in that they spent part of their time in Italy and part in their native land, probably owning property in both countries. Resulting both from deliberate policy and from a natural eugenic process, this participation by distinguished and able provincials in the central administration was the greatest psychological unifying force in the Roman empire.

Dio was born probably around A.D. 163, and came some sixteen years later to Rome, where he completed his education by a course in rhetoric, which in his case included special study of the Atticists, and presumably the Attic authors themselves. This suggests an early intention to write, and a desire to imitate the best models. But most of his energies at this time were probably directed towards his political career. No office earlier than his praetorship in 194 can be firmly dated, though a quaestorship or a tribunate, or both, must have fallen to him between 188 and 191. The emperor at this time was Commodus, son of Marcus Aurelius and a replica of Domitian without that emperor's sense of responsibility. He was murdered in 192, and after the disappointingly brief reign of Pertinax, five years of civil war ended in 197 with the enthronement of the aptly-named Septimius Severus. Dio's first consulship probably fell in the year 205 or 206, having been preceded by a provincial governorship in Asia. Under Septimius he does not appear to have been an active participant in debates, and was not among the foremost senators, at least in the matter of wealth. The following reign of Severus Alexander, however, brought him considerable distinction, which included the governorship of the important province of Pannonia Superior (which included parts of modern Austria and Czechoslovakia south of the Danube). There his essentially civilian talents may have caused him some embarrassment at the hands of an unruly garrison and a barbaric native population. Nevertheless, his sojourn passed without any major disaster, and, returning to Rome as a senior citizen and a pillar of senatorial respectability, he was an obvious choice for a second consulship at a time when the principate itself was in some danger of collapse. The date of his death is quite uncertain.

Dio's first literary essay centred on contemporary affairs, in particular the civil wars after the death of Commodus. It was the success of this work (now lost) which induced him to embark upon a history of Rome from her foundation, which he began in the year of Septimius's accession (A.D. 197), and which occupied him for most of his remaining life. We can, in fact, be more precise, for he tells us that he was occupied in compiling his information between 197 and 207, and in composing his history from 207 to 219. Considering that the coverage was nearly 1,000 years, and the author was not exclusively occupied with his literary work, the time he allowed for it seems too short. Of the original eighty books only Books 36–54 (covering 68–10 B.C.), considerable fragments of Books 55–60 (9 B.C.–A.D. 46) and parts of Books 79 and 80 (the first half of the reign of Elagabalus) survive in their original form. With the many excerpts and epitomes scattered throughout later Byzantine literature we are not here concerned, except as an indication of the esteem in which Dio's work was held by these historians. The first fifty books covered 723 years of republican history, the last thirty the 250 years of the empire, a fair division considering the uncertainties of the early period.

Unfortunately, like other historians who owe their minor status to their subordination of truly historical to rhetorical requirements, Dio often deliberately avoids precision and detail on the ground that it would tend to inhibit the flow of his narrative. Again, though in theory annalistic, Dio's history proves an unreliable guide to dates, on account of his inconsistent methods. He is less interested in constitutional antiquities than Dionysius, and even on occasion dismisses important legislation of recent times, like that of Julius Caesar in 59 B.C., with the statement that they 'contribute nothing to this narrative'.[34] For his purposes it was more important to elaborate upon material which illustrated virtue and vice, or characterized an historical personality.

But this approach to history leads Dio to some pronouncements on matters of perennial interest which should not go unrecorded. On the subject of the ideal form of government he shows himself to be a man of his times: democracy is good in theory, but in practice it brings strife because it is unstable; while monarchy has an evil reputation, but works in practice because one good man is easier to find than many. The disturbing feature of monarchy is the curtailment of freedom which it usually demands. A balance by which a degree of freedom was achieved at no expense of order and security was discovered for the first time by Augustus, and his example is a permanent justification of the principate. Most of Dio's more interesting statements concern the autocratic power of one or a few men. He observes, for example, that two or three men holding joint power are unlikely to agree,[35] that king-makers cannot always switch to the role of king-destroyers,[36] and that rulers are often better informed of external affairs than of those of their own household.[37] These are observations made in the light of comparatively recent historical, and perhaps personal experience. Others have no such association, and of these many bear signs of the writer's immersion in the political thought of Thucydides.[38]

The greatest concentration of Dio's political thought is to be found in a debate attributed to Augustus's advisers Agrippa and Maecenas on the subject of the principate.[39] In this the balance of the argument weighs in favour of a monarchy in which the *princeps* regularly consults a senior chamber, which also plays a positive part in the administration. A regular sequence of promotion, by which knights and freedmen are excluded from higher offices, is recommended; while those within the hierarchy are virtually assured of preferment, thus permanently safeguarding the dignity of the senatorial class. Also recommended is the institution of a new office, that of *sub-censor* (apparently an original idea of Dio himself), whose function would be to assume the censorial powers hitherto exercised by the emperor (an anachronism when referred to Augustus, but intermittently applicable to Vespasian and his successors). This office would confer a degree of independence upon the senatorial class.

It is in such practical ideas as these, the fruits of his own experiences in public life, rather than upon his grasp of historical causality that the merit of Dio's history chiefly lies. As a narrator, he weaves the main thread of his story too narrowly and with a wayward contempt for detail. The polymathy of the second-century Greek world, which saw a rebirth of intellectual and literary activity in several of the fields that were explored so thoroughly in classical times, rubbed off on to Dio, the preoccupied administrator, only to a limited extent. He knows something of geography; but a little learning is a dangerous thing, and his description of Britain, like that of some of his predecessors, is a model of inaccuracy.[40] References and discussions on the subjects of philosophy and religion betray a similarly sketchy knowledge. Dio reveals a Roman rather than a Greek temperament in his deliberate limitation of the scope and depth of his knowledge to what he needed as an administrator of an empire whose greatness and permanence he took for granted, and of which he considered himself an honoured and useful part.

The last historian of considerable stature under the Roman empire, and the one least deserving relegation to a chapter on minor historians, is Ammianus Marcellinus. With him the history of Graeco-Roman influences has run its full course of reciprocation: born of good parentage around A.D. 330 in the flourishing Syrian city of Antioch, he wrote in polished Latin for a Roman public. His active life, in the course of which he probably saw more military service than any of the other historians in this book, was passed during the latter half of the fourth century, and his death is probably to be assigned to its closing years. This is one of the few important biographical details on which we are ill-informed, but this deficiency becomes understandable when it is realized that most of what we know comes from the pen of the historian himself.

In the course of his career, which began, unusually for a person of his favoured background, with seven years of military service, he was on intimate terms with some of the men who shaped history. It is also fair to say that certain of his acquaintances, like his first commander Ursicinus, occupy a place in his narrative that is disproportionate to their importance. This worthy but unspectacular officer, like other men of rank in this troubled age, became involved in the intrigues and quarrels which inevitably surround an unstable throne, and his friend and chronicler, who was a man susceptible to strong personal attachments and antipathies, felt forced to take sides in his support. It is this too-easy involvement, which we must suspect in other parts of his narrative where authenticity and truth cannot be checked, that undermines our confidence; while the heady exuberance of his style, which is so much given to superlatives and is otherwise the most attractive feature of his work, only adds to our doubts as to his capacity for cool and impartial judgment.

On the other hand, Ammianus's personal participation in events which are undoubtedly worthy of inclusion in a serious history enabled him, like Xenophon, to supplement his literary gifts by the spontaneity of an eyewitness. In the year 355 a Frankish prince named Silvanus assumed the title of Emperor in the city of Cologne. Ursicinus was appointed to suppress this revolt, and the faithful Ammianus accompanied him. The historian proved to be an observant traveller, both in regard to natural phenomena, like the Alps and the Rhine, whose elemental strength he describes in colourful language,[41] and in regard to people. Many of his predecessors had described the Gallic national character. For a time after his work in Germany had been finished, Ammianus sojourned in Gaul and had the leisure to observe it. His description contains an unexpected twist:[42]

> Almost all the Gauls are of tall stature, fair and ruddy, terrible for the fierceness of their eyes, fond of quarrelling, and of overbearing insolence. In fact, a whole band of foreigners will be unable to cope with one of them in a fight, if he should call in his wife, stronger than he by far and with flashing eyes; least of all when she swells her neck and gnashes her teeth, and poising her huge white arms, begins to rain blows mingled with kicks, like shots discharged by the twisted cords of a catapult . . .

'The female of the species . . .'; a description by which modern French womanhood would not be flattered, but one which perhaps explains the sequel, in which Ammianus notes the willingness of the Gallic men to serve on arduous military campaigns! This passage displays the intoxicating vigour of Ammianus's style to good effect, and conjures up in the imagination some particular situation in which he found himself, and which he can scarcely forbear to describe.

The next theatre in which we find Ammianus is the East, whither he accompanied Ursicinus in order to prevent a Persian invasion of the eastern borders. The whole of Ammianus's description of this campaign is worth reading as an example of animated narrative, full of topographical detail and violent changes of fortune, and including a personal hairsbreadth escape. Seven Roman legions found themselves besieged in the small city of Amida. Ursicinus (who is likened to 'a lion of huge size and terrible fierceness which did not dare to go to save from danger his whelps that were caught in a net, because he had been robbed of his claws and teeth')[43] was powerless to relieve them against the full might of the Persian host with its king Sapor at its head. The horror of the experience, of which as one of those besieged Ammianus retained vivid memories, is fully reproduced in his narrative. But it also exhibits the control of art in its exploitation of contrasting action within a single episode:[44]

> Accordingly, after two days had been given to rest, a large force was sent to devastate the rich, cultivated fields, which were unprotected as in times of peace; then the city was begirt by a five-fold line of shields, and on the morning of the third day gleaming bands of horsemen filled all places which the eye could reach, and the ranks advanced at a quiet pace and took the places assigned to them by lot. The Persians beset the whole circuit of the walls. The part which faced the east fell to the lot of the Chaonitae, the place where the youth so fatal to us was slain, whose shade was destined to be appeased by the destruction of the city. The Gelani were assigned to the southern side, the Albani guarded the quarter to the north, and to the western gate were opposed the Segestani, the bravest warriors of all. With them, making a lofty show, slowly marched the lines of elephants, frightful with their wrinkled bodies and loaded with armed men, a hideous spectacle, dreadful beyond every form of horror, as I have often declared.
>
> Beholding such innumerable peoples, long enrolled to set fire to the Roman world and bent upon our destruction, we despaired of any hope of safety and henceforth strove to end our lives gloriously, which was now our sole desire. And so from sunrise until the day's end the battle lines stood fast, as though rooted in the same spot; no sound was heard; no neighing of horses; and they withdrew in the same order in which they had come, and then refreshed with food and sleep, when only a small part of the night remained, led by the trumpeter's blast they surrounded the city with the same awful ring, as if it were soon to fall. And hardly had Grumbates hurled a blood-stained spear, following the usage of his country and the custom of our fetial priest, than the army with clashing weapons flew to the walls, and at once the lamentable tempest of war grew fiercer, the cavalry advancing at full speed as they hurried to the fight with general eagerness, while our men resisted with courage and determination.

Waiting and watching as the enemy prepare for their destruction, the besieged historian has time to think of the universal hostility against the Roman empire, a prophetic idea at this time, and not unconnected with the reference to the ritual casting of the first spear. Here was an enemy with a civilization similar, and by implication equal to that of Rome (Ammianus never calls the Persians barbarians, reserving this appellation for the Germans, whom he hates); this idea will be returned to and amplified later. After the pregnant silence, sensed even by the animals, the noise of battle is the more fraught with terror.

As the fortunes of the garrison sink to their lowest point, another passage of an entirely different character appears, dividing and relieving, and also characterizing the historian. It examines the causes of the plague which struck the garrison, setting forth ancient philosophical and scientific opinions about it in a cool, didactic tone.[45] The narrative which follows describes a temporary revival of the fortunes of the besieged before the city is finally stormed. Ammianus thus shows an extraordinary mastery of structure, and incidentally reveals one of his distinguishing qualities, his extraordinary breadth of reading.

We leave his biography to look at this quality more closely. Throughout his history are scattered references, allusions and quotations derived from most of the important authors of antiquity. Allowing for the fact that it was fashionable in this age to display erudition, the range of Ammianus's knowledge is astounding, and would do credit to any modern scholar. But not all Ammianus's contemporaries shared his cultural accomplishments. His own city of Antioch, although it could boast the philosopher Libanius and John Chrysostom as its sons, was somewhat too frivolous for Ammianus's taste. More serious, however, was the same fault when found in the chief city of the empire, and in the administration and judiciary elsewhere. In a digression which, significantly, precedes the arrival on the scene of the Huns and the Goths, whose incursions reached their climax with the battle of Adrianople in 378, Ammianus scathingly outlines the corruption and philistinism of these officials, who can nevertheless exercise considerable power for evil. After comparing modern legal functionaries with the cultured men of old, the Attic orators and Cicero, he goes on to deplore their ignorance, which undermines the law, their mendacity and their venality. Then:[46]

And if in a circle of learned men the name of an ancient writer happens to be mentioned, they think it is a foreign word for some fish or other edible; but if any stranger asks for the orator Marcianus ['so-and-so', any person by that well-known name], at once they all pretend that their own name is Marcianus. [In other words they all like to be thought of as accomplished orators.]

With vital parts of the administration in the hands of such men, the empire is hardly better organized than the roving hoards of the barbarians, and is doomed to fall.

Ammianus is thus a fitting author with whom to end this survey of the historians of Greece and Rome. Starting off as a continuator of Tacitus's *Histories* with the year 97, he covered the following 255 years in thirteen books (now lost), while the surviving eighteen books cover a mere twenty-five years. Biography and autobiography colour these eighteen books to a high degree. But since characterization is his strongest point, it is possible to stomach the sometimes excessive hyperbole and over-sensuality of his style and to enjoy the minutiae of his personal portraits. His broad cultural interests, and his prophetic lamentation of their absence in many of his contemporaries, are an authentic reflection of a world on the point of cataclysmic change.

Notes

Numerical references are, successively, to book, chapter in book, and section in chapter. The latter are found in the Greek and Latin texts, but not in the majority of translations.

Chapter 1

p.3 1. For a full presentation of the surviving tradition concerning these writers, see L. Pearson: *Early Ionian Historians.* (Oxford, 1939)

p.4 2. 1.1.1

p.5 3. 2.123.1
4. 7.152.3

p.6 5. 8.8
6. 3.116
7. 4.25.1
8. 1.172.1
9. 3.2.1
10. 1.216.1
11. 6.121–124
12. 7.54
13. 1.1–5
14. This number has been computed from the catalogue in 7.60–99
15. 5.92.6–7

p.7 16. 3.108
17. 7.21. 109
18. 3.60
19. 1.178–181
20. 3.40–43
21. 1.23–24
22. 2.121
23. 3.85–87

p.9 24. 7.102
25. 7.103.3–4
26. 7.104.4–5

p.10 27. 1.30–33
p.11 28. 8.26.3
p.12 29. 9.122
30. 4.127
31. 9.82.3
p.13 32. 8.118
33. 8.119–120
34. 8.67–69
35. 8.86–88
36. 9.62–63
p.14 37. 6.21
38. 5.78
39. 5.90–91
40. 3.81–82
41. 7.38–39
p.15 42. 8.69
43. 7.11.1
44. 8.118.4
p.16 45. 5.105
46. 5.67.1
p.17 47. 8.112.1
48. 7.45–46.2. But such feelings also show materialism
49. 8.60
p.18 50. 8.77
51. 7.57
52. 36.1
53. 8.37
p.19 54. 9.100
p.20 55. A good example of the recourse to supernatural explanation after reason has

failed to make sense is to be
found in the discussion of the
cause of the Trojan War in
2.120
56. 3.40

p.21 57. 1.66–67
58. 7.35
59. *Olympian Ode*, 1.87
p.22 60. 7.136
61. 7.50

Chapter 2

p.28 1. 1.20–22
2. 1.20
p.29 3. 2.47–53
4. ch. 82–84
p.30 5. 4.61
6. 4.62
p.31 7. 6.24.1–3
8. 8.2.3–4
8(a). 1.42.2–3
9. 3.38
p.32 10. 2.65
11. 8.1.1
12. 2.65.10–12
p.33 13. 8.97.2
14. 6.39.1
p.34 15. 1.2–17
p.37 16. 1.90.1
17. 1.90.2
18. 1.95
19. 1.95.2
p.38 20. 1.96.1
21. 1.98.4
22. 1.99.3
23. 1.68–71
p.39 24. 6.16–18
25. 6.20
26. 2.35–46
p.40 27. 8.68.4
28. 1.23.6
p.41 29. 1.139.1
p.42 30. 7.71
p.44 31. 2.83–84
32. 4.32–36
33. 1.82.4
p.45 34. 4.65
35. 6.23.4
36. 3.53–68
37. 5.87–112

p.46 38. 1.22.1
p.48 39. 1.32–36
40. 1.37–43
p.49 41. 3.36
42. 3.37–40
43. 2.63
p.50 44. 3.42–48
p.51 45. 3.49.4
p.52 46. 6.12.2
47. 6.15.2–4
48. 6.16–18
p.53 49. 6.18.6–7
50. 1.68–71
p.54 51. 1.73–78
52. 1.80–85
53. 1.86
54. 1.120–124
55. 1.139–144
p.55 56. 2.41.1
57. 2.43.3
p.56 58. 4.126
59. 6.68
p.57 60. 2.89
61. 7.66–68
p.58 62. 2.65
63. 8.68.1–2
p.59 64. 1.138
65. 1.128–134
66. 3.36.6
67. 4.27–28
68. 4.39.3
69. 4.28.5
70. 5.10–11
71. 5.16.1
p.60 72. 6.15
73. 5.16.1
p.61 74. 7.86.5
p.62 75. 2.52.1–2, 54

p.62 76. 7.50.4
      77. 7.79.3
      78. 1.23
p.65 79. See the chapter on

Thucydides in H. D. F. Kitto. *Poiesis: Structure and Thought.* (Berkeley and Cambridge, 1966)

Chapter 3

p.67 1. Diogenes Laertius. *Lives of the Philosophers* 2.48
p.68 2. *Anabasis* 3.1.4–8
p.69 3. Diog. Laert. *id.* 2.49
p.70 4. *Hellenica* 2.4.2–43
p.71 5. *id.* 1.4.2–7
p.72 6. *Anab.* 1.5.1–3
p.73 7. *id.* 1.8.8–10
p.74 8. *id.* 2.5.31–33
      9. *id.* 1.9
      10. *id.* 2.6.1–15
p.75 11. *id.* 2.6.16–20
      12. *id.* 2.6.21–29
p.76 13. *id.* 3.1.4
p.77 14. *id.* 3.1.37
p.78 15. *id.* 3.2.7–32
      16. *id.* 3.2.18
      17. *id.* 3.2.19
      18. *id.* 3.2.25
      19. *id.* 3.2.26
p.79 20. *id.* 4.4.11–13
p.80 21. *id.* 4.7.24
      22. *id.* 5.1.2
      23. 8.1.1
      24. *Anab.* 5.7.5–12
      25. *id.* 6.1.20
p.81 26. *id.* 7.7.20–47
      27. *id.* 7.8.6
      28. *id.* 7.8.23
p.84 29. Pseudo-Lucian, *Longaevi* 21
p.87 30. *Hell.* 1.4.13

      31. *id.* 1.1.27–31
      32. *id.* 1.6.5, 8
      33. *id.* 1.5.5
p.88 34. *id.* 1.1.35
      35. *id.* 1.5.9
      36. *id.* 1.1.14
p.89 37. *id.* 2.2.3–4
      38. *id.* 2.2.23
      39. *id.* 1.7.16–23
      40. *id.* 2.3.24–34
      41. *id.* 2.3.35–49
p.91 42. *id.* 2.3.55–56
p.92 43. *id.* 4.3.10–12
      44. *id.* 5.1.36
      45. *id.* 6.2.1
      46. *id.* 5.2.7
p.93 46(a). *id.* 5.4.1
p.94 47. *id.* 3.4.17–18
      48. *id.* 4.1.32
p.95 49. *id.* 6.2.29–30
      50. *id.* 6.2.39
      51. *id.* 6.1.4–15
p.96 52. *id.* 7.1.41
      53. *id.* 5.1.4
      54. *id.* 7.2.1.
p.97 55. *id.* 4.8.1
      56. *id.* 4.1.32–3
      57. *id.* 6.5.38–48, 7.1.1–11
p.98 58. *id.* 6.3.7–9
      59. *id.* 7.1.23
      60. *id.* 5.1.29

Chapter 4

p.101 1. *Panegyricus* 8
p.107 2. 32.9–11
p.108 3. 3.1
       4. 1.1
p.110 5. 12.25(b)

p.112 6. 38.6
p.113 7. 3.6
p.114 8. 8.11–13
       9. 9.21–26
p.115 10. 10.2–3

p.115 11. 10.21
p.116 13. 6.5
p.117 14. 6.19–36
15. 6.37–39
p.118 16. 6.52–53
p.119 17. 37.9
18. *ibid*
p.120 19. 2.23
20. 3.118

21 1.71
p.121 22. 12.25(a)
23. 2.56.10
24. 36.1.6–7
25. 3.64
26. 15.10
p.122 27. 5.104
28. 9.28–31

Chapter 5

p.130 1. *Epistles* 2.1.156–157
p.131 2. There is a tradition that the Gauls destroyed the records of early Roman history when they sacked the city in the invasion of 390–386 B.C.
p.138 3. He did, however, attempt to glorify his consulship in verse; but such is the quality of his poetry that he might have done less harm to his literary reputation if he had attempted to write a history in prose
p.139 4. *Gallic War* 7.46–47
p.140 5. *Catiline* 3.3–4
p.142 6. *Institutiones Oratoriae* 2. 5.19
7. *Annals* 3.30.1
8. 14.191.2
p.145 9. *Catiline* 5.1–8
10. *id.* 14
11. *id.* 15.4–5
12. *id.* 22
p.146 13. *id.* 23.1–4
14. *id.* 23.5–24.1
15. *id.* 24.2–4
16. *id.* 36.4ff
17. *id.* 39.6ff
p.147 18. *id.* 48.1–2
19. *id.* 51
20. *id.* 52

21. *id.* 55
22. *id.* 56–60
23. *id.* 46.5
24. *id.* 49.4
25. *id.* 60.7
26. *id.* 31.1–3
27. *id.* 48–1.2
p.148 28. *id.* 23.6
p.149 29. e.g. *Cat.* 26.2
30. *id.* 31.6
31. *id.* 43.1
32. *id.* 53.6
p.152 33. *Jugurtha* 5.1
p.153 34. *id.* 35.10
35. *id.* 44–45
36. *id.* 85
37. *id.* 64
p.154 38. *id.* 95
39. *id.* 102–113
40. *id.* 42.1
41. *id.* 41.1–5
42. *id.* 64.1
p.155 43. *id.* 6.1
44. *id.* 8.1–2
45. *id.* 10.4–6
46. *id.* 63.1–2
p.156 47. *id.* 64.5
48. *id.* 85.29–34
49. *id.* 84.2
p.157 50. *id.* 95.2–4
51. *id.* 92.5–94.7
p.160 52. *Anabasis* 5.2.28–32

Chapter 6

p.164 1. Thuc. 1.17
p.166 2. *Annals* 2.34
p.167 3. *Preface* 9–12
p.168 4. 26.41.12
p.169 5. 21.11.2
    6. 21.7.2
    7. 6.40
    8. 28.40ff
    9. 28.41
    10. 28.43–44
    11. 28.44.18
p.170 12. 8.7.15–19
p.171 13. 9.17–19
    14. 22.47–49
    15. 22.46.6–9
    16. 27.48ff
p.172 17. 24.34
    18. 24.10
p.173 19. 43.13.1–2
    20. 1.19.4–5
p.174 21. 8.30.1, 27.23.4
p.175 22. 2.34.12
    23. 2.1.4, 28.25.8
    24. 3.16.5

    25. 6.31.4
    26. 22.13.11
    27. 21.1ff
    28. 21.4
p.176 29. 9.22–26
    30. 22.1–7
    31. 22.30
    32. 28.40ff
p.177 33. 26.45.9
    34. 28.45.1
p.178 35. 26.45.9
    36. 38.53.9
    37. 39.40
p.179 38. 1.3.2, 3.5.12, 5.1.2
    39. 21.28.11
    40. 37.7.10
p.182 41. 21.34–37
p.185 42. 30.32.4–35.3
p.190 43. 22.7.10–13
p.191 44. 3.17.2–6
p.192 45. 21.40
p.196 46. 7.30
    47. 5.3–6
    48. 7.35.2–12

Chapter 7

p.204 1. *Histories* 1.1 (cf. *Annals* 1.1.6)
p.206 2. *Annals* 1.72
    3. *id.* 4.35 (cf.14.50)
    4. *Agricola* 2.3–3.2
p.207 5. *Annals* 3.65
p.208 6. *id.* 4.33
    7. *id.* 16.18
p.210 8. *id.* 3.53–54
p.211 9. *id.* 4.37–38
    10. *id.* 4.40
    11. *id.* 11.31
p.212 12. *id.* 12.3
    13. *id.* 15.57
p.213 14. *id.* 11.38
    15. *id.* 13.45
p.215 16. *id.* 6.45
p.217 17. *id.* 14.51

p.218 18. *id.* 1.6
    19. *id.* 13.1
    20. *id.* 1.6.6
    21. *id.* 11.38
    22. *id.* 15.47
p.219 23. *id.* 1.16
p.220 24. *id.* 6.51
p.221 25. *id.* 13.3
    26. *id.* 13.4
    27. *id.* 13.6
    28. *id.* 14.9
p.222 29. *id.* 14.38
p.223 30. *id.* 14.43–44
p.225 31. *id.* 14.51–59
    32. *id.* 14.65
p.226 33. *Histories* 2.35
p.227 34. *id.* 3.25
    35. *id.* 1.4

p.228 36. *id.* 1.51–52
      37. *id.* 2.70ff
      38. *id.* 1.53
p.229 39. *id.* 1.62
      40. *id.* 1.76

p.230 41. *id.* 3.85
      42. *id.* 2.37
p.231 43. *id.* 3.56
p.232 44. *Annals* 1.74
      45. *id.* 4.34

Chapter 8

p.236 1. 1.5.2
      2. 1.3.6
      3. 3.12–14, 5.35–38
p.237 4. Books 11–12
      5. 1.89–118
      6. M.I. Finley, *The Greek Historians* (London, 1959), p.16
      7. J. Palm, *Über Sprache und Stil des Diodoros von Sizilien* (Lund, 1955). A similar conclusion was reached independently by S. Usher in *Development of Post-Attic Prose Narrative Style* (Dissertation, University of London, 1955)
p.238 8. *Antiquitates Romanae* 1.7.2
p.239 9. *id.* 1.6.5
      10. *Letter to Pompeius* 3
p.240 11. *Ant. Rom.* 8.5–8, Thuc. 6.89–92
p.241 12. Livy 2.34.7–12, *Ant. Rom.* 7.20–67
      13. Livy 7–12; Dionysius 15–18
p.242 14. 2.41
      15. A rhetorical exercise or composition, usually exploring the arguments for or against a course of action known to have been followed or contemplated by a famous historical or mythological person
      16. 2.68

p.243 17. 2.44
p.245 18. Books 13–17
      19. 8.81
p.246 20. 8.45
p.247 21. e.g. *Tactics against the Alani*, 28.8; *Circumnavigation of the Euxine*, 1.1, 12.5, 25.1
      22. 1.12.1–5
      23. Introduction 2
      24. e.g. 5.14
      25. 5.26.1.
p.248 26. 5.26.4
      27. 3.3.2
      28. 3.10
      29. e.g. 1.15.6
      30. 3.18.12
      31. 6.13.4
      32. 4.8.
p.249 33. 7.29
      34. 38.7.6
p.251 35. 48.1.2
p.252 36. 61.7.3
      37. 55.10.13
      38. See F. Millar, *A Study of Cassius Dio* (Oxford, 1964), pp. 42, 76, 177
      39. 52.1–40
p.253 40. 76.11ff
p.254 41. 15.4.2–6
      42. 15.12
p.255 43. 19.3.3
      44. 19.2.2ff
      45. 19.4
      46. 30.4.17

Bibliography

The following list is intended for the guidance of the general reader. The specialist will need no prompting to consult *Fifty Years (and Twelve) of Classical Scholarship*, edited by M. Platnauer (Oxford, 1968), and the other standard bibliographies. The series *Greece and Rome New Surveys in the Classics* includes Thucydides, Livy and Tacitus among the authors surveyed.

TRANSLATIONS

All the ancient historians whose works have survived in quantity have been translated, with parallel text, in the Loeb Classical Library series. There are translations in the Penguin Classics series of Herodotus, Thucydides, Xenophon (*Anabasis* and *Hellenica*), Caesar (*Civil War* and *Gallic War*), Sallust (*Catiline* and *Jugurtha*), Livy (Books 1–10 and 21–30) and Tacitus (*Annals, Histories, Agricola* and *Germania*). Polybius was translated many years ago by E. S. Shuckburgh, and his version was reprinted by the Indiana University Press in 1962.

GENERAL STUDIES

BURY, J. B. *The Ancient Greek Historians* (London, 1909; repr. Dover Books, New York, 1958).

WILAMOWITZ-MOELLENDORFF, U. VON. *Greek Historical Writing* (Oxford, 1908).

FINLEY, M. I. *The Greek Historians: the essence of Herodotus, Thucydides, Xenophon, Polybius* (London, 1959).
    (A short introductory chapter followed by selections from the four historians, Xenophon being represented by the *Anabasis* only).

LAISTNER, M. W. L. *The Greater Roman Historians* (Berkeley, 1947. Paperback repr. 1963).

DOREY, T. A. (Ed.) *Latin Historians* (London, 1966).
    (Chapters by E. Badian, F. W. Walbank, G. M. Paul, T. A. Dorey, P. J. Walsh, E. A. Thompson and J. Campbell.)

LOFSTEDT, E. (trans. P. M. FRASER) *Roman Literary Portraits* (Oxford 1958). (Essays on Sallust and Tacitus).

VON FRITZ, K. *Die Griechische Geschichtsschreibung I* (Berlin, 1967).

GRANT, M. *The Ancient Historians* (New York, 1970).

LESKY, A. *A History of Greek Literature* (London, 1966).

WESTLAKE, H. D. *Essays on Greek Historians and Greek History* (Manchester, 1969).

CHAPTER 1

PEARSON, L. *Early Ionian Historians* (Oxford, 1939).
GLOVER, T. R. *Herodotus* (Berkeley, 1924).
MYRES, J. L *Herodotus, Father of History* (Oxford, 1953).
IMMERWAHR, H. R. *Form and Thought in Herodotus* (Cleveland, 1966).
SELINCOURT, A. DE *The World of Herodotus* (London and Boston, 1962).
FORNARA, C. W. *Herodotus, an interpretative essay* (Oxford, 1971).
BENADETE, S. *Herodotean Inquiries* (The Hague, 1969).
BURN, A. R. *Persia and the Greeks* (London and New York, 1962).
HIGNETT, C. *Xerxes's Invasion of Greece* (Oxford, 1963).

CHAPTER 2

ABBOTT, G. F. *Thucydides: a study in historical reality* (London, 1925).
CORNFORD, F. M. *Thucydides Mythistoricus* (London, 1907).
LAMB, W. R. M. *Clio Enthroned* (Cambridge, 1914).
COCHRANE, C. N. *Thucydides and the Science of History* (Oxford, 1929).
GRUNDY, G. B. *Thucydides and the History of his Age* (2 vols. London, 1911).
ADCOCK, F. E. *Thucydides and his History* (Cambridge, 1964).
ROMILLY, J. DE (trans. P. THODY) *Thucydides and Athenian Imperialism* (Oxford, 1963).
ROMILLY, J. DE *Histoire et Raison chez Thucydide* (Paris, 1956).
GOMME, A. W., ANDREWES, A., DOVER, K. J. *A Historical Commentary on Thucydides* (5 vols. Oxford, 1945–81).
HENDERSON, B. W. *The Great War between Athens and Sparta* (London, 1927).
FINLEY, J. H. *Thucydides* (Ann Arbor Paperbacks, 1963).
WESTLAKE, H. D. *Individuals in Thucydides* (Cambridge, 1968).
WOODHEAD, A. G. *Thucydides on the Nature of Power* (Harvard, 1970).

CHAPTER 3

GRANT, A. *Xenophon* (Edinburgh, 1914).
DELEBECQUE, E. *Essai sur la Vie de Xenophon* (Paris, 1957).
HENRY, W. P. *Greek Historical Writing* (Chicago, 1966).
    (On the composition of the *Hellenica*).
JACKS, L. V. *Xenophon, Soldier of Fortune* (London, 1930).
UNDERHILL, G. E. *A Commentary on Xenophon's Hellenica* (Oxford, 1900).
LUCCIONI, J. *Les Idées politiques et sociales de Xenophon* (Paris, 1947).
ANDERSON, J. K. *Xenophon* (London, 1974).
HIGGINS, W. E. *Xenophon the Athenian* (New York, 1977).

CHAPTER 4

WALKER, E. M. *The Hellenica Oxyrhynchia* (Oxford, 1913).
BARBER, G. L. *The Historian Ephorus* (Cambridge, 1935).

CONNOR, W. R. *Theopompus and Fifth-Century Athens* (Washington, 1968).

VON FRITZ, K. *The Theory of the Mixed Constitution in Antiquity* (New York, 1954).

PEARSON, L. *The Lost Histories of Alexander the Great* (New York, 1960).

BROWN, T. S. *Onesicritus* (Berkeley, 1949).

BROWN, T. S. *Timaeus of Tauromenium* (Berkeley, 1958).

PÉDECH, P. *La Méthode historique de Polybe* (Paris, 1964).

WALBANK, F. W. *A Historical Commentary on Polybius* (3 vols. Oxford, 1957–).

WALBANK, F. W. *Polybius* (Los Angeles & London, 1972).

WALBANK, F. W. *The Hellenistic World* (Glasgow (Fontana), 1981).

TARN, W. and GRIFFITH, G. T. *Hellenistic Civilisation* (London, 1959).

ROSTOVTZEFF, M. *Social and Economic History of the Hellenistic World* (Oxford, 1941).

CHAPTER 5

EARL, D. C. *The Political Thought of Sallust* (Cambridge, 1961).

SYME, R. *Sallust* (Berkeley and Cambridge, 1964).

McGUSHIN, P. A. *Commentary on Sallust Bellum Catilinae* (Leiden, 1977).

ADCOCK, F. E. *Caesar as a Man of Letters* (Cambridge, 1956).

RICE HOLMES, T. *Caesar's Conquest of Gaul* (Oxford, 1931).

SMITH, R. E. *The Failure of the Roman Republic* (Cambridge, 1956).

SYME, R. *The Roman Revolution* (Oxford, 1939. Paperback repr. 1960).

SCULLARD, H. H. *Roman Politics 220–150 B.C.* (Oxford, 1951).

SCULLARD, H. H. *From the Gracchi to Nero* (Oxford Paperback, 1963).

CRAWFORD, M. *The Roman Republic* (Glasgow (Fontana), 1978).

CHAPTER 6

WALSH, P. E. *Livy: his historical aims and methods* (Cambridge, 1963).

OGILVIE, R. M. *A Commentary on Livy Books 1–5* (Oxford, 1965).

BRISCOE, J. *A Commentary on Livy Books 31–33* (Oxford, 1973) and *34–37* (Oxford, 1981).

ULLMAN, R. *La Technique des discours dans Salluste, Tite-Live et Tacite* (Oslo, 1927).

ULLMAN, R. *Etude sur le style des discours de Tite-Live* (Oslo, 1929).

CHARLESWORTH, M. P. *The Roman Empire* (Oxford, 1951).

HAMMOND, M. *The Augustan Principate* (Cambridge Mass. 1933).

RICE HOLMES, T. *The Architect of the Roman Empire* (Oxford, 1931).

BUCHAN, J. *Augustus Caesar* (London, 1937).

DOREY, T. A. (ed.) *Livy* (London, 1971).

CHAPTER 7

SYME, R. *Tacitus* (Oxford, 1958, 2 vols.)

MENDELL, C. W. *Tacitus: the man and his work* (Yale and London, 1957).

WALKER, B. *The Annals of Tacitus* (Manchester, 1952).

DOREY, T. A. (ed.) *Tacitus* (London, 1969).

BENARIO, H. W. *An Introduction to Tacitus* (Athens, Georgia, 1975).

MARSH, F. B. *The Reign of Tiberius* (Oxford, 1931).

ROGERS, R. S. *Studies in the Reign of Tiberius* (Baltimore, 1943).

BALSDON, J. P. V. D. *The Emperor Gaius* (Oxford, 1934).

MOMIGLIANO, A. D. (trans. HOGARTH, W. D.) *Claudius: the emperor and his achievement* (Oxford, 1934).

SCRAMUZZA, V. M. *The Emperor Claudius* (Harvard and Cambridge, 1940).

BISHOP, J. *Nero: the man and the legend* (London, 1964).

HENDERSON, B. W. *The Life and Principate of the Emperor Nero* (London, 1903).

WARMINGTON, B. H. *Nero, Reality and Legend* (London, 1969).

GARZETTI, A. *From Tiberius to the Antonines* (London, 1976).

CHAPTER 8

FARRINGTON, B. *Diodorus Siculus: universal historian* (Univ. of Wales, 1937).

BONNER, S. F. *The Literary Treatises of Dionysius of Halicarnassus* (Cambridge, 1939).

MILLAR, F. *A Study of Cassius Dio* (Oxford, 1964).

THOMPSON, E. A. *The Historical Work of Ammianus Marcellinus* (Cambridge, 1947).

SYME, R. *Ammianus and the Historia Augusta* (Oxford, 1968).

WRIGHT, F. A. *A History of Later Greek Literature* (London, 1932).

DEN BOER, W. *Some Minor Roman Historians* (Leiden, 1972).

WISEMAN, T. P. *Clio's Cosmetics* (Leicester, 1979).

Index

Histories, vii, 203–5, 211, 226–31, 234, 257
  Livy and, 215, 218, 231
  Sallust and, 207, 234
  speeches in, 231–3
Teleutias, 96
Tellus, 10
Themistocles, 16, 17, 37, 59, 61
Theognis, 69
Theopompus, 100–3, 109, 114
  Hellenica, 101
  Philippica, 101
Theramenes, 89, 91
Thibron, 81, 82, 94
Thrasybulus, 6
Thucydides, 15, 23–65, 80, 100, 108, 109, 110, 112, 122, 190, 196, 197, 217, 226, 227, 231, 232, 237
  Archaeologia, 34, 35–6
  as historian, ix, 23–9, 45–6, 63–5
  Dionysius and, 238–9, 240
  Herodotus and, 23, 24, 28, 40, 43, 45, 46
  Peloponnesian War, 23–65, 85–7, 89, 90
  Pericles and, 31–2, 34, 37, 41, 58
  Sallust and, 142, 147, 151, 160
  speeches in, 45–58
  Xenophon and, 71, 85–7, 89, 90–1, 97–9
Tiberius, 200–1, 206, 207, 208, 209–11, 212, 214, 215–16, 217, 218, 219–21, 232, 234
Tigellinus, 209, 217, 225
Timaeus, 103–4, 109, 237
  History, 103
Tissaphernes, 74, 79, 83, 88, 94
Titus, 202, 205
Torquatus, Manlius, 151, 170
Trajan, 203, 205, 244, 249
Tritantaechmes, 11

Tubero, Aelius, 179

Ursicinus, 253–5

Valens, 228, 230
Valerius, Publius, 191
Varilla, Appuleia, 219
Velleius, vii, 241–4, 245
Vespasian, 142, 202, 205, 229–30
Vinicius, Marcus, 241
Vinius, Titus, 204
Virgil, 166
  Aeneid, 165, 180
  Georgics, 165
Vitellius, 202, 205, 211, 228–31

Xanthus, 3
Xenophon, vii, 66–100, 109, 113, 123, 160, 178, 240, 254
  Agesilaus and, 82–3
  Agesilaus, 83–4
  Anabasis, 69, 70–82, 83, 99, 135, 155, 247
  Apology, 84
  Cyropaedia, 84, 105, 135
  Diodorus Siculus and, 236–7
  Equitation, 83
  Estate Management, 83, 135
  Hellenica, 69, 70–1, 77, 84, 85–96
  Hiero, 84
  Hipparchicus, 84
  Memorabilia, 67–8, 84
  Revenues, 83, 84
  Socrates and, 67, 68, 69, 70
  Spartan Constitution, 83
  speeches in, 89
  Symposium, 84
  Thucydides and, 71, 85–7, 89, 90–1, 97–9
Xerxes, 4, 6, 7, 8–10, 12–15, 16, 17, 18, 19, 21, 22, 113